World Disasters Report

2004

Focus on community resilience

International Federation
of Red Cross and Red Crescent Societies

The opinions expressed in this publication do not necessarily represent the official policy of the International Federation of Red Cross and Red Crescent Societies or of individual national Red Cross or Red Crescent societies. The designations used do not imply the expression of any opinion on the part of the International Federation or National Societies concerning the legal status of a territory or of its authorities.

Editor: Jonathan Walter

Managing Editor: Eva von Oelreich

Design and Production Team: Jean-Charles Chamois, Aradhna Duggal-Chadha and Serge Marin-Pache

External Reviewers: Yasemin Aysan, Tony Beck, Ailsa Holloway and Mark Pelling

We would also like to thank all those who assisted contributors during travel and research for this issue.

Baseline maps by Geoatlas® – ©GRAPHI-OGRE, Hendaye, France
Typesetting by Strategic Communications SA, Geneva, Switzerland
Printed by ATAR Roto Presse, Satigny/Vernier, Switzerland

Contact details:
International Federation of Red Cross and Red Crescent Societies
17, chemin des Crêts, P.O. Box 372
CH-1211 Geneva 19, Switzerland
Tel.: + 41 (0)22 730 4222. Fax: + 41 (0)22 733 0395
E-mail: secretariat@ifrc.org; wdr@ifrc.org
Web: http://www.ifrc.org

To order the *World Disasters Report*, contact:

Kumarian Press Inc
1294 Blue Hills Ave
Bloomfield CT 06002, USA
Tel.: +1 860 243 2098
Fax: +1 860 243 2867
E-mail: kpbooks@aol.com
Web: http://www.kpbooks.com

Eurospan
3 Henrietta Street, Covent Garden
London WC2E 8LU, UK
Tel.: +44 (0)20 7240 0856
Fax: +44 (0)20 7379 0609
E-mail: orders@edspubs.co.uk
Web: http://www.eurospanonline.com

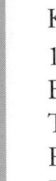
International Federation
of Red Cross and Red Crescent Societies

The International Federation of Red Cross and Red Crescent Societies would like to express its gratitude to the following for committing to and supporting this publication:

AUSAID

British Red Cross

CIDA

DHL

Governement of Ireland through Development Cooperation Ireland

Japanese Red Cross

Netherlands Red Cross

Norwegian Red Cross

SIDA/Swedish Red Cross

Spanish Red Cross

Contents

Section One
Focus on community resilience

Section Two
Tracking the system

Building the capacity to bounce back

The face of disasters is changing. Soaring urban populations, environmental degradation, poverty and disease are compounding seasonal hazards such as droughts and floods to create situations of chronic adversity. Old ways of coping are proving inadequate. But equally, people at risk are finding new ways to respond on their own initiative.

Aid organizations must keep up. We need new approaches that boost people's resilience to the full spectrum of physical, social and economic adversities they face. By resilience, I mean people's ability to cope with crisis and bounce back stronger than before. If we fail to shift from short-term relief to longer-term support for communities in danger, we risk wasting our money and undermining the resilience we seek to enhance.

Top-down interventions may prove less effective than many assume. Following last December's devastating earthquake in Bam, 34 search-and-rescue teams from 27 countries flew to the city and saved 22 lives. Meanwhile, local Red Crescent teams pulled 157 people alive from the rubble, using far fewer 'sniffer' dogs. Investing in local response capacities saves lives and money.

However, 'natural' disasters are not the biggest killers. In sub-Saharan Africa last year, 2.2 million people died from HIV/AIDS, while 25 million live with the infection. Disease, drought, malnutrition, poor healthcare and poverty have together created a complex catastrophe, demanding a more integrated response than simply food aid or drugs.

Meanwhile, the unplanned acceleration of urban areas is concentrating new risks. Diseases from filthy water and sanitation kill over 2 million people a year – many of them slum children. So why have national governments and aid organizations barely addressed the issue?

The developed world faces new threats, too. Five degrees more summer heat than usual triggered a disaster that shamed modern, wealthy societies across Europe in 2003. Up to 35,000 elderly and vulnerable people suffered silent, lonely deaths, abandoned by state welfare systems in retreat.

Europe was caught off guard. Humanitarian organizations are more prepared for sudden-impact, high-profile disasters. But as the nature of disaster changes, we must change too. Instead of imposing definitions and solutions on people we consider vulnerable, we should ask them what they define as a disaster. How are they adapting to the new risks facing them?

International Federation
of Red Cross and Red Crescent Societies

The answers can be surprising – and inspiring. In Swaziland, HIV/AIDS and drought are conspiring to leave many perpetually hungry. But Chief Masilela informs us that his community wants irrigation and seeds – not food aid – so they can grow crops, craft their own recovery and retain their dignity. His government, meanwhile, is expanding access to life-lengthening drugs and recruiting 10,000 women as 'surrogate parents' for thousands of AIDS orphans.

Across the Indian Ocean in Mumbai, one woman we report on has rented out her comfortable apartment and moved into a shack beneath a bridge, at risk of flooding and fire. That way, she can pay for her daughter's education. She's decided the family's long-term resilience depends on investing in her daughter rather than living somewhere safer. To the south, the low caste women of Andhra Pradesh have rediscovered indigenous, hardy seeds to help farmers recover from debt and despair as their cash crops – recommended by experts in distant capitals – wither in the drought.

The capacity for resilience in the face of adversity shines through all this year's stories. People continually adapt to crisis, coming up with creative solutions. They prioritise livelihoods and household assets rather than the quick fix. Supporting resilience means more than delivering relief or mitigating individual hazards. Local knowledge, skills, determination, livelihoods, cooperation, access to resources and representation are all vital factors enabling people to bounce back from disaster. This implies a paradigm shift in how we approach aid. We must focus on the priorities and capacities of those we seek to help. Mapping vulnerabilities and meeting needs is no longer enough. The idea is not new – it's been enshrined in *The Code of Conduct for the International Red Cross and Red Crescent Movement and NGOs in Disaster Relief* for the past 10 years. So why do humanitarian organizations still fail to assess – let alone harness – the capacities of those at risk?

Three things need to happen. First, we must understand what enables people to cope with, recover from and adapt to the risks they face. Second, we must build our responses on the community's own priorities, knowledge and resources. Third, we must scale up community responses, by creating new coalitions with governments and advocating changes in policy and practice at all levels.

If we focus only on needs and vulnerabilities, we remain locked in the logic of repetitive responses that fail to nurture the capacities for resilience contained deep within every community. We have talked about building capacity and resilience for decades. It is now time to turn rhetoric into reality: to dispel the myth of the helpless victim and the infallible humanitarian, and to put disaster-affected people and their abilities at the centre of our work.

Markku Niskala
Secretary General

**Focus on
community
resilience**

International Federation
of Red Cross and Red Crescent Societies

From risk to resilience – helping communities cope with crisis

To read the headlines, one would think that most disaster-affected communities are paralysed and helpless – saved only by the aid of outsiders, whether from national capitals or abroad. Yet the television images of disasters from Bam's earthquake to New York's collapsed twin towers reveal, on careful inspection, what is concealed in most headlines: survivors, family members and neighbours saving people from under the rubble with their bare hands, salvaging what is left and counselling each other. When all seems lost, the capacity of disaster-affected people to pull together and not give up is both amazing and humbling.

Factors that enable people to cope with hardship and survive trauma have long been of interest to social and behavioural scientists, covering a wide range of situations, whether the death of a loved one, surviving an accident or the adaptation of Latino immigrant teenagers to the United States. In the last two decades, 'resilience' has become the 'buzz' word to describe this capacity to survive, adapt and bounce back – applied freely to anything from ecosystems to business, at any level from households to countries and global communities (see Box 1.1).

For example, battered by dramatic changes in markets, technology, environmental legislation and the resource base, residents of the hundreds of small towns in the Canadian province of British Columbia that owe their existence to harvesting, extracting and processing natural resources found themselves presented with a stark choice: change or die. Many, especially the young, abandoned their towns. A few, however, bounced back. They formed a 'community resilience project' to assess and strengthen their own capacity to adapt to these changes.

Since the attacks on New York on 11 September 2001, notions of corporate resilience have been radically reappraised to take into account catastrophic events that had previously not been contemplated. Often described as 'business continuity' planning, senior executives from all over the world periodically discuss new models of resilience to unexpected events and shocks, from economic downturn to terrorist attacks and natural disasters.

The Resilience Alliance, a multidisciplinary research group, explores solutions to coping with change and uncertainty in complex social-ecological systems through an international programme connecting regional case studies. The idea is to contribute

Photo opposite page: Creating resilience includes enhancing the knowledge and skills of everyone in the community to cope with and adapt to disasters. This Red Cross board game aims to enhance disaster awareness among children in Latin America.

© Marko Kokic/ International Federation.

"Resilience is the capacity to cope with unanticipated dangers after they have become manifest, learning to bounce back."
Wildavsky, A. Searching for Safety. New Jersey, USA: Transaction Publishers, 1991.

"Researchers at the Disaster Research Center and the Multidisciplinary Center for Earthquake Engineering Research... have identified several dimensions along which resilience can be measured. These are robustness, resourcefulness, redundancy, and rapidity."
Kendra, J. and Wachtendorf, T. Elements of Community Resilience in the World Trade Center Attack. Newark, USA: Disaster Research Center, University of Delaware, 2002.

"Resilience, for social-ecological systems, is related to (a) the magnitude of shock that the system can absorb and remain within a given state, (b) the degree to which the system is capable of self-organization, and (c) the degree to which the system can build capacity for learning and adaptation."

Government of Sweden. Resilience and Sustainable Development: Building Adaptive Capacity in a World of Transformations. Scientific background paper on resilience for the World Summit on Sustainable Development on behalf of the Environmental Advisory Council to the Swedish Government (April 2002).

"A resilient ecosystem can withstand shocks and rebuild itself when necessary. Resilience in social systems has the added capacity of humans to anticipate and plan for the future... 'Resilience' as applied to ecosystems, or to integrated systems of people and the natural environment, has three defining characteristics:

- The amount of change the system can undergo and still retain the same controls on function and structure
- The degree to which the system is capable of self-organization
- The ability to build and increase the capacity for learning and adaptation."
Resilience Alliance, http://www.resalliance.org ■

to sustainable development through better management of nature and people as an integrated system. Meanwhile, small island developing states consider that, to implement a programme for sustainable development agreed in Barbados in 1994, building social, economic and environmental resilience is at the core of sustaining progress in fragile island communities.

Resilience is sometimes achieved over the long term at the expense of resilience in the short term. The extreme tenacity of the poor in taking the long view to preserve the basis for their future livelihood is starkly exemplified in a story related by development analyst Alex de Waal. He told of a woman in Sudan's Darfur province who, during the 1985 famine, preserved her millet seed for planting by mixing it with sand, to prevent her hungry children from eating it. During the same disaster, famine-affected people were also reported to have left food-aid centres to return home in time for planting. However, 20 years later, such coping strategies are being corroded across sub-Saharan Africa as the impacts of

HIV/AIDS force families to sell or eat the very assets that could enable them to recover.

At the individual level, resilience is a common characteristic of all human beings. Yet what is regarded as hardship in one context may be simply a way of life in another. For example, power cuts across Europe and North America during the summer of 2003 created serious disruptions to everyday life. Those who depend on electricity for cooking or cooling had no alternative provisions and found it difficult to adjust. In many other parts of the world, however, searching for the raw materials with which to cook a meal is a daily chore rather than a disaster. Clearly, supporting disaster resilience requires different kinds of intervention in different contexts.

These varying examples point towards a common issue: the importance of understanding the ability of individuals, communities or businesses not only to cope with, but also to *adapt* to adverse conditions and to focus any interventions at building on these strengths. The development community has made significant shifts towards people-centred policies and approaches based on local capacities. Yet, how far has the disaster community – in its delivery of humanitarian assistance or promotion of disaster risk reduction – moved in this direction?

While conceptually the importance of people and their strengths are understood, there is little analysis of how people survive in the face of disasters. And there is even less programming that builds on the resilience strategies of disaster-prone communities. Afghanistan is a case in point. Despite 25 years of conflict and four years of drought, Afghans have dispelled the myth, subscribed to by many in the West, that they are helpless victims, and have shown astonishing resilience in the face of crisis (see Box 1.2).

This edition of the *World Disasters Report* examines community resilience with specific reference to disasters, case studies and good practices. It advocates a stronger emphasis on approaches to humanitarian, risk reduction and development work which put *resilience*, rather than just need or vulnerability, at the heart of the debate.

Shift from vulnerability to capacity

Emergency appeals inevitably concentrate on identifying the vulnerable and their needs. Far less attention is given to what affected communities can do for themselves and how best to strengthen them. This lack of interest is not surprising given the complexity of resilience strategies, which require in-depth research to understand. Equally complex are the ways of linking household and community coping mechanisms to national and international policy and practice. Many countries or organizations do not have inclination or capacity for such research and most humanitarian operations do not allow time for much beyond the traditional needs assessment approach. This is equally true of

Box 1.2 Part 1: Afghan farmers recover more quickly than expected

After the fall of the Taliban regime it was assumed that Afghanistan was a food security 'basket case', and that massive support would be required from the international community for a number of years to prevent famine. Since then, however, experience has shown that although there are still a number of areas of acute vulnerability, rural Afghans have rebuilt their livelihoods far ahead of schedule.

As the Taliban were leaving Kabul in late 2001, a 'crisis narrative' dominated the contingency planning under way among donors and operational agencies waiting at the border. They expected that farmers had 'eaten their seeds', lost all productive capacity or were simply too weak to farm.

They were wrong. By 2003, Afghanistan's cereal production was estimated to be one of the largest ever recorded. Even other crops, such as potatoes and melons, were extremely successful. Seed distributions and other aid programmes helped, but the vast majority of farmers undoubtedly ploughed, sowed and harvested without ever seeing any aid. The assumption that food security would require massive aid interventions for a number of years ignored the extraordinary latent dynamism among Afghanistan's farmers. Agencies found it easier to speculate about losses than to try and understand how people pull together to rebound in the wake of a crisis.

The current version of the 'crisis narrative' focuses on the threat of too much agricul- tural production – in the form of opium. Afghanistan is said to be in danger of becoming a 'narco-mafia state'. The establishment of a strong licit economy and a modestly well-functioning government are essen-tial bulwarks to protect Afghanistan from again degenerating into a rogue and dangerous state, threatening its citizens and the world at large. Agricultural recovery has been portrayed as both the fundamental problem and the essential solution for Afghanistan. The recovery of poppy production is the primary threat, but it is at the same time acknowledged that alternatives to the illicit economy will primarily need to be found in agriculture.

So far, however, the experience of Afghan reconstruction does not support this 'either-or' narrative of a strong, healthy, licit economy or the emergence of a narco-mafia state. Afghanistan has proven surprisingly capable of developing both licit and illicit agricultural economies. It is apparent that rural people have been getting on with bridging the relief/development continuum themselves, by rapidly increasing their production of wheat, poppies and other cash crops. The sum result shows that none of the assumptions of outsiders, be they of food security, community resilience or agriculture-based growth are really in tune with the efforts of millions of Afghan farmers getting on with their lives.

What then is the role of the international community to support these processes? Studies of rural livelihoods by the Kabul-based Afghanistan Research and Evaluation Unit and an international review of agricultural rehabilitation programming by the United Kingdom's Overseas Development Institute point to the importance of focusing interventions much more on supporting the markets and institutions through which rural people rebuild their farming livelihoods. Simply handing out seeds is not enough.

International Federation
of Red Cross and Red Crescent Societies

Box 1.2 Part 2: Afghan children dispel myths of war trauma

What has been the impact of 24 years of war on children's mental health? How can they be healed when there are so few psychiatrists? Is Afghanistan now burdened with a generation of children who know only what it is to kill and take revenge? These questions – frequently asked by international journalists and aid workers alike – spring from assumptions that reflect only a fraction of the reality in Afghanistan.

Of course, Afghan children have lived through events that most of us would not wish upon any child. There is something about children that makes us want to protect them and assume that any harm will affect them negatively. But, as I work with Afghan children, I am constantly amazed at their resilience and fortitude. They have experienced terrible suffering but are still able to live as children, to play, to learn and to laugh. I do not, generally, find children overwhelmed by trauma but children who have come through suffering with their humanity and hope intact. Much of the credit must go to Afghan parents. They bear the brunt of difficult events to shield their children, while teaching them how to cope when bad things do happen. Research among children and their families in Kabul during 2002 revealed that children are taught several key qualities to help them cope:

■ First is courage. Children are expected to learn how to overcome fear – by confronting their fears and by being reassured when they are afraid.

■ Second, they are taught how to be thankful – for still being alive after an attack or for being better off than others around them.

■ Third, children are encouraged to be happy through playing, joking, picnicking, going to school, being with friends. Afghans understand that if children have happiness in their life, they are much more able to cope with sadness.

■ Fourth, children are expected to have religious faith. They are taught prayers to say when they are scared. They are encouraged to understand that everything that happens to them is in the hands of God, beyond their control and therefore to be accepted.

■ Finally, children are taught morality. As parents in Kabul note, it is one thing to be exposed to bad events but it is another to know right from wrong. Children need not automatically follow the paths of the wrong.

Afghans know that children who have such qualities will be affected by violence but not permanently scarred by it. Exposure to war might even enhance these positive traits. Certainly in Afghanistan, the thirst for peace, the hunger for knowledge, the strength and motivation among young people will prove to be a major resource in a country struggling to get back on its feet for many years to come. ■

the consolidated appeals of the United Nations Office for the Coordination of Humanitarian Assistance (OCHA) as it is for the emergency appeals of the International Federation of Red Cross and Red Crescent Societies.

It is no surprise that opportunities to go beyond needs assessment exist in recurrent, seasonally predictable or slowly changing situations such as droughts or food security crises. International and local development actors have found a balance between the anthropology on the one hand and more 'quick and dirty' methods (through participatory rural appraisal) on the other. Rural development and famine studies of the 1970s and 1980s have pioneered this approach in identifying how households survive and how their resilience gradually breaks down. Strategies employed by poor families to protect their assets by adapting to changing conditions formed the focus of this work. Influenced by a people-centred approach to development, particularly in the field of food security, the emphasis shifted from what people lacked towards what actions they took, what their priorities were and how to build on what was already there.

In the field of disasters, especially rapid-onset events such as earthquakes, windstorms and floods, most emphasis has remained on needs assessment and risk-based approaches. Identifying, assessing, recording, mapping and ranking hazard characteristics, vulnerability indicators and risk factors still dominate the disaster community's practices – at the expense of analysing the strengths, skills and resources available within communities to build resilience in the face of hazards. Even practice concerned with mitigating, preventing or preparing for disasters is often defined under the general rubric of *disaster risk reduction*, implying a certain level of risk and ways of lowering it, rather than an equally explicit identification of levels of resilience and ways of strengthening it.

In practice, vulnerability also means the deficit of capacities to cope with hazards, and resilience exists only in the context of adversity, so these two concepts co-exist. But capacities and resilience are often only implicitly assumed and not disaggregated or analysed as systematically as needs, vulnerabilities or risks. For example, characterizing Bangladesh as being at high risk from cyclones and floods conceals what has been achieved and why life losses from disasters there have been reduced significantly over the last ten years. Speculations are made, from the nature of cyclones to the role of improved early warning systems or community-based disaster preparedness as significant contributing factors. But even in a country like Bangladesh, where there is a considerable amount of community development work, what has contributed to increased resilience to cyclones is not analysed or understood nearly as thoroughly as the hazard events themselves and vulnerabilities to those hazards.

Following on from earlier work in rural development, the systematic assessment of capacities and vulnerabilities under the same framework was introduced into the field of disasters at the end of 1980s, principally by Mary B. Anderson and Peter J. Woodrow in their 1989 publication *Rising From The Ashes*. Their framework, known as Capacities and Vulnerabilities Analysis (CVA), aimed to address the more positive attributes of people caught up in disasters and developed a systematic way of looking at physical, institutional, social, economic and gender-based strengths.

A number of organizations, particularly non-governmental organizations (NGOs) and the International Federation, have been employing frameworks that are fundamentally based on the CVA approach. In practice, these assessments use variations of the earlier 'quick and dirty' community-based appraisal methods which place people, their participation and their priorities at the centre of development work. Like its predecessors, the CVA framework – and the local capacities for peace or 'do no harm' approach also promoted by Anderson – calls for an understanding and recognition of what is already in place and why, before any external interventions are foreseen.

It is noticeable, however, that humanitarian actors hardly ever use the CVA approach – whether in preparing for disasters, alongside needs assessments to promote a better-informed relief strategy or to inform appropriate post-disaster interventions. Outsiders often admit much later that people have apparently demonstrated their coping strategies and resilience. Of course they have been resilient – that is why they are still there. But many more may have perished, the coping process may have collapsed and resilience may mean bouncing back to a situation that is far worse than before the disaster. Ideally, we need to know whether people can cope or be resilient *before* the situation turns into a disaster.

Despite best intentions, however, identifying what is missing in a crisis situation (i.e., needs and vulnerabilities) is both more tempting and perhaps better rationalizes the intervention than identifying what is already in place (i.e., capacities). This applies to both humanitarian aid and community-level disaster preparedness and mitigation. A recent meeting of international and local NGOs on CVA methods, organized by the ProVention Consortium, once again highlighted the weakness of many programmes in systematically identifying capacities, while mapping of hazards, risks and vulnerabilities are routine work.

Meanwhile, just as dangerous as ignoring coping and adaptive capacities completely is the danger that outsiders, impressed by the mere fact of survival, romanticize community resilience. To some extent, this was the case in southern Africa over much of the past decade, where the breakdown (due to many complex and new factors) of traditional strategies for coping with droughts went unrecognized by the aid community. The task is not to marvel at what communities can accomplish even under the most adverse conditions, but rather to create the conditions that make coping less destructive and resilience much more than simply a return to vulnerability.

It is an indictment of the disaster management system that it has not been able to reorient itself in this way over the last 20 years, despite all the rhetoric and policies to the contrary. While concepts have moved on, disaster management has little more knowledge of how to build on livelihoods than it did during the first wave of livelihoods research in the 1970s and 1980s. The question now is: what is needed for that kind of shift to take place and what are the best examples of building on the strengths of disaster-affected communities?

Sustainable livelihoods: 'layers of resilience'

The renewed emphasis on identifying and building strengths, rather than just examining deficits, represents a paradigm shift in how to address issues of concern to communities living with risk. In the development field, the sustainable livelihoods (SL) approach – first promoted by Chambers and Conway in 1992 – has become an important organizing framework for the efforts of a wide range of multilateral agencies, donors, NGOs and government bodies. Based on the earlier work of the 1970s and 1980s in rural development, SL is concerned with the potential, competence, capacities and strengths – rather than weaknesses and needs – of communities. This does not mean that only the more able members of the community get recognized. Rather, the assumption is that even the worst-off may have some potential, so the focus of interventions must be on removing constraints to the realization of this potential.

The SL approach recognizes a range of strengths or assets – which it calls 'capitals' – as essential to sustain a livelihood. These include:

- **natural** capital: water, land, rivers, forests and minerals;
- **financial** capital: savings, income, remittances, pensions, credit, state transfers;
- **human** capital: knowledge, skills, health, physical ability;
- **social** capital: networks, relations, affiliations, reciprocity, trust, mutual exchange; and
- **physical** capital: infrastructure, shelter, tools, transport, water and sanitation, energy.

In the SL approach, coping with adversities and change is seen as a normal part of life that involves adapting to anything from seasonal floods or droughts to changing family circumstances, economic cycles or political upheaval. As such, disasters – including the capacity to resist their impact and bounce back – are part and parcel of a wider development framework. This is a significant change from the traditional risk reduction approach, which takes as its starting point hazards, vulnerability and disaster risk – then looks for relationships and linkages with development and ways of mainstreaming disasters into development.

These complex webs of assets, capacities, resources and strengths together provide people with what Glavovic and others have called 'layers of resilience' to deal with 'waves of adversity' – including disasters. For the purpose of protecting people from various adversities, each kind of capital has something vital to offer, although different combinations of capital will be called upon to cope with and recover from different kinds of risk and adversity.

Natural capital

Natural capital is essential for the survival of both rural and urban populations. These assets are compromised by many factors, including population increase, deforestation, overgrazing, climatic variability, ownership issues, poor water and soil management, industrial and household waste, pollution, inadequate drainage and sanitation, and poor governance. The relationship between hydro-meteorological disasters and natural assets is well recognized. Environmental degradation can increase the impact of floods and landslides. On the other hand, disasters such as fires, droughts and floods can cause serious damage to forests, farmland and livestock.

Increasing environmental resilience is not an easy task as it takes a very long time and the benefits may not be easily or quickly visible. Nevertheless, there are many small-scale measures that can be taken at the community level to try and increase environmental resilience, in turn reducing the impact of future disasters. Case studies from rural India in Chapter 3 relate the work of local NGOs in supporting communities' own ideas for creating social forestry and fish-farming projects to recover from the impact of the 'supercyclone' that hit Orissa in 1999; rediscovering indigenous, drought-resistant seeds and traditional farming techniques to boost resilience to drought and debt in Andhra Pradesh; and rainwater harvesting as part of post-earthquake reconstruction in Gujarat, to help address the problems of ongoing drought.

Meanwhile, Chapter 5 presents an innovative joint venture in the Philippines between the government, a Filipino NGO and a local 'people's organization' to establish a community-based forestry project. The aim is to prevent illegal logging and soil erosion, thereby protecting villagers from the threat of landslides while providing them with an income from sustainable timber harvesting.

These examples of strengthening resilience highlight the importance of both helping affected populations bounce back from disaster and building a stronger natural resource base to prevent future disasters.

Financial capital

Access to financial capital such as income, savings, remittances and credit is a critical resilience factor. However, accurately assessing and boosting financial capital in aid programmes requires a great deal of skill and experience – as well as gender sensitivity, since women and men access and control financial capital in different ways. The availability of economic assets undoubtedly increases the resilience of people to disasters and helps them recover more quickly. Aid organizations are increasingly experimenting with post-disaster micro-finance and cash aid, instead of simply distributing relief items. The advantage of cash is that disaster-affected people can direct it towards their own highest recovery priorities.

However, cash does not always protect people if the risks are not understood. Our analysis of December 2003's Bam earthquake in Chapter 4 reveals how money alone did not make people safer: both rich and poor, the powerful and the powerless, suffered during the quake, losing homes and family members. But during the post-disaster period, the wealthier could access financial resources to recover faster. Meanwhile, for the poor, aid handouts were soon replaced by cash-vouchers – an innovative approach for Iran, which helped to speed up recovery and boost the local economy at the same time.

Following the Gujarat earthquake of January 2001, one group of very poor craftswomen found a way to make their lives even better than before the disaster. Key to their success was membership of a union supported by the Self-Employed Women's Association (SEWA), an Indian NGO whose aim is to help its 220,000 members strengthen their livelihoods. This enabled the craftswomen to access credit to buy raw materials for their embroidery and tarpaulin covers under which to work. It also helped them invest in rebuilding safer houses. Meanwhile, a recent survey in the Gujarati town of Bhuj, at the epicentre of the quake, found that 9,800 slum-dwelling families had invested nearly US$ 300,000 of their own money into improving their homes and livelihoods in the two years following the disaster (see Box 1.3).

Supporting local commitment to recovery is one of the most useful contributions that aid agencies can make. Lending money to communities at risk – or at least guaranteeing loans – can prove more productive than simply building physical structures. For example, rather than funding and implementing recovery projects themselves, several local NGOs working in disaster-stricken parts of Gujarat and Orissa have ensured that affected villagers can access government compensation schemes and soft loans to help them rebuild their homes and lives themselves (see Chapter 3).

During times of crisis, most of those at risk prioritize their ability to earn an income above all else. Field research in the Philippines shows that when rural farming communities and the agricultural labour on which they depend are hit by floods, female household members will often seek paid employment in the cities or even abroad, sometimes for years at a time, to enable their families to recover (see Chapter 5). However, during the recent drought in southern Africa, the migration of seasonal labourers to farms in Zimbabwe from neighbouring countries (a well-known coping strategy in times of drought) was not widely possible, due to political tensions and changes in the ownership of farmland.

Remittances from relations living and working in other parts of the country and abroad are known to play a significant role in building resilience back home, as was the case after both the Gujarat and the Turkey earthquakes. Migrant workers remit about US$ 80 billion per year to developing countries – considerably more than the

International Federation of Red Cross and Red Crescent Societies

Box 1.3 Gujarat's poor invest to recover

The poor were the first and most active investors in their own coping and recovery after the earthquake that shattered the Indian town of Bhuj, Gujarat, in January 2001. Based on a study of 14 low-income areas in Bhuj, the Ahmedabad-based Disaster Mitigation Institute (DMI) found that slum dwellers made rapid, cash investments to replace earthquake-damaged homes and revitalize their livelihoods.

The DMI study encompassed 9,800 families (42,000 people), of whom 40 per cent depended for their livelihoods on casual labour, while the remainder earned a living through home-based work, vending or small businesses. As well as losing their homes, many families also lost small shops and essential equipment, such as handcarts.

During the two years following the earthquake, these families alone invested a total of 13 million rupees (about US$ 289,000) into post-disaster recovery. Of this figure, they spent just over half on improving their shelters and invested the remainder into their livelihoods and businesses. Shelter improvements ranged from adding reinforcement walls or extending roof beams to rebuilding entire dwellings. Their investment in economic recovery included buying raw materials or new tools and spending money on better marketing.

One Bhuj resident, Mohangar Goswami, sold iced drinks before the earthquake. After the disaster, he invested 2,000 rupees (around US$ 44) in his business and now earns 3,000 rupees a month. "I do not want relief or compensation," says Goswami, "if I can run my business well, that is my best coping."

Another slum dweller, Keshubhai Maheshwari, invested 5,000 rupees into his shoe-making business in the two years following the quake. "Whatever I save, I invest in my business – to buy tools, raw materials and produce in bulk – to stand up on my two feet," he says with pride.

The study also found that the poor from these 14 slums were willing to invest up to 20 million rupees (around US$ 444,000), over a period of time, to repay the costs of providing community infrastructure such as clean water and sanitation facilities, domestic electricity connections and primary health care. However, they need a cost-recovery mechanism to pool their resources.

The personal investments in recovery made by the slum dwellers of Bhuj were timely, came in suitable amounts and – most remarkable of all – were in the form of up-front cash. They also brought other advantages:

- The investments directly targeted recovery and therefore helped alleviate poverty.
- The returns on these investments helped to stimulate the local economy.
- The investments cost the Indian taxpayer almost nothing.

The Asian Development Bank, the government of Gujarat, businesses and individual citizens are also investing significant resources in the recovery of Gujarat's towns. However, if the investment climate could be improved to encourage poorer investors, then far more local resources could be attracted to promote recovery in earthquake-struck towns across the state. ■

US$ 55 billion of aid from rich countries – although not all remittances are used for humanitarian or development purposes.

Human capital

Human capital in the form of knowledge, skills, health and physical ability determine an individual's level of resilience more than any other asset. Ill-health or lack of education are recognized as core dimensions of poverty as well as of vulnerability to disaster.

Our analysis in Chapter 6 of the crisis gripping southern Africa shows how the HIV/AIDS pandemic has combined with drought and destitution to render traditional ways of coping with food insecurity inadequate. As the virus targets Africa's most productive adults, rural households find it hard to continue farming. And the burden of caring for sick family members means that otherwise healthy adults are not free to seek wage labour in nearby towns. The hunger and poverty, which inevitably follow, lower people's resistance to opportunistic infections and force them to sell vital livestock and even sex for food or cash. Children drop out of school, as their parents cannot afford the fees or have already died, leaving the orphans to fend for themselves. So the disease undermines the human capital of the next generation too.

Breaking this vicious downwards spiral and strengthening resilience to HIV/AIDS is a colossal task, cutting across many different sectors. At an individual level, antiretroviral drugs can prolong the lives of infected people by up to 20 years. Governments in the region, such as Botswana, South Africa and Swaziland, are now beginning to make such treatment available to those who could not normally afford it. However, ensuring that the drugs are effectively and safely administered requires investing in health-care facilities and trained professionals.

In addition, programmes that focus on boosting awareness of HIV/AIDS and knowledge of its causes and consequences are particularly important to help break down stigma and prevent the disease's spread. In the Kenyan town of Mombasa, for example, local Islamic leaders now raise HIV/AIDS issues in public at evening prayers. In Swaziland, the World Food Programme is providing schools with food to encourage children from families weakened by disease and poverty to return to education.

People at risk from disasters may sometimes view education as more important than other, traditional risk reduction measures. Chapter 7, which analyses urban risk and resilience in the slums of India, describes how one woman, interviewed in her poorly-built shack under a bridge in Mumbai, appeared to be living at great risk from floods and water-borne diseases. However, it emerged that she owned an apartment in another part of the city, which she rented out so that she could afford to give her daughter a good education. She decided her family's long-term resilience was best served by investing in the human capital of her only child.

International Federation
of Red Cross and Red Crescent Societies

Our case study in Chapter 3 of drought-affected communities in India's Andhra Pradesh (AP) state reveals that the knowledge vital for resilience is not necessarily related to power or wealth. A combination of drought and pest attacks has decimated cash crops – such as wheat, rice and cotton – across the state, leading to widespread destitution and thousands of farmer suicides. This prompted a local NGO to promote community 'gene' funds, to rediscover and store local varieties of drought-resistant food grains. They found that *dalit* (low-caste) women had a detailed knowledge of indigenous sorghum and millet seeds. The women were put in charge of the gene funds and soon found that both their livelihoods and their status in the community were improving, as farmers – including wealthy and high-caste men – approached them to purchase the seeds.

Knowledge and well-being are equally important assets in developed countries. Chapter 2 analyses the impact of heatwaves that killed up to 35,000 mainly elderly people across Europe in summer 2003 in one of the continent's most deadly disasters of recent decades. Yet a little basic knowledge – such as wrapping yourself in damp cloths or drinking enough cold water – could greatly boost the resilience of elderly people to excess heat. Knowledge in the form of early warning about unusually hot weather from meteorologists could help medical staff and carers prevent tragedies like this from happening again.

In all this report's case studies, knowledge of risks and responses provides a vital underpinning to resilience. Adaptive capacity is closely related to learning, but the knowledge generated must be relevant. Often, it is international aid organizations themselves that must listen to communities at risk and learn the ways in which they cope with crisis, so that programmes to create resilience can build on those human skills and resources. The World Bank's *Voices of the Poor* project was one such approach, which chronicled the struggles and aspirations of more than 60,000 poor women and men from 60 countries. The next challenge is ensuring that surveys like this feed into policy and influence practice.

Social capital

There is much debate about what exactly is meant by the term 'social capital'. In the sustainable livelihoods context it is taken to mean the forms of mutual social assistance upon which people draw. These include networks such as clan or caste; membership of more formalized groups such as women's associations; or affiliations of religion or ethnicity. These social networks can provide an informal safety net during difficult times and often play a pivotal role in helping people access resources urgently needed after disaster, such as credit or labour.

One of the most significant characteristics of resilient communities is the extent to which they work together towards a common aim – a function of their social cohesion.

It is important not to romanticize the extent to which all communities share this characteristic. What makes a community cohere has long been the subject of debate. Groups that are homogenous in terms of class, ethnicity, livelihood or wealth are more likely to cooperate in building resilience to disaster than communities divided by those attributes. Community cohesion may be a function of individual education. Or it may derive from the extent to which the group is aware of a common threat which galvanizes them to seek a common response – as is the case for inhabitants of flood-threatened Tuti island on the River Nile in Khartoum, Sudan (see Box 1.4).

Box 1.4 Tuti islanders fight floods together

Tuti island lies in the heart of the Sudanese capital Khartoum, at the confluence of the White Nile and the Blue Nile. Around 15,000 residents live on the 8-square-kilometre island, including farmers, businessmen and government employees. People have lived on Tuti for more than five centuries and the inhabitants have a strong sense of community identity and independence from Khartoum. A ferry is the only link with the mainland.

Tuti is highly flood-prone. Floods in 1946, 1988, 1998 and 2001 engulfed parts of the island, destroying homes, farms and livelihoods. The Sudanese government has repeatedly urged the Tuti islanders to move permanently to higher ground on the mainland, but they have always vehemently resisted relocation. Not only has Tuti been the ancestral home for many generations of islanders, it is a rural, tranquil haven in the centre of a busy city. Yet it is also a high-risk environment. To protect themselves, islanders have developed a number of ingenious coping strategies, spanning the whole disaster management cycle, from mitigation and preparedness to response and reconstruction.

The islanders practise various traditional mitigation measures. To prevent flood waters entering their houses, they elevate the walls and entrances to their homes. External walls are plastered to make them waterproof. To prevent erosion, villagers join forces to shore up the riverbanks with sandbags and tree saplings. The community is responsible for planting and taking care of the trees, as well as for maintaining the river banks.

Villagers have developed a sophisticated system of disaster planning and preparedness. When the flood season approaches, local leaders set up a flood-control committee which is in charge of contingency planning, coordinating emergency operations and providing material assistance. Local subcommittees deal with aid stocks and disbursement, communications and coordination, food supplies, health and finance. Volunteers run all these committees. The flood-control committee classifies risk areas on the island according to three categories: high, medium and low risk.

The island is also subdivided into river observation units (*tayat*), to which volunteers are assigned. Each *taya* has a leader, some of whom are chosen by the people while others are appointed by the flood-control committee. Every *taya* consists of a headquarters tent and two auxiliary tents, one for providing health services and the other for preparing meals. *Taya* leaders identify the needs of the group they are in charge of and supervise the work of their volunteers, reporting back to the flood committee on a regular basis. In

International Federation
of Red Cross and Red Crescent Societies

addition, schools and clubs in Tuti are used as stores – complete with storekeeper – to stock sackcloth for sandbags, shovels and hoes. Food stores are established, and the local branch of the Sudanese Red Crescent Society stocks medicines, particularly anti-malaria tablets.

When river levels start to rise, the flood committee coordinates 24-hour river patrol teams. Residents heap up sandbags along the shore to keep the floods at bay. Youth teams distribute hoes, shovels and sackcloth for sandbags to the most threatened parts of the island. When the Nile threatens to break through the first defences, river patrol volunteers use drums and the megaphone on the mosque's minaret to warn the population of impending disaster. If parts of the island succumb to the flood waters, local Red Crescent volunteers organize search and rescue, provide first aid, conduct disease surveillance and distribute drinking water.

Those affected by floods will usually be sheltered by family members who live on higher ground. Others seek refuge in the mosque or primary school or live on the roofs of their flooded homes until the river waters recede. Local inhabitants shoulder the bulk of post-disaster reconstruction. Homes are often rebuilt through mutual assistance, while public buildings are reconstructed through collective action.

Using inventive, well-organized coping mechanisms, the people of Tuti have managed to withstand the major floods in Sudan's recent history without suffering major casualties. External assistance has been limited to an absolute minimum. Tuti island may not be a unique case in Sudan, but certain specific conditions have undoubtedly contributed to the effectiveness of local flood resilience:

■ The island's population is culturally very homogeneous. Families have lived here for many generations and the strong social cohesion of these closely-knit groups greatly contributes to resilience and resourcefulness in the face of floods.
■ The islanders' independence and pride – as well as fear of eviction – has stimulated them to find local solutions to the threats they face without depending on external assistance.
■ The islanders' detailed knowledge of their specific local environment plays a large part in explaining their ability to resist recurrent hazards.
■ The constant risk of flooding and seasonal fluctuations in river levels have made islanders highly risk-aware and committed to maintaining successful coping mechanisms.

Although the Tuti island experience may not easily be replicated in other flood-prone areas, this case study shows that under particular circumstances it is possible for highly risk-prone communities successfully to mitigate, prepare for, cope with and recover from the impacts of natural hazards without being dependent on external aid.

Learning the lessons of Tuti, the Sudanese Red Crescent, with support from the ProVention Consortium and the International Federation, is introducing a community-based self-reliance training programme in Khartoum and Kassala states. The training provides local leaders with the knowledge to develop effective disaster preparedness plans, committees and risk reduction activities in their communities. The programme helps communities put these plans into practice using locally available resources and promotes coordination among local organizations and individuals involved in disaster management. The long-term aim is to strengthen community resilience and reduce the level of external assistance required to protect these communities each time disaster strikes. ■

One Indian NGO engaged in supporting the resilience of rural villages in Orissa puts so much emphasis on the need to create social cohesion that they insist on working with everyone in the community or no one (see Chapter 3). The months of village meetings it can take to create the required consensus are considered to be as valuable as any subsequent investments in physical infrastructure.

Equally, however, community cohesion can be undermined by poorly conceived aid interventions – whether by governments or NGOs. Recent evidence from Santa Fe province in Argentina, following the worst floods there for a century, suggests that too much in the form of state welfare handouts, combined with too little progress or transparency in the authorities' rehabilitation plans, generated a sense of dependency among flood-affected working-class people, as they waited – with mounting expectation and frustration – for the government to deliver on its promises. Meanwhile, middle-class residents who received few state benefits organized themselves into mutual support groups (see Box 1.5).

The critical role of social networks in coping with hazards is evident in all our case studies. Elderly people in close social contact with their friends and neighbours are more likely to survive heatwaves, as their vulnerability is recognized earlier, while those people 'invisible' to society suffer most (see Chapter 2). Social cohesion erodes more easily in urban areas, where extended family structures fragment and the bonds of common livelihoods break down. Research into slum dwellers in Mumbai reveals both the breakdown of social resilience in urban settings and its possible re-creation through joint ownership and protection of physical assets, such as pottery kilns needed to generate a communal income (see Chapter 7, Box 7.2).

Following December 2003's colossal earthquake in Bam, the whole relief and recovery process depended on traditional, informal social networks: city groups of 'notables' or 'white beards' proved a useful medium for distributing aid, while every province in Iran adopted a neighbourhood in Bam to help meet the needs of survivors (see Chapter 4). The experience of Bam also reveals the importance of the *cultural* dimension of resilience, which, although often neglected in the SL approach, can prove to be one of the strongest assets in creating mutual support. Within a month of the earthquake, for example, 90 per cent of the 1,850 children orphaned by the disaster had been taken into the homes of their extended families.

In some societies, culture and religion can create complacency and fatalism, leading people to regard a disaster as an act of God rather than the result of human negligence. But fatalism and religious faith can also be comforting and healing when hope has diminished, giving survivors the strength to externalize the tragedy and face up to its consequences – as was the case in Bam. Hence, faith is a form of psychological and communal resilience in times of hardship.

International Federation of Red Cross and Red Crescent Societies

Physical capital

Physical capital comprises the basic infrastructure, goods and services needed to support sustainable livelihoods, including secure shelter and buildings, clean water supply, sanitation, adequate tools, affordable transport and energy, and access to information and communications. 'Lifeline' infrastructure in disaster-prone areas, such as hospitals, government offices, emergency services' headquarters and stores, schools and cyclone shelters, needs to be strong enough to withstand any natural hazards. However, Bam's three hospitals collapsed or were badly damaged during the earthquake, which meant injured people had to be airlifted to other hospitals – costing more lives and money (see Chapter 4).

Building stronger homes in Orissa *before* the 'supercyclone' struck in 1999 proved life-saving for the people of Samiapalli, while investing in a water harvesting and irrigation system in the Gujarati village of Patanka has greatly improved community recovery and livelihoods since the earthquake of 2001 (see Chapter 3). Meanwhile, more than 2.2 million people a year, in urban and rural areas, die from water and sanitation-related diseases – many of them children in urban slums. Improving physical infrastructure such as piped clean water, covered toilets and sewage disposal could save thousands of lives (see Chapter 7).

Physical mitigation measures – such as seawalls, dykes to contain flooding rivers or terraces to prevent soil erosion – are particularly popular with donors keen to display the visible effects of their aid. While such 'hardware' measures should always be accompanied by 'software' measures (e.g., training, awareness, strengthening social cohesion), physical structures serve important protective and symbolic purposes. In the Philippines, for example, concrete walls built to reduce the impact of coastal storm surges are seen as embodying the achievements of participating villagers as well as providing a focus around which to build cooperation with local authorities (see Chapter 5).

Challenges of community-level action

Most poverty analysis, including the sustainable livelihoods framework, starts with the household as the basic unit of analysis. While the concept of resilience applies to every level from individual to global, the main focus of our case studies is on the community level. Understanding how communities work is considered key to understanding resilience and a precondition for helping strengthen people's capacities to cope with and recover from disaster.

But how valid is this level of analysis, how true is the notion of 'community' as a homogeneous, caring, moral and cooperative group of people attached to a place? Is it just wishful thinking? Are there dangers in assuming that such communities exist, that they are the 'place' or 'group' of people where something should be done? Where

Box 1.5 Argentine floods: state aid saps resilience

Torrential rains during April 2003 precipitated the worst floods Argentina has witnessed for a century. The poorer farming provinces in the north were hardest hit and a third of Santa Fe city was inundated, forcing 150,000 people to evacuate their homes within the space of a few hours. The disaster followed close behind a four-year economic and social crisis, which plunged 22 million Argentinians – more than half the population – into poverty and saw unemployment soar to 25 per cent.

During the flooding, the Argentine public showed great solidarity in their concern for those affected. Some 6,000 Red Cross volunteers and staff helped rescue survivors and distribute supplies of food and clothing donated from across the country. In Santa Fe itself, fellow citizens used their boats and canoes to help over 75,000 people to safety. The rising waters had, in just a few hours, equalized a socially stratified population of business people, intellectuals, workers, impoverished middle classes, the 'structurally' (long-term) poor and the unemployed.

What prompted this display of solidarity? Was it simply momentary human compassion in the face of sudden flooding, or were other factors at work? Did the social cohesion displayed in the face of disaster develop into longer-term resilience or did it subside as swiftly as the flood waters?

Resilience among the newly impoverished middle classes continued to be evident as people began to rebuild their homes. Much of their cooperation in recovery could be attributed to the solidarity developed during the years of social crisis. Following the country's financial collapse in December 2001, there was unprecedented and almost constant social mobilization across different sectors. Both the unemployed and the middle

classes took to the streets. The *cacelorazos*, groups of the urban middle class who lost their savings due to devaluation, were largely responsible for bringing down the government of Fernando de la Rúa. These groups then transformed themselves into neighbourhood associations and new organizations for the unemployed. The number of NGOs soared and a nationwide network of over 500 bartering clubs sprang up. Social resilience flourished in the arid soil of a failing economic and political system.

After the 2003 floods, the government offered the newly poor middle classes little in the way of financial aid. So with support from family, friends and neighbourhood associations, they began the process of physical, emotional and financial recovery themselves. They improved their organizing capacity and demanded that the government answer why there was so much destruction in Santa Fe and what it was doing to ensure that such floods would never affect the city again. The provincial authorities have been forced to both listen to their citizenry and be much more accountable in their decisions and actions.

However, the structurally poor did not display the same levels of resilience and organization. A visit to the district of San Lorenzo, where the Red Cross and other NGOs were working in reconstruction projects, proved revealing. Several community members criticized Red Cross volunteers for not caring about their well-being – even though they were standing in the doorways of new homes that had just been built for them. One woman shouted at two Red Cross volunteers: "We are not dogs. We have rights." Rubbish was strewn across the streets

International Federation of Red Cross and Red Crescent Societies

around her and children were playing in stagnant, dirty water – but she did nothing about it. People were simply waiting for aid distributions or for someone else to come and solve their problems.

Volunteers recalled similar attitudes in some of the emergency shelters. They described how survivors waited for volunteers to arrive to cook and clean. Teachers complained that schools used as shelters were left in disarray, while chairs and desks were stolen.

So, despite the solidarity shown during the height of the floods, why did the newly impoverished middle classes continue to display such resilience in the aftermath of disaster, while the poor felt like the victims of injustice? One could argue that the middle classes are better educated and have more opportunities. But there are countless examples throughout the world of marginalized, 'uneducated' people organizing themselves to improve their quality of life. Why did some Argentinians complain about the treatment they received, while not taking steps to improve their own lives?

In the aftermath of the Santa Fe floods, the government took a leading role in providing for the poorest sectors of society. "Along the way," says Liliana Pantano, an Argentine sociologist, "the traditional solidarity was weakened as the government began to institute social programmes." For example, every poor family waiting for new or rehabilitated homes in the disaster-struck districts of La Tablada and San Lorenzo received monthly government subsidies through a programme, created in April 2002, which gives 150 pesos (about US$ 50) per month to unemployed heads of households who have families with children. Although the subsidy is supposed to be in return for working on community projects, the programme compares favourably with the 120 pesos per month that most families in La Tablada used to earn through the laborious process of brick-making.

However, the risk of creating dependency is very real when communities become used to receiving generous, ongoing state subsidies. The incentive for working together to solve common problems is undermined by social welfare programmes and handouts. Furthermore, the poorest members of society lack the skills or education needed to enter the mainstream economy. Many of those hardest hit by the floods now sit and wait. The government's welfare programmes provide them with more than they had in the past – as well as the prospect of receiving better housing.

A lack of transparency and urgency in the government's response has further embittered many of those affected by the Santa Fe floods. "Everything was politicized – who got what and even where houses were built," complains Jorge Fernández, director of programmes for the Argentine Red Cross. The flood occurred in the middle of elections and was used by candidates for criticizing opponents. Once the media spotlight on the disaster faded, government rehabilitation programmes were slow to unfold.

A year after the disaster, land allocation and housing construction for the poor have not been finalized. In La Tablada, 20 homeless families are still living in tents. Entering one, the smell of rotting canvas is almost overbearing. The children and elderly are suffering from respiratory illnesses. The look on most of their faces is one of defeat rather than defiance. Resilience often thrives when people are forced to assume responsibility for their own well-being. But a combination of joblessness, government subsidies and unfulfilled promises following disaster has sapped community resilience among Santa Fe's poorest. ■

social ties are bound tightly together by common history and interest, then disparities of class, gender and income seem to matter less. But in many cases of community-based disaster preparedness (DP) and mitigation, the idea of community is reduced simply to those people who *will* cooperate and doesn't necessarily include everyone in a particular location.

One DP project in Cambodia, described by a researcher from the United Kingdom's Coventry University, found considerable difficulties dealing with the internal tensions in the 'community'. As the project leader said: "The more powerful in society may not want the most vulnerable to participate. Therefore changing this may require advocacy by the NGO, which is not really compatible with a participatory research methodology, or bypassing the more powerful in society, which is not sustainable once the NGO has left. Doing this may actually endanger the most vulnerable, putting them at risk of reprisals."

In sociology, the problem has been known for many years, as sociologist Steven Brint pointed out recently: "An often repeated message of the community studies' literature is that communities are not very community-like. They are as rife with interest, power, and divisions as any market, corporation, or city government." Brint reports on sociological studies from more than 50 years ago that show "the comforting image of community-centred governance" was acknowledged to be an illusion and that, instead, supposed communities had "a self-interested and self-reproducing power structure ruling from behind the scenes".

Communities may well encompass areas of common interest, but power relations and existing structures of inequality must also be understood. In southern Africa, for example, the impacts of the HIV/AIDS pandemic are aggravated by people neglecting or abusing spouses or orphans within their own extended families (see Chapter 6, Box 6.1). And people living in urban slums are perpetually exposed to risk as long as they remain outside the system of legal governance. For example, the fear of eviction is a major disincentive for slum dwellers to invest in measures to disaster-proof their homes or improve their environments. Any capacity-building approach has to recognize that existing community structures do not necessarily provide the most amenable contexts within which to improve disaster resilience for all.

Sometimes it takes the wider 'community' of outsiders to break down the barriers to change which keep communities vulnerable. Outside organizations can act as *catalysts* for creating resilience by building awareness and consensus for action through meetings with community members, engaging local government and inspiring others to act by celebrating the examples of individuals or communities who have embraced change for the better.

However, community work like this may only be possible in situations where the poor and less powerful feel safe from reprisal. Approaches that do not aim to enhance social

International Federation
of Red Cross and Red Crescent Societies

status and representation as an integral part of the programme are likely to reinforce the position of those already in power. Either that, or there will be a rapid return to the status quo once the outsiders have left.

Putting the capacities of people and communities first may (erroneously) suggest that all relationships and progress can happen in political isolation. However, understanding resilience also requires understanding the policy and institutional environment, how people relate to it, where power lies, and what influences decision and change. Significantly, most of the advances in community-level work have been in areas where local empowerment has taken root, for example in the Philippines, Bangladesh, South Africa and parts of India and Latin America.

Another major concern arising from community-level work is how to 'scale up' isolated good practices to the national level, through promoting change in governmental policies and institutions. One Indian NGO in Orissa has begun scaling up its programmes for safer housing and cleaner water supply and sanitation by clustering new projects around villages that have already implemented projects (see Chapter 3). The aim is to create a 'critical mass' of practice sufficient to influence both governmental and aid agency policy. Meanwhile, in southern Africa, for example, it has taken years of lobbying from pressure groups to persuade national governments and drugs companies to provide antiretroviral drugs free of charge to poor HIV/AIDS sufferers.

After December 2003's massive earthquake hit Bam, the relief and recovery process depended on traditional social networks, including groups of 'notables' or 'white beards' who helped allocate aid.

© Christopher Black/ International Federation.

Conclusions

The pro-poor focus of the recent aid policies of most donor governments, and the shift towards identifying and supporting livelihoods, makes it timely to re-explore both the concept of resilience and the ways in which outsiders can build on the strengths of at-risk women and men for improved disaster preparedness, mitigation and response. If we, as outsiders, cannot understand these capacities and build on them, then we perpetuate the idea that 'we know best' and that only 'risk' matters. We thereby ignore the most important resource that currently exists in managing disasters and risks: people's own strategies to cope and adapt. Understanding and enhancing local resilience to risks is a responsibility for all actors in the aid community. It is not a question of leaving it to either humanitarian or development agencies. Rather, it is about a people-centred, developmental way of working – in relief, recovery, disaster risk reduction or development. Six key conclusions – relevant for local, national and international actors – can be drawn:

1. Sytematic assessment of what enables people to cope with, recover from and adapt to various risks and adversities – at household and community level – is badly needed. This will provide emergency planners, disaster risk managers and development actors with a clearer understanding of the foundations on which to build interventions that support resilience. Coping strategies of at-risk populations are poorly understood. Many people, especially the poor, tend to focus on their problems and weaknesses – as evident from the personal accounts reported in our case studies. But through confronting crisis or engaging in communal activities, people can begin to see their strengths in helping themselves and their neighbours. Equally, outsiders – even those working at community level – may recognize people's capacities without really understanding them. Our knowledge of what makes up resilience, how it can be measured and, above all, how it can be strengthened is still limited compared to our understanding of what constitutes need, hazard, risk or vulnerability.

2. Strengthening social capital should be the key objective of all disaster interventions, whether in relief, recovery or risk reduction – rather than a by-product. Our case studies reveal that unlocking the potential of communities to overcome traditional barriers and work together for a common cause is the key to increasing disaster resilience. But there is a lack of systematic analysis of how humanitarian aid and longer-term community programmes can either erode or enhance resilience. Building the social capital needed to ensure the success of any community action is often treated as an after-thought or by-product of programmes supporting risk reduction, rather than the main objective. The fundamental challenge is to change the mindsets of all actors in this field to prioritize strengthening social capital as the key objective of all interventions.

3. People-centred approaches to development provide models that can improve humanitarian aid and disaster risk management. In the field of development, there has been a significant paradigm shift over the last two decades towards a much more people-centred approach to aid that builds on strengths at household and community levels. The sustainable livelihoods framework incorporates shocks and disasters as part of the wider challenges facing development, rather than as adjuncts to it. Key assets that help poor people lift themselves out of poverty are also the basis for increasing their capacities to reduce, cope with and recover from the impacts of disaster. More systematic work is required to assess the value of these developmental approaches in improving humanitarian aid as well as disaster risk management.

4. New institutional strategies and cross-sectoral coalitions are required to boost the resilience of local livelihoods in the face of multidimensional risks. Recent research – including that from our case studies – suggests that people living with risk do not necessarily regard one-off disasters as the greatest hazard facing them. The security of their livelihoods is usually paramount. Threats to those livelihoods come in many forms – not only natural hazards, but also ill-health, lack of infrastructure, social discrimination and stigma, unaffordable credit or misguided government policies. So any attempts to increase community resilience to such a complex range of risks need to enhance the full range of natural, financial, human, social and physical assets. No single agency or institution – whether at local, national or international level – can deliver in all these areas. Hence, new context-specific coalitions between different actors (e.g., government, municipality, private sector, NGOs, community groups) and cutting across different sectors must be formed to meet the challenge.

5. Good governance is essential to create the environment in which more resilient communities can thrive. Just as many communities are vulnerable to risks across a range of sectors, so all communities are inevitably caught up in a larger web of relationships, where actions taken by different actors at different levels can hinder or help the resilience of their livelihoods. No community is an island. Some government policies can limit community empowerment while, conversely, an active civil society can invigorate community resilience. At-risk households need to gain access to political representation – at every level from community upwards – in order to influence the decisions that affect their lives. Aid organizations can facilitate this process by creating opportunities for dialogue between communities, local government, urban municipalities and the private sector, to ensure that the voices and needs of those at greatest risk are not marginalized.

6. Scaling up strategies based on the aspirations and capacities of people at risk remains the greatest challenge. The key to ensuring people's lives and livelihoods are resilient over the long term is through detailed assessment and people-centred programming at the community level. But replicating this approach across all communities and groups at risk is a colossal challenge. The incorporation of disaster risks into development planning through the sustainable livelihoods framework offers a promising way of scaling up issues of resilience into policy. The role for both domestic and international aid organizations is twofold: to ensure their humanitarian and development strategies are informed by the experiences and priorities of those at risk; and to represent those priorities at international and national levels to influence the policies of donors and national governments for the better. Ultimately, however, the successful scaling-up of programmes to promote community resilience depends on national actors taking a lead role.

Policy and practice that aim to build proactively on people's strengths – rather than simply targeting their vulnerabilities – could offer the positive paradigm shift badly needed to help the world's poor and marginalized cope with today's increasingly complex and interrelated risks and adversities.

Principal contributor was Yasemin Aysan, independent analyst of humanitarian and development issues, with additional contributions from Terry Cannon, co-author of At Risk: Natural hazards, people's vulnerability and disasters, *and Jonathan Walter, editor of the* World Disasters Report. *Box 1.1 was contributed by Jonathan Walter; Box 1.3 by Mihir R. Bhatt, Honorary Director, Disaster Mitigation Institute, Ahmedabad, India; Box 1.4 by Bruno Haghebaert, Senior Officer, ProVention Consortium Secretariat; and Box 1.5 by Jan Gelfand, an independent humanitarian and development consultant based in La Paz, Bolivia. Part 1 of Box 1.2 was contributed by Ian Christoplos, a consultant specializing in humanitarian and rural development issues; part 2, which first appeared in the* Crosslines Essential Field Guide to Afghanistan, *was contributed by Joanna de Berry, Save the Children (USA), Kabul.*

Sources and further information

Adger, Q.N. 'Social and ecological resilience: Are they related?' in *Progress in Human Geography*, vol. 3, no. 24, pp. 347-364.

Anderson, M.B. and Woodrow, P.J. *Rising from the Ashes: development strategies in times of disaster.* Boulder, CO: Intermediate Technology Publications/Lynne Rienner, 1998 (reprint).

Bebbington, A. 'Capitals and capabilities: a framework for analysing peasant viability, rural livelihoods and poverty' in *World Development*, vol. 27, no. 12, pp. 2021-2044, 1999.

Berkes, F., Colding, J. and Folke, C. (eds). *Navigating Social-Ecological Systems: Building Resilience for Complexity and Change.* Cambridge: Cambridge University Press, 2003.

Blaikie, P., Cannon, T., Davis, I. and Wisner, B. *At Risk: Natural hazards, people's vulnerability and disasters.* London: Routledge, 2004 (second edition).

Brint, S. '*Gemeinschaft* revisited: a critique and reconstruction of the community concept' in *Sociological Theory*, vol. 19, no.1, pp. 1-23, 2001.

Cannon, T., Twigg, J. and Rowell, J. *Social Vulnerability, Sustainable Livelihoods and Disasters.* Report to DFID Conflict and Humanitarian Assistance Department (CHAD) and Sustainable Livelihoods Support Office, 2003.

Carney, D. *Livelihood Approaches Compared.* London: Department of International Development (DFID), 1999.

Carpenter, S., et al. 'From Metaphor to Measurement: Resilience of What to What?' in *Ecosystems*, no. 4, pp. 765-781, 2001.

International Federation
of Red Cross and Red Crescent Societies

Chambers, R. (ed.). 'Vulnerability: How the Poor Cope' in *IDS Bulletin*, vol. 20, no. 2, April 1989.

Chambers, R. and Conway, G. R. *Sustainable Rural Livelihoods: Practical Concepts for the 21ˢᵗ Century*. IDS Discussion Paper No. 296, Institute for Development Studies, University of Sussex, 1992.

Christoplos, I. *Out of Step? Agricultural Policy and Afghan Livelihoods*. Kabul: Afghanistan Research and Evaluation Unit, 2004.

Comfort, L. *Shared Risk: Complex Systems in Seismic Response*. New York: Pergamon, 1999.

De Waal, A. *Famine that Kills: Darfur, Sudan, 1984-1985*, Oxford: Clarendon Press, 1989.

Dreze, J. and Sen, A., *Hunger and Public Action*, Oxford: Clarendon Press, 1989.

Girardet, E. and Walter, J. *Crosslines Essential Field Guide to Afghanistan*. Geneva: Media Action International, 2004 (second edition).

Glavovic, B.C., Scheyvens, R. and Overton J. 'Waves of Adversity, Layers of Resilience: Exploring the Sustainable Livelihoods Approach' in *Proceedings of the 3rd Biennial Conference of the International Development Studies Network of Aotearoa New Zealand*, Massey University, 5–7 December 2002.

Holling, C.S., 'Resilience and Stability of Ecological Systems' in *Annual Review of Ecological Systems*, no. 4, pp. 1-23, 1973.

Kendra, J. and Wachtendorf, T. *Elements of community resilience in the World Trade Center attack*. Newark, NJ: University of Delaware, Disaster Research Center, 2002.

Klein, R.J.T., Nicholls, R.J. and Thomalla, F. 'Resilience to natural hazards: How useful is this concept?' in *Environmental Hazards*, no. 5, pp. 35-45, 2003.

Narayan, D. et al., *Voices of the Poor: Can Anyone Hear Us?* New York: Oxford University Press/World Bank, 2000.

Scoones, I. *Sustainable Rural Livelihoods: A Framework for Analysis*. Institute of Development Studies, Sussex, 1998.

Twigg, J. 'Disaster risk reduction: Mitigation and preparedness in development and emergency planning' in *Good Practice Review*, No. 9, March 2004. Humanitarian Practice Network, Overseas Development Institute, London.

Williams, A. *The viability of integrating community based disaster management within NGO strategic management*. Unpublished coursework, Coventry University, 2003.

Web sites

Downtown Community Resource Center, New York City
http://www.communityresilience.org
Livelihoods Connect **http://www.livelihoods.org**
ProVention Consortium **http://wwwproventionconsortium.org**
Resilience Alliance **http://www.resalliance.org**
Small island developing states **http://www.sidsnet.org**
World Bank *Voices of the Poor* **http://www.worldbank.org/poverty/voices**

Focus on community resilience

Heatwaves: the developed world's hidden disaster

How does one of 2003's most fatal disasters occur in one of the most developed regions in the world? During August 2003, between 22,000 and 35,000 people died across Europe as a result of a scorching heatwave (see Box 2.1). Lives lost were calculated using the average number of deaths for that month of the year and attributing excess deaths to the heat.

In France, the national health ministry put the death toll at 14,802. In England and Wales, authorities estimated over 2,000 people died. In both Portugal and the Netherlands, the heatwave claimed at least 1,300 lives, while authorities in Italy and Spain indicated that 4,000 people died in each country. Reports in the press estimated that Germany suffered some 7,000 heat-related deaths.

On top of this catastrophic death toll, economic losses to agriculture and business from the summer drought totalled in excess of US$ 13 billion, according to the global reinsurance group, Munich Re.

Many government figures throughout Europe sought to shift responsibility for the heatwave onto global warming and nature's unpredictability. But for public health professionals, the heatwave served as a natural trigger for a disaster which exposed a breakdown in social networks, political failure to support an ageing population, and overwhelmed and run-down public health services.

This chapter will analyse the unnatural root causes behind one of Europe's worst disasters for decades. Why were authorities and communities so poorly prepared? How likely are more heatwaves in the future? What can be done to support those most at risk?

Silent, invisible killer

People in temperate countries find it hard to imagine heat as a disaster. With floods or hurricanes you can see the damage in a matter of minutes or hours. With heat, usually the worst to happen is that roads buckle, trains derail and livestock die. So who would have thought a bit of summer heat would kill so many people and cost so much in Europe? As the Associated Press wrote: "Europe's heatwave of 2003 stands as one of the deadliest weather phenomena in the last century. The intense heat caused billions of euro in damage, withering crops, sparking wildfires, decimating livestock and melting Alpine glaciers. But the greatest loss was human, mostly the frail and elderly who died alone in their homes because they were unable to cope with the temperatures."

Photo opposite page: A street thermometer in Bucharest, Romania. Europe's summer heatwave was the continent's most deadly disaster for at least a decade.

Radu Sigheti/Reuters,

Europe is not alone. Heatwaves kill more people in the United States than hurricanes, tornadoes, earthquakes and floods combined. The heatwave that hit Chicago in 1995 killed 739 people. In Australia, heatwaves are the most underrated natural disaster. According to government figures, they caused more deaths there than any other natural hazard during the 20th century. But response programmes are limited and few people are aware of the widespread dangers of heatwaves.

Heatwaves are not a typical natural hazard. The response is not high profile or high tech, as in the case of earthquakes, floods, hurricanes or even prolonged droughts. It is very much low profile – home visits and bottles of water. It falls into the gap between short-term emergency relief and long-term social care. As a result, heatwaves trigger unrecognized disasters, which explains why most governments and public health authorities frequently fail to raise the alarm in time. They are silent disasters in which those who suffer are the elderly and the marginalized. As Eric Klinenberg, author of *Heatwave: A social autopsy of disaster in Chicago,* writes: "Heatwaves are slow, silent, and invisible killers of silent and invisible people."

The dread factor

Why are heatwaves missing from disaster or public health policies? Klinenberg points out: "The introduction to a recent anthology of essays on urban disasters, for example, lists the most deadly urban events in the 1980s and 1990s, but inexplicably excludes the Chicago heatwave – and indeed all other American heatwaves – even though the 1995 catastrophe killed more than ten times the

---

Box 2.1 Heatwaves: facts at a glance

Deaths from Europe's 2003 heatwave
(heatstroke and excess mortality)

	WHO	EPI
France	14,802	14,802
Germany	—	7,000
Spain	59*	4,230
Italy	3,134	4,175
Portugal	2,106	1,316
England and Wales	2,045	2,045
Netherlands	—	1,400
Belgium	—	150
Total	**22,146**	**35,118**

*According to WHO, more than 6,000 excess deaths were informally reported during the heatwave in Spain, but only 59 were accepted as being caused by the heatwave.
Sources: World Health Organization (WHO), 2004; Earth Policy Institute (EPI), 2003

Financial cost of Europe's 2003 heatwave: US$ 13 billion
Source: Munich Re

Summer 2003 was the hottest in Europe for at least 500 years
Source: Juerg Luterbacher, University of Bern, Switzerland

Heatwaves kill roughly 1,500 Americans a year; the combined toll from hurricanes, tornadoes, earthquakes and floods is less than 200
Source: Eric Klinenberg, The Guardian, 20 August 2002

International Federation of Red Cross and Red Crescent Societies

number of people as the deadliest disaster in the table, the 1989 San Francisco earthquake."

In India, the National Disaster Management Cell does not categorize a heatwave as a natural disaster. This is despite mounting evidence that, as India's population rises and climate change sets in, thousands of people are dying each year from heatwaves. In May 2003, for example, temperatures reached between 45 and 49 degress Celsius in the Indian state of Andhra Pradesh, claiming some 1,200 lives. The chief minister of Andhra Pradesh at the time, Chandrababu Naidu, said the tragedy was unparalleled in the state's history, although 1,000 people died a year earlier during another one-week heatwave.

More widely, the lack of public recognition of the dangers of extreme temperatures has led to increasing losses. As witnessed in Europe, heatwave warnings received less attention than other natural disaster alerts. And, as Klinenberg points out, most health professionals fail to identify heat-related deaths, while local authorities rarely keep records of them.

Risk perception studies over the past 20 years have provided some insight into why heatwaves fail to register as a devastating natural disaster or serious public health threat. These studies showed an apparent contradiction in the perceived level of threat posed by different risks. In the 2002 *World Health Report*, the World Health Organization (WHO) explained: "An early approach to study and map people's understanding of risks was to ask them to estimate the number of deaths for 40 different hazards and to compare these with known statistical estimates. This showed that people tend to overestimate the number of deaths from rarer and infrequent risks, while underestimating considerably those from common and frequent causes, such as cancers and diabetes."

To measure it better, the United Nations (UN) Disaster Management Training Programme (DMTP) identifies in its training module, *Vulnerability and Risk Assessment,* four factors that influence human perceptions of risk:
- **Exposure:** Actual quantitative risk level.
- **Familiarity:** Personal experience of the hazardous event.
- **Preventability:** The degree to which the hazard is perceived as controllable or its effects preventable.
- **Dread:** The horror of the hazard, its scale and its consequences.

The 'dread factor', according to the DMTP, has the greatest impact on perceptions of risk, with exposure levels or personal familiarity affecting perceptions on a less direct and more general level. For instance, earthquakes tend to evoke a higher dread factor than road accidents, despite the scientific evidence that more people are injured or killed in road accidents annually than in earthquakes.

The higher the dread factor and the higher the perceived unknown risks, the more people want action to reduce those risks, including through stricter government regulation and legislative controls. However, such action can divert limited resources towards perceived risks that are actually remote and infrequent, rather than addressing more urgent social problems.

The challenge for health professionals and disaster mitigation specialists is to begin working together and raising awareness, among themselves and the general public, of the potential harm caused by extreme temperatures. One lesson learned in Europe is that heatwaves can kill thousands of people and destroy livelihoods when insufficient attention is paid to the underlying vulnerabilities of those most affected.

The next step is to take this knowledge about at-risk communities and develop programmes to prevent losses when nature's sometimes-harsh climate sets in motion a catastrophe. But in order "to develop effective information and communication strategies and policies about natural risks, the perception and evaluation of these risks and influencing factors should be known," explains WHO.

A future summer

Over the last 25 years, according to the UN's Intergovernmental Panel on Climate Change, the average global surface temperature rose by 0.56°C. By the end of the century, it is projected to rise by a further 1.4–5.8°C. As the mercury rises, heatwaves are set to become more common and severe.

For the WHO, the public health implications are worrying. By 2030, "we see an approximate doubling in deaths and in the burden in healthy life years lost," says WHO scientist Diarmid Campbell-Lendrum. The World Meteorological Organization believes that in the United States alone, the number of annual heat-related deaths could rise from 1,500 (in 2000) to 3,000–4,000 by 2020.

The summer of 2003 was a record-breaker in Europe. The average temperature was more than 3.5°C above normal for that time of year. "From a statistical point of view such a summer should never have happened," says Christoph Schär, professor at the Institute for Atmospheric and Climate Science in Zürich, Switzerland. But what is abnormal now may become the norm within the near future.

As part of a national research project, Schär and his colleagues compared the temperatures from 2003 with data from the past 150 years. The results of their research, published in the journal *Nature*, indicate that summer 2003 provided clear evidence that the climate is changing. "Since 1975," they note, "we have observed a pronounced warming of the climate in the northern hemisphere. If we assume a not-too-optimistic scenario, based on a doubling of the current level of the concentration

International Federation
of Red Cross and Red Crescent Societies

of greenhouse gases in the Earth's atmosphere, average summer temperatures in central Europe will be around 4.6°C higher at the end of the century."

Another factor, more important than an average rise in temperature, will be the increase in temperature *variability*. As Schär says, "The past two summers were very different. While drought was very widespread last year, floods grabbed the headlines in the summer of 2002. According to our results the standard variation of summer temperatures in central Europe will increase by up to 100 per cent. This means that towards the end of the century the climate in summer will be extremely different from year to year."

The kind of uncertain climate that Schär predicts would cause major problems for central Europe in particular. "In principle one can become accustomed to a warmer climate if it's more or less constant. Farmers, for example, can cultivate other plants that do well in a warmer climate," he says. "But if mean temperatures become erratic and change greatly from one year to the next, it can be far more difficult to adjust to the unpredictable conditions."

Is the future already here? Thomas Loster, a geographer and expert in weather-related losses with Munich Re, explains: "We used to talk in terms of floods and heatwaves being one-in-100-year events, but in the south of France this year [2003] we have had a one-in-100-year heatwave, and in December one-in-100-year floods – all in the same year. This is climate change happening now and a big headache for the insurance industry." He adds: "The summer of 2003, with its extensive losses, is a glimpse into the future, a 'future summer'."

Europe bakes and burns

Sudden variations in temperature can prove more deadly than sustained heat, as the human body needs time to acclimatize. "A heatwave is a very relative factor," explains Laurence S. Kalkstein, a climatologist at the University of Delaware Center for Climatic Research, in an interview with the *New York Times*. A heatwave in Riyadh, Saudi Arabia is different from a heatwave in London. As Dr Kalkstein points out: "We respond to the normal weather conditions of wherever we live."

A heatwave is a deviation from average temperatures. According to Kalkstein, people living in areas with occasional but intense variability – like Paris or New York, where summer and winter temperatures can change significantly in a few days – suffer more than in places like Miami or Rio de Janeiro, where the weather is warmer but with fewer fluctuations.

It does not take a lot of extra heat to kill the vulnerable. In extreme heat, the body maintains its temperature of 37°C by circulating blood to the skin and perspiring.

As the body temperature rises, the heart has to work harder, putting it and other vital organs at risk. This is why anyone who tries to do too much in the heat is vulnerable to heatstroke. However, elderly people are particularly at risk, since they may already suffer from cardiovascular disease – which hot weather further exacerbates.

August 2003 was the hottest August on record in the northern hemisphere, according to the Earth Policy Institute, a US-based environmental group. The heatwave in Europe officially began in June when the mercury exceeded average temperatures by 4–5°C and remained very high until mid-August. Drought-parched countries stretching from Russia to Portugal suffered the consequences, as forest fires spread and agricultural output tumbled.

In Spain, more than 12,000 hectares of woodland were reportedly destroyed by fire. In Portugal, the prime minister declared a state of emergency after 60 forest blazes scorched the country. Wildfires regularly flare across Portugal during the summer, but in 2003 unusually hot, dry air and strong winds combined to make many unmanageable.

Volunteers from the Portuguese Red Cross (CVP) took part in government-led emergency operations. When the fires first broke out, 100 volunteers used 25 ambulances to help evacuate victims in the Castelo Branco, Portalegre, Santarém and Lisbon regions, transporting them to hospitals or temporary shelters.

On 6 August temperatures from London to Lisbon exceeded 37°C. Over the next week, the heat baked most of central Europe. Worse still, temperatures did not drop during the night. The cooling-off period after sunset usually allows the body to recuperate. As temperatures remained above 30°C at night, people were not able to recover, setting in motion the catastrophe.

Urban disaster

Heatwaves are primarily an urban disaster. In cities, the dominant features are heat-absorbing black roofs and pavements, rather than cool green areas. These 'heat islands' can be as much as 5–6°C warmer than rural areas.

In 2003, people in Paris and surrounding urban areas suffered significantly more than those in rural regions, with the bulk of the 14,800 deaths taking place in and around the capital. According to figures from France's National Institute for Public Health Surveillance, there was a 130 per cent increase in death rates in Île-de-France (Paris and surrounding suburbs) over the same time the previous year. Meanwhile, in the southern rural region of Languedoc-Roussillon, for example, death rates were just 20 per cent higher than in 2002.

The majority of deaths in the United Kingdom took place in London and in the densely populated areas of the south-east and east. From 4 to 13 August, 1,314 deaths more than the five-year average for that time of year were recorded in these areas – 28 per cent higher than normal. Of this figure, 900 died in London alone.

Climate scientists and meteorologists have long understood that cities compound the difficulties, costs and pain of a summer heatwave. To offset this effect and as part of a micro climate change study, the New York Climate and Health Project is identifying the local heat sources that aggravate summer temperatures in New York. The aim is to look at the smaller-scale impact of climate change and develop local methods of reducing it.

According to project mangers, the heat islands in New York are a collection of industrial areas in New Jersey and Long Island. To counteract these islands, the project is planting a 'green roof' of drought-resistant grasses, and is measuring its impact. The goal is to create a model that can be replicated and even to foster a new industry. Long Island City is one of New York's last industrial strongholds – but it has

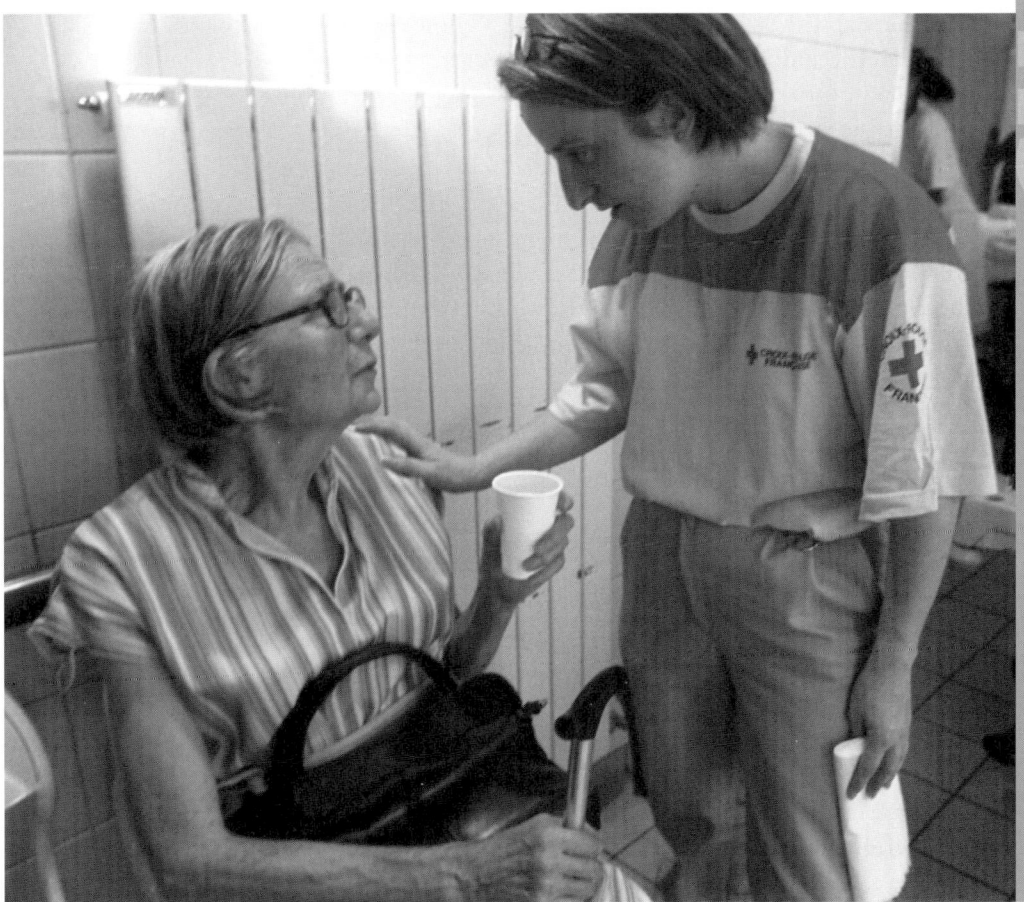

The elderly are at greatest risk during heatwaves. Daily home visits or phone calls from carers can prove life saving for those living alone.

J.-P. Porcher/ French Red Cross.

enough flat roof space to build a green roof almost the size of Brooklyn's Prospect Park. This, say the project leaders, could form "a huge heat-absorbing sponge of roughly 500 acres [200 hectares], all at roof height".

However, while climate scientists debate what impacts climate change will have, where and when, it is crucial to view heatwaves as more than simply a climate issue. They are first and foremost a health and care issue. As Eric Klinenberg explains: "Heatwaves are like urban particle accelerators. They speed up and make visible conditions that are always there but are difficult to perceive. Living and dying alone is one of those conditions." The social ecology of an urban area often has a far greater impact on death rates than the effect of physical structures.

In his study of the Chicago heatwave of 1995, Klinenberg found that not all urban communities suffered equally. One poor neighbourhood, with a high percentage of violence and abandoned buildings, had a death rate ten times higher than that of a similarly poor adjacent area (with the same proportion of elderly, solitary residents), which had a more active street life. "The areas of the city that had high concentrations of deaths are areas that had lost the viable public spaces, the busy sidewalks, the commercial streets," Dr Klinenberg says. "Those are the things that draw people out of the home and into social contact."

Isolated elderly suffer most

Those worst affected by heatwaves live in urban areas, and for complex and often different reasons, elderly people tend to make up the bulk of them. In many cases, they are likely to be disproportionately invisible to researchers and aid workers alike, rarely willing or able to call much attention to their plight. As proof of this, a study of the 1995 Chicago heatwave confirmed that those people most at risk were in poor health, unable to care for themselves, isolated and lacking air-conditioning (see Box 2.2).

The 2003 heatwave in France affected primarily those over 75 years of age, who accounted for 70 per cent of the 14,802 deaths. But the 45- to 74-year-old age group also suffered, accounting for 30 per cent of deaths. Women died in higher proportions than men, as they form the largest part of this population group. But in most studies on heatwaves, gender has little impact on who is at risk.

Researchers from other countries have confirmed the high vulnerability of the elderly to heatwaves. The National Institute of Environmental Health in Hungary studied heatwaves in Budapest from 1993 to 2000. They found that mortality was highest among the population aged over 75 years. And in Chicago in 1995, government authorities indicated that 73 per cent of the 739 heat-related victims were older than 65 years. In contrast to Europe, men in the Chicago heatwave were more than twice

International Federation
of Red Cross and Red Crescent Societies

Box 2.2 Who is most at risk?

The World Health Organization, in its 2004 publication *Heat-waves: risks and responses*, explains that vulnerability to heat depends on "climate factors (such as the frequency of heat-waves) and on individual risk factors, including medical, behavioural and environmental factors". It lists a number of situations or characteristics that are predictive of heatstroke and heat-related death and illnesses:

■ being elderly, overweight, unfit or tired;

■ impaired cognition, such as dementia;

■ pre-existing disease, especially cardio-vascular;

■ use of certain medications, which affect the body's temperature regulation;

■ dehydration;

■ living alone;

■ housing (such as living in a certain type of building or on a higher floor); and

■ absence of air-conditioning in the home or residential institution. ■

as likely to die as women. The reason for this, according to some experts, is the higher number of elderly men living isolated from social contact. Several studies have shown a direct correlation between levels of social contact and heatwave vulnerability.

Europe's population is ageing. According to the UN's Population Division (UNFPA), by 2050 there will be 2.4 older persons for every child, and more than one in three people will be aged 60 years or over in the region. UNFPA points out that the fastest-growing segment of the global population in 2000 was aged 80 or over. In France, government figures show that the segment of the population aged 75 and over is increasing by 3 per cent each year.

As the world grows older, more people will become vulnerable to heatwaves. UNFPA estimates that, globally, the number of older people (60 years or over) will nearly triple, from 606 million today to almost 2 billion by 2050. By then, the number of older people in the world will exceed the number of young. Europe is particularly threatened, as climate predictions indicate that the frequency and severity of heatwaves are likely to increase, and it is home to the world's largest aged population.

But what matters is not only who dies. How and where they die point to the social failures that lead to disaster. In France, according to the National Institute for Public Health Surveillance, more than 60 per cent of those who lost their lives in the 2003 heatwave died in hospitals, private health-care institutions and retirement homes. In Chicago in 1995, most died alone, locked in their apartments, forgotten by family, friends and neighbours.

Death and illness from heatwaves are, as sociologist Paul Farmer notes, "biological reflections of social fault lines". Events in Chicago and Europe signify a catastrophic failure in the care and treatment of the elderly. And as Klinenberg writes: "We have collectively created the conditions that made it possible for so many Chicago residents to die in the summer of 1995… We can collectively unmake them too, but only once we recognize and scrutinize the cracks in our social foundations that we customarily take for granted and put out of sight."

Hot climate, cold society

The high human toll of 2003's heatwave caused a public uproar in France. In a commentary entitled "French barbarity", the French newspaper *Le Figaro* said the country had witnessed during the summer of 2003, "such a reversal of values that vacations have become more sacred than the respect we owe our elders". The article was referring to the habit of French officials, professionals and their families to take summer holidays *en masse* during August. This left government departments and public health and emergency services poorly equipped to deal with the emergency.

More in France than other places, the heatwave made visible cultural attitudes that isolate the elderly. "Here, the status of an elderly person is very bad," Jean-François Lacan, a French author and nursing home industry watchdog, is quoted as saying. "They're basically rejects of society." During the heatwave, French health professionals repeatedly tried to point out that the problem was less the heat and more an elderly care system in crisis, with services habitually underfunded and understaffed, combined with, as one report notes, "a national habit of shutting senior citizens out of sight and mind".

And why in other European countries, particularly in the south, was the loss of life considerably less? Most experts attribute it to the fact that elderly people are more integrated into the daily life of a family. As Stéphane Mantion, an official with the French Red Cross, is quoted as saying in *Time* magazine: "The French family structure is more dislocated than elsewhere in Europe, and prevailing social attitudes hold that once older people are closed behind their apartment doors or in nursing homes, they are someone else's problem. These thousands of elderly victims didn't die from a heatwave as such, but from the isolation and insufficient assistance they lived with day in and out, and which almost any crisis situation could render fatal."

As Klinenberg notes in his study of the Chicago heatwave, the considerable loss of life there was a result of "an increasingly hot climate and a cold society that turns its back on the vulnerable, threatening the growing population of elderly and isolated urban residents".

Crucially, the problem is less about the hazard and more about vulnerability. The marginalization and poverty of the elderly are the root causes of disaster – extreme temperatures are simply the natural trigger. Cold waves can be even deadlier than heatwaves. The UK-based charity Help the Aged is running a campaign to raise awareness of the toll that cold weather takes on the elderly there. According to government statistics, each winter over the last five years in England and Wales, between 21,000 and 50,000 people aged 65 and over suffered avoidable winter deaths (see Box 2.3).

Box 2.3 Cold waves in the UK: the other extreme

Every winter for the past decade, an average of 33,600 people – mainly the elderly – have died as a result of the cold in England and Wales alone, according to the Office of National Statistics (ONS). During the winter of 2002–03, 21,800 people over the age of 65 died from the cold, prompting Mervyn Kohler, head of public affairs for the NGO Help the Aged, to ask: "Why has there been no outcry about these latest figures like that witnessed in France when some 15,000 older people died in this summer's heatwave?"

These 'excess winter deaths' (as the ONS terms them) are defined as the increase in deaths during the four winter months (December to March) compared to the average number of deaths for the remainder of the year. According to Help the Aged, mortality data are "the tip of the iceberg" compared to the additional burden, borne disproportionately by the elderly, of poor health in winter and the discomfort and stress of coping with cold, damp homes.

In comparable north European countries such as Finland and Germany, the numbers of excess winter deaths are "proportionately much lower than in the UK", says Help the Aged. The European Union-funded Eurowinter study found that the avoidance of 'cold stress' (by restricting outdoor excursions, wearing warmer clothing and increasing activity when outdoors) is associated with less cold-related mortality in those countries which had the most severe winters. Risk of illness or death appears to be equally related to exposure to indoor or outdoor cold.

Other research has firmly linked winter deaths with poor, energy-inefficient housing. A London School of Hygiene and Tropical Medicine study found that the temperature of the home and its age and energy efficiency are important factors in determining winter deaths. Living in cold and damp houses increases the risk of strokes, heart attacks and respiratory illnesses.

Fuel poverty makes matters worse. A household is defined as being in fuel poverty when it has to spend more than 10 per cent of its income on fuel to heat the home to World Health Organization standards. Help the Aged's research found that 22 per cent of older people living in poverty in Britain were "sometimes forced to choose between heating and eating". Around half of the UK's 3.5 million fuel-poor households are estimated to contain older people.

As part of its November 2003 campaign, Help the Aged's Kohler argues that: "By failing to properly address fuel poverty and by failing to coordinate help across departments, the Government is letting people die of cold." While the NGO welcomes the government's commitment to tackle cold homes and end fuel poverty for older people by 2010, much remains to be done. Help the Aged has called on the government to commission further research on 'excess' winter deaths, so that the causes can be better understood and a strategy put in place to reduce death rates at least to levels of comparable European countries. ■

While the trigger for 80 per cent of those deaths was cold weather, the root causes of vulnerability remain much the same as for heatwaves. The elderly are too poor to take preventive measures, whether to pay for air conditioning during hot weather or for heating during cold weather. They are often poorly informed about what to do to mitigate the effects of extreme temperatures. Many suffer and die invisibly, being isolated and neglected by society.

Political denial and neglect

Government officials rarely react well to heatwaves. In Chicago, Mayor Richard M. Daley queried the integrity of autopsy reports following 1995's heatwave and said the crisis was being blown out of proportion. A leading newspaper columnist even played down the claims of one advocacy group, saying that "trying to blame the mayor for an act of God is not only unfair, it also does an injustice by wrongfully framing the debate".

In France, the health minister Jean-François Mattéi is quoted as saying, in response to questioning from a government committee: "In fact, the silent, unimaginable catastrophe of this summer's heatwave was really pretty well managed by the health ministry… There was no malfunction, no failing, no shortfall on its part, on the part of its staff or of any of its dependent services... France, it seems, was the only country in Europe to have actually reacted to the crisis. We should probably be congratulating ourselves." However, a subsequent parliamentary commission into the tragedy concluded that poor political management of the emergency had contributed to the scale of the disaster (see Box 2.4).

Box 2.4 Heatwave exposes public health failures

The heatwave of summer 2003 will be remembered in France as a disaster without precedent. From 1 to 20 August, average mortality rates for that time of year soared by 60 per cent, which meant nearly 15,000 people died as a result of the extreme heat. The national meteorology service forecast a heatwave on 1 August. A week later, the Ministry of Health warned of potential health risks. By 11 August, temperatures in Paris reached levels not seen since records began in 1873. On 13 August, with hospitals overflowing, city authorities activated an emergency plan to provide hospitals with as many staff and resources as possible.

On 11 August, the French Red Cross (FRC) launched its own 'extreme heat' plan. Volunteers were summoned for duty, with many cutting short or delaying their holidays. A national crisis centre was set up, with a dual coordination unit to cover both inside and outside the Île-de-France (the administrative zone centred on Paris). Twenty first-aid workers were immediately sent to hospitals in Paris and the suburbs. In 41 *départements* (administrative zones) across France, 750 Red Cross volunteers helped ambulance and fire services to identify and evacuate heatwave victims. Teams were dispatched to 52 hospitals and 72 retirement homes to help staff cool and rehy-

International Federation
of Red Cross and Red Crescent Societies

drate their patients. Red Cross members also identified and visited individuals living alone, to ensure they didn't die avoidable deaths. On 17 August, as temperatures subsided, the FRC's mobilization came to an end. Volunteers had worked flat out for nearly ten days, undertaking many different tasks – a baby was even delivered in one Red Cross vehicle.

According to a report by a special parliamentary commission, published on 3 March 2004, the heatwave was unprecedented anywhere in the world in terms of its intensity, geographic spread and death toll. Across 61 of France's 95 *départements*, temperatures exceeded 35°C or even 40°C. Urban areas were hit hardest and, as temperatures remained high at night, the vulnerable had little chance to recover. At greatest risk were people aged over 75 and those in poor health.

While poor housing conditions in the capital and the isolation of elderly people were important factors, the commission concluded there were also major failings in the political management of the disaster. The commission heard that, before August 2003, the health authorities had not anticipated the consequences of extremely high temperatures. The dangers of a heatwave were not the subject of specific early warning procedures, in the way that severe winter conditions were. This failure to anticipate possible disaster, combined with poor information, health monitoring and early warning systems, contributed to the scale of the tragedy.

Worse still, the monitoring and early warning information that was available was not shared outside the government's public health department. Yet the crisis showed that others not directly involved in health monitoring could also make significant contributions – fire fighters, paramedics, ambulance staff and emergency services were among the first to assist victims. The crisis demonstrated that hospital emergency services are central to identifying major health alerts.

However, measuring the scale of such a crisis in real time remains challenging. Experience from other cities that have suffered heatwaves, such as Chicago, Athens or Marseilles, reveals that an early warning system will not sound the alarm until a health disaster has already taken place. Nevertheless, the demographic background of an ageing population should have given particular cause for concern in France, when temperatures rose and remained extremely high.

Despite its unprecedented nature, such a heatwave is likely to occur again, given the global warming predicted by many scientists. The ageing of the population will exacerbate the climate's potential impact on health. To try and prevent a similar disaster recurring, the government has allocated 9.38 billion euros to fund a 20 per cent rise in staff and 10,000 new residential places at care homes. All homes for the elderly will have to provide at least one air-conditioned room between now and 2007.

Meanwhile, a new heatwave early warning programme has been initiated, which will become the responsibility of the prefect in each *département*. An early warning link will be set up between the meteorology and health services, and individuals living alone will be identified and monitored in their own homes. The government also announced the creation of a new social protection agency, which will aim at addressing the dangers faced by those unable to care for themselves.

For its part, the French Red Cross has set up a working group of retirement home directors, with a view to offering temporary accommodation for old people in times of crisis; providing residents with an air-conditioned communal room; and introducing specific training on how to assist elderly people. Red Cross teams must also strengthen their own local capacities to identify frail and isolated individuals, so they can help prevent future disasters happening on such a scale again. ■

Throughout central Europe, strong state welfare systems have traditionally provided extensive social and medical protection. But as economies stagnate and as the proportion of old people to working tax-payers increases, these systems are becoming increasingly difficult and expensive to sustain. Today, many European countries are facing serious choices about the future of their economies and welfare systems.

In France, the disaster sounded the alarm on the state of the country's care system for the elderly. There are fears that it might happen again because of a massive and unwieldy government system unable to change and a public health system chronically underfunded.

"What the heatwave made transparent are all the inefficiencies," says nursing home expert, Jean-François Lacan. Investigations established that although France has a highly centralized form of government, its bureaucracy is very fragmented, preventing it from recognizing the extent of the disaster until it was too late. As soon as officials identified the problem, there was no way for them to respond effectively and alert the appropriate local authorities in a coordinated manner.

Pascal Champvert, a labour leader who represents workers in public retirement homes, is quoted as saying the long-term care system needs more money. He points out that the ratio of staff to residents is far higher in other European countries, such as Austria, Germany and the Netherlands, than it is in France. "What we need now in France is a Marshall Plan for the elderly," he says. "We're not looking for little steps or symbolic concessions," he adds, but rather for concrete, substantial reform.

Preparing for next time

In 2003, we saw the consequences of a slow response to a heatwave. Emergency rooms reached capacity, refusing to accept new patients in the Paris region, despite the fact that heat-related illnesses need immediate attention. In both Paris and Chicago, morgues were overwhelmed and refrigerated trucks were called in to house temporarily the overflow of corpses. Eric Klinenberg acidly points out that in Chicago, once they had died, "the victims had accessed the two forms of assistance that would have saved them, artificial cooling and medical attention".

Many individuals can take measures to protect themselves. Klinenberg highlights the story of one elderly resident in Chicago. To survive the summer heat, she established a specific time during the day when she phoned her best friend. And at least once a day she went on a 'summer holiday', which consisted of soaking towels in cold water and wrapping herself in them to relieve the heat. These simple precautions, notes Klinenberg, helped save this woman's life. As well as remaining in phone contact with friends or family, ensuring a sufficient supply of liquids is another obvious precaution (see Box 2.5).

Box 2.5 Prevention tips in a heatwave

Although anyone at any time can suffer from heat-related illness, some people are at greater risk than others. Check regularly on:
- infants and young children;
- people aged 65 or older;
- people who have a mental illness; and
- those who are physically ill, especially with heart disease or high blood pressure.

  Visit adults at risk at least twice a day and watch them closely for signs of heat exhaustion or heatstroke. Infants and young children, of course, need much more frequent watching. If you must be out in the heat yourself:
- Limit your outdoor activity to morning and evening hours.
- Cut down on exercise. If you must exercise, drink two to four glasses of cool, non-alcoholic fluids every hour. A sports beverage can replace the salt and minerals you lose in sweat. *Warning:* if you are on a low-salt diet, talk with your doctor before drinking a sports beverage and limit your outdoor activity during the heat of the day.
- Try to rest often in shady areas.
- Protect yourself from the sun by wearing a wide-brimmed hat (also keeps you cooler) and sunglasses and by putting on sunscreen of SPF 15 or higher (the most effective products say 'broad spectrum' or 'UVA/UVB protection' on their labels). ∎

Source: World Health Organization, 2004.

However, for many elderly people, their vulnerability arises because they are incapacitated or poorly informed. It is in these cases that the community, which includes family, friends, public health authorities and elderly-care professionals, must intervene to ensure the safety of elderly people.

Mitigating and preparing for the effects of extreme temperatures require a multi-dimensional approach, with action at both a practical and a policy level. A 'lessons learned' exercise is going on throughout Europe among climate specialists, disaster response organizations, governments and public health institutions as a result of the 2003 heatwave. While few conclusions are being drawn at this point, it is apparent that practical preparedness measures need to take place in conjunction with a fundamental change in attitudes towards the elderly.

On a practical level, communities and individuals can prepare for a heatwave, as long as they are warned in time. "Information about an oncoming heatwave is available as much as three days in advance, and they take two days to start killing," says Dr Lawrence Robinson, deputy health commissioner of the US city of Philadelphia, in the *New York Times.* Heat-related death rates there have dropped since an early warning system was established seven years ago.

Philadelphia's Hot Weather Health Watch and Warning System is one of the most effective of its kind. An evaluation found that from 1995 to 1998, the system is believed to have saved 117 people. Its effectiveness stems from close coordination between different meteorological and health agencies, both public and private. The system includes:

- promoting a 'buddy' system through mass media announcements, which encourage friends, relatives, neighbours and other volunteers to make daily visits to elderly people during hot weather;
- activating a 'heat' telephone hotline to provide information and counselling to the general public on how to avoid heat stress;
- visits by local health authorities to people requiring attention that cannot be provided over the phone;
- directly informing care and nursing home facilities of a high-risk heat situation;
- increasing fire department and hospital emergency staffing during heatwaves; and
- implementing daytime outreach services to homeless people.

In general, most specialists agree that preparedness plans must be tailored to local needs and should involve multiple public and private authorities, including city managers, public health and social services workers, and emergency medical officers.

In Europe, preparedness measures are being established and strengthened. French hospitals and residences for the elderly are installing air-conditioning in selected rooms to provide momentary relief for the most acute cases. "Ultimately, faced by extreme heat, air-conditioning in hospitals and old people's homes is the only solution – just as heating is the only solution in winter," explains Lucien Abenhaim, France's former director general for health.

In addition, holidays for medical and residence care staff are to be better managed to prevent the mass exodus in August, which in the past left a significantly reduced staff on duty to respond to emergencies. Local authorities are now required to establish lists of particularly vulnerable elderly and disabled people and to ensure regular personal contact, especially during a heat or cold wave.

A 'heatwave action plan' has been drawn up which includes a heat watch warning system, using historical data on mortality rates as indicators in 13 French cities. The plan will also try to calculate the impact smog levels had on the death rate in 2003, and build models to predict mortality under extreme weather conditions.

In Italy, the Ministry of Health has initiated a pilot 'buddy' programme in three Italian cities: Turin, Milan and Genoa. Within two years, an analysis will be made of the programme by studying its impact on those people who took part, compared to others who did not. The German government has developed a more sophisticated approach to issuing heat warnings that now takes into account the human body's short-term acclimatization to heat.

International Federation
of Red Cross and Red Crescent Societies

For its part, the Red Cross, whose staff and volunteers comprise the largest humanitarian network on the ground, is looking at ways to reinforce and expand its programmes for the elderly. As a vulnerable group, elderly people benefit from numerous Red Cross initiatives. But while there was widespread praise for the work of European National Societies during the heatwave, there is agreement among Red Cross leadership that stronger preparedness measures should be put in place.

One model could be that of the Swedish Red Cross, which assists elderly people who are isolated and housebound, by offering social activities and home visits. This programme and others like it in Sweden and beyond have systematically proven that efforts to reduce the isolation of the elderly have a direct impact on their quality of life and health. Interventions during heatwaves that use both mass media and local networks to inform and contact vulnerable residents directly are the most effective form of disaster prevention.

Politics of ageing

The heatwave of August 2003 has served as a catalyst in France to bring about change in care for the elderly from practical to policy levels. Previously, government officials were looking at ways to reduce the cost of health care, including for the elderly. While financial pressures to reduce staffing and restructure the system remain, there is recognition of the chronic shortage of space in and staffing for retirement homes. As a result, within the heatwave action plan, French authorities will hire 13,200 more care workers and add 10,000 new places by 2007. Additionally, the government is planning on upgrading retirement home buildings, which in many instances are poorly constructed and maintained.

But this falls short of Pascal Champvert's call for a Marshall Plan. Hindering efforts in France and elsewhere are the lack of civil society organizations advocating on behalf of the elderly. In the UK, Help the Aged is raising awareness on issues of concern, as well as leading campaigns to pressure governmental authorities for action. In the US, AARP (formerly known as the American Association of Retired Persons) is a major non-governmental organization (NGO), influencing legislation and policy related to ageing. In central Europe, however, NGOs advocating on behalf of the elderly are noticeably few. But this is set to change. The heatwave last year served as a wake-up call to Europe's ageing population, and to those who care for them, that all is not well. And it is not just Europe that is facing a crisis. Events in Chicago in 1995 clearly showed the failure of certain US policies related to ageing.

When heatwaves become human-made disasters in some of the richest countries on Earth, it is time for the developed world to reconsider its policies and values. There is little doubt that, as governments struggle to balance shrinking health budgets with rising costs for elderly care, the politics of ageing are becoming a global concern. The heatwave of 2003 highlighted what happens when the problem is ignored.

Jean Milligan, a freelance writer specializing in humanitarian and development issues, was the major contributor to this chapter and Boxes 2.2 and 2.5. Jonathan Walter, editor of the World Disasters Report, *contributed Boxes 2.1 and 2.3. Box 2.4 was contributed by Pierre Kremer and Marie Gustin of the French Red Cross.*

Sources and further information

Abenhaim, Lucien. *Canicules: La santé publique en question.* Paris: Arthème Fayard, 2003.

Abenhaim, Lucien. *Decision under uncertainty. Lessons from the heatwave epidemic in France.* Presentation at the World Health Organization meeting, Bratislava, 9 February 2004.

Bahrampour, Tara. 'Most deadly of the natural disasters: The heat wave' in *New York Times*, 13 August 2002.

Crumley, Bruce. 'Elder careless' in *Time*, 25 August 2003.

Department of Environmental Health and the French Institute of Public Health. *Health impact of 2003 heatwave in France.* Presentation at the World Health Organization meeting, Bratislava, 9 February 2004.

Farmer, Paul. *Infections and inequalities: The modern plagues.* Berkeley and Los Angeles: University of California Press, 1999.

Help the Aged. *Cold homes: The UK's winter death scandal.* Help the Aged Policy Statement. London, 2003.

Klinenberg, Eric. 'Baked to death' in *The Guardian*, 20 August 2002.

Klinenberg, Eric. 'Victims of a hot climate and a cold society' in *International Herald Tribune*, 22 August 2003.

Klinenberg, Eric. *Heat Wave.* Chicago: University of Chicago Press, 2002.

Larsen, Janet. *Record heat wave in Europe takes 35,000 lives.* Earth Policy Institute. 9 October 2003.

Paldy, Anna, Bobvos, Janos and Kovats, Sari. *Heat waves in Hungary.* Presentation at the World Health Organization meeting, Bratislava, 9 February 2004.

United Nations Disaster Management Training Programme. *Vulnerability and Risk Assessment Training Module.* Module prepared by A.W. Coburn, R.J.S. Spence, A. Pomonis at the Cambridge Architectural Research Limited, UK, 1994.

United Nations Population Division. *World Population Prospects: The 2002 Revision.* New York: United Nations, 2002.

World Health Organization (WHO). *The World Health Report 2002.* Geneva: WHO, 2002.

WHO Regional Office for Europe, German Weather Service and London School of Hygiene and Tropical Medicine. *Heat-waves: Risks and responses*. Copenhagen: WHO/Europe, 2004. Available at http://www.who.dk/ccashh/HeatCold/20040331_1

Würsten, Felix. *Harbinger of climate change*. Swiss Federal Institute of Technology Zurich (ETH Life) weekly web journal, Zurich, 15 January 2004. Available at http://www.ethlife.ethz.ch

Web sites

French Institute of Public Health **http://www.invs.sante.fr**
French Red Cross **http://www.croix.rouge.fr**
Help the Aged, UK **http://www.helptheaged.org.uk**
United Kingdom Office of National Statistics **http://www.statistics.gov.uk**
United Nations Disaster Management Training Programme
    http://www.undmtp.org
United Nations Population Division
    http://www.un.org/esa/population/unpop.html
World Health Organization **http://www.who.int**

Focus on
community
resilience

International Federation
of Red Cross and Red Crescent Societies

Harnessing local capacities in rural India

Disasters are posing an ever-greater threat to the lives and livelihoods of millions of people in India. Droughts and floods, earthquakes and cyclones hit the country with grim regularity year after year. Between 1994 and 2003, disasters – both 'natural' and technological – claimed 68,671 Indian lives and affected an average of 68 million people every year of the decade, according to the Belgium-based Centre for Research on the Epidemiology of Disasters (CRED). This toll is worse than for the previous ten years, from 1984 to 1993, when disasters claimed 42,171 lives and, every year, affected an average of 55 million people. Meanwhile, catastrophes in India during the 1990s claimed US$1.9 billion annually in direct economic costs alone.

In the face of such devastating impacts, the task of supporting the resilience of Indian communities to disasters has never been more urgent. Resilience is taken to mean the capacity to mitigate, prepare for, respond to and recover from the impacts of disaster – in a way which leaves communities less at risk than before. This chapter presents three case studies from across the subcontinent, illustrating ways of enhancing resilience before, during and after disaster. Although the case studies themselves are small scale, they reveal the potential to be 'scaled up' across the region.

Our first study, which focuses on the village of Samiapalli in the highly disaster-prone state of Orissa, reveals how prioritizing risk reduction before disaster strikes pays dividends in the future. During the 1990s, the people of Samiapalli, with the help of a local non-governmental organization (NGO), embarked on a long process of development, one element of which was to construct disaster-proof homes. When the 'supercyclone' of October 1999 struck the village, these houses saved both lives and livelihoods, while tens of thousands of people in weaker homes perished around them.

Our second study highlights the plight of subsistence farmers in the drought-stricken, semi-arid Zaheerabad region of Andhra Pradesh. Since at least the mid-1990s, the area has been suffering an ongoing disaster of chronic food insecurity, driven by drought and the failure of pest-prone cash crops such as wheat, rice and cotton. However, inspired by a local development agency, some of the state's poorest and most marginalized communities have rediscovered traditional, drought-proof seeds and farming techniques in a bid for self-sufficiency. This initiative has now spread to 65 villages.

Our third study describes how, following the devastating earthquake of 2001, villagers from Patanka in the state of Gujarat rebuilt their homes stronger than before, with the

Photo opposite page: Orissa is prone to both floods and cyclones – and it is the state's poorest people who are hit hardest.

Bijoy Patro/ International Federation.

help of a partnership of local and international aid organizations. Farmers, left unemployed by three years of intense drought, retrained as masons and helped build earthquake-resistant houses for every family in the village. Building on the success of this initiative, villagers were able to access government funds to create a new rainwater-harvesting system to improve both their health and their crop yields.

Each case study is unique and each is presented here in compressed form, leaving out many of the daily challenges that had to be overcome. However, some common obstacles, principles and success factors emerge. The role of aid organizations is very much that of a catalyst for a community-led process of self-transformation from vulnerability to resilience. Some villagers proved hostile to change and had to be won over through a process of consensus building. The ideas, resources and motivation to increase resilience to disaster are often there within the community, but lie hidden or unrecognized. The challenge for aid organizations is to create the right environment within which these local resources can flourish. That may mean helping to improve the confidence and status of more marginalized groups. Or connecting villagers with the financial and technical resources needed to help realize their plans. Meanwhile, to have any impact, individual projects must be linked to wider processes of creating resilience and reducing risk. In this respect, successful, locally-led initiatives are more likely to catch on and be replicated elsewhere than 'top-down' projects imposed and funded by external agencies.

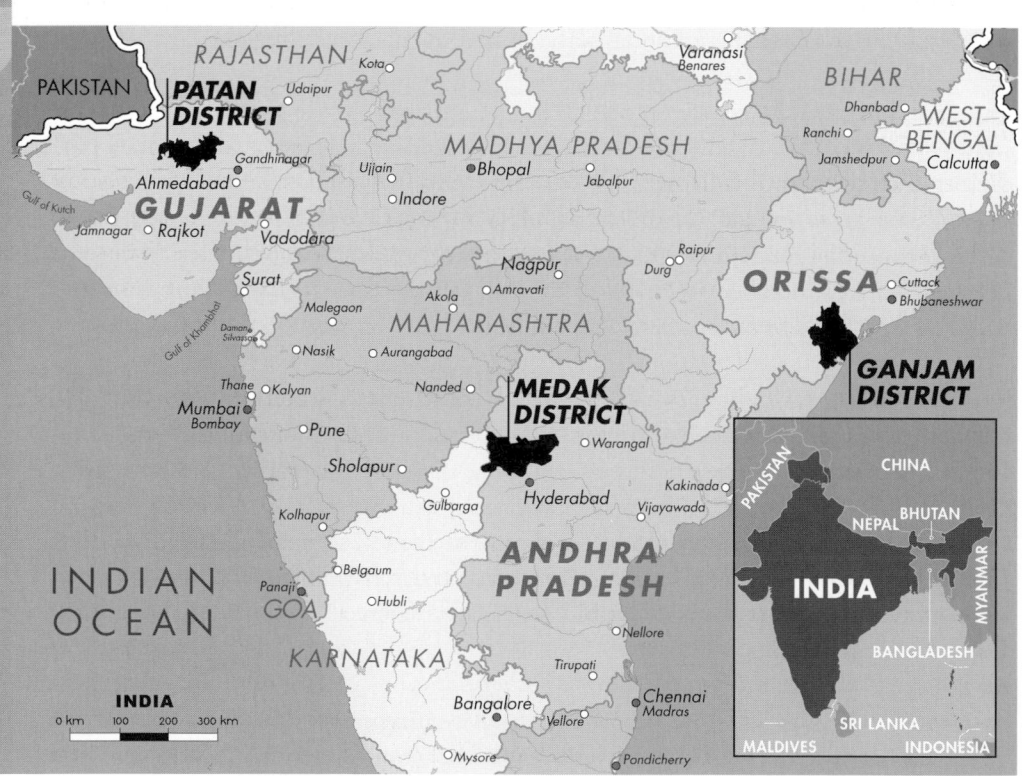

International Federation
of Red Cross and Red Crescent Societies

But first of all, any organization arriving from 'outside' must recognize that their presence may destabilize the existing balance of power in the community. Including the powerful, so as not to alienate them, while boosting the capacities of those less powerful, is a delicate balancing act. So finding the right entry-point is essential: what is needed is an approach that builds community-wide trust and meets the real needs of those at risk. Whatever that entry-point is – whether improving water and sanitation or building disaster-proof homes – long-term success seems to depend on including the entire village community in the process. This can be challenging if the community is divided along ethnic or caste lines.

Similarly, the process of enhancing resilience cannot limit itself to one particular hazard. Each of the communities analysed is prone to a range of different natural hazards and to the chronic risks of disease, food insecurity and poverty. A multidimensional approach, which strengthens livelihoods and skills as much as it strengthens physical infrastructure, is essential.

For this reason, the only sustainable way to boost resilience is to integrate disaster risk reduction within the wider development process. Such an approach mirrors the outlook of vulnerable people, who are often more concerned about reducing chronic, long-term risks like poverty or ill health, than they are about mitigating one-off disasters. This approach also entails working in cooperation with local government wherever possible. Sometimes, as we shall see, initiatives started at a local level are so good that the government will pick them up and apply them elsewhere.

Samiapalli case study

Samiapalli village, in the district of Ganjam, Orissa, lies just five kilometres from the coast of the Bay of Bengal, the most cyclone-prone region in the world. The east coast of Orissa suffers a major cyclone every two to eight years, the most recent being the 'supercyclone' of 1999, which killed between 10,000 and 40,000 people – no one knows for sure to this day. In rural parts of Orissa, 80 per cent of the population live below the poverty line, less than one-fifth have access to clean water and under 5 per cent have access to adequate sanitation. Apart from periodic cyclones, the population is plagued by regular floods and chronic water-borne diseases, causing widespread illness and death.

In the early 1990s, an Orissa-based development NGO, Gram Vikas, decided to initiate a rural health and environment programme (RHEP) to help tackle the state's water and sanitation problems. Gram Vikas selected Samiapalli as one of the five villages in which to begin its programme – based both on need and on the villagers' enthusiasm to participate. The village consists of 76 families belonging to one of India's most marginalized and exploited groups, the *dalits* (literally, 'the oppressed', previously known as 'untouchables'). Their caste status meant they were

Stronger homes save lives and livelihoods

Samiapalli's new water and sanitation system was not the end of the story. The villagers now decided that they needed stronger homes. They lived in mud and thatch houses of less than 10 square metres, which had to be repaired each year. Four months of torrential monsoon rain and wind would destroy the leaf and grass roofs. Recurrent floods would inundate living quarters. Termites would nibble through the timber frames. Their new toilets were better than their houses.

The villagers decided to rebuild their homes on a larger site nearby. Gram Vikas helped them raise a bank loan to buy the land, which they repaid from their community fund. Armed with loan support arranged by Gram Vikas of Rs 22,500 (about US$ 700 at the time) per house, the villagers built their own permanent, disaster-proof homes, with new water and sanitation facilities. These houses, around 40 square metres in area, are brick built with reinforced concrete roofs to ensure they are resistant to cyclones and floods. Since local masons already knew the necessary construction techniques, Gram Vikas' role was to help villagers access loans from the government's Housing Development Finance Corporation and to act as guarantor of those loans. As a result, the formerly impoverished *dalit* stone-crushers began a new life in new, safer homes.

When the one of the most powerful cyclones in India's history slammed into Orissa in October 1999, its 300 km/h winds whipped up a tidal surge seven metres high which swept 20 km inland. The mud and thatch houses across most of Orissa's coastline collapsed. Tens of thousands lost their lives. Millions more people lost all their possessions – cows, pigs, chickens, tools, cooking utensils – their livelihoods swept away in a single storm. But Samiapalli was prepared. Villagers sought safety in their new houses. No one died. And, as survivors in neighbouring villages waited for relief supplies in makeshift shelters, the people of Samiapalli were able to resume their lives and livelihoods with far less disruption. Their water tank and piped supplies ensured that, unlike in neighbouring villages, their drinking water supply was not contaminated by dead bodies or detritus. The community proved equally resilient to the 2003 floods.

Today, the village committee, which Gram Vikas helped create, has replaced the NGO as the villagers' interface with the outside world. They have learned to use the savings in the village community fund as collateral to obtain loans for more development projects, such as raising cattle and selling cashew and coconuts grown on 12 hectares of social forestry. They are now represented at local government level, through which they were able to access public funds to build a village road and a temple. They have turned the village pond – no longer contaminated by bathing – into a profitable fish farm. Some previously landless *dalit* families have purchased land for cultivation. Villagers do not depend on contractors or stone-crushing to earn a living. The committee even supervises village education, which has led to an increase in school attendance. With these developments, a new sense of dignity has begun to emerge.

International Federation
of Red Cross and Red Crescent Societies

Inspiration to others

Samiapalli's safer homes and watsan programmes have proved very powerful in their demonstration effect with other communities. Villagers who worked with Gram Vikas have become ambassadors for the programme, motivating and influencing other communities to start similar initiatives. Whereas in the past, Gram Vikas would be engaged in dozens of meetings spread over several years to encourage villagers to improve their infrastructure, now communities are approaching the NGO directly to get involved. Local families even want their daughters to marry into villages with improved watsan facilities. By 2004, around 12,000 families in more than 150 villages across Orissa had cooperated with Gram Vikas on projects to build clean water facilities and disaster-resistant homes. Meanwhile, nearly 5,000 people (mostly women) had formed 319 savings groups in 91 different villages.

Gram Vikas has realized that in order to scale up such initiatives across a wider range of communities, it is essential to integrate their interventions with similar government schemes (see Box 3.1). The NGO's aim is to reach 100,000 poor families across rural Orissa (about 1 per cent of the state's population) by 2015. Safer housing, water supply and sanitation are now developed simultaneously. By clustering new projects in villages around communities that have already implemented projects, Gram Vikas hopes to create a 'critical mass' of practice sufficient to influence policy at government level as well as among NGOs and the private sector.

Zaheerabad case study

The following example from Andhra Pradesh in southern India reveals how, with the right help, rural communities can build their resilience in the midst of ongoing disaster, in this case drought. Zaheerabad, in Medak district, is one of the most neglected areas of Andhra Pradesh, close to the Karnataka state border. Low rainfall and deforestation have left soils arid and eroded. Unemployment and indebtedness are rife. Many of the region's poor people – especially the *dalit* communities – suffer from chronic food insecurity.

As with many other crises, man-made factors have turned hazard into disaster. The 'green revolution' technology, advocated by the Indian government (and Andhra Pradesh's state government in particular) in a bid to 'modernize' agriculture, has been heavily biased in favour of wheat, rice and cotton. These cash crops were assumed to be more profitable, but they are prone to pests and require expensive fertilizers and pesticides to succeed. Moreover, their introduction has come at the expense of food grains like sorghum and millet, which are native to the rain-fed regions of India and have traditionally been the primary source of nutrition for over 40 per cent of the rural population. The dominance of rice and wheat has eroded the food culture of 'dryland' India, which constitutes almost 70 per cent of all agricultural land.

Box 3.1 Scaling up disaster resilience beyond the community

Building disaster resilience at community level is only a start. To have widespread impact on mitigating the impact of disasters on lives and livelihoods, the message – and practice – of risk reduction needs to spread beyond the confines of individual villages. The challenge is to scale up micro-level initiatives to the point where the policies and practices of government and the wider public are influenced.

The concept of community-based disaster mitigation task forces, launched by some NGOs in India's Orissa state, provides one example of how this challenge was addressed. One of the NGOs is CASA (Church's Auxiliary for Social Action), an Indian NGO with a nationwide relief, rehabilitation and development remit, which works with the poor irrespective of creed.

With 10 to 15 years' development experience in Orissa, CASA provided emergency relief following the 'supercyclone' that devastated the state in 1999. The CASA team realized that, in such a disaster-prone region, much of their development work could prove futile without appropriate disaster preparedness and mitigation measures. So the organization set up a disaster mitigation training centre at Banamalipur in coastal Khurda district. Over one year, it provides a seven-phase training programme for rural community members and local NGOs. The training covers disaster awareness, formation of disaster mitigation task forces (DMTFs), capacity building, income generation, mitigation measures, advocacy, lobbying and maintaining data banks.

The newly trained participants then return to their villages to set up DMTFs, which in turn run training programmes for villagers on disaster early warning, rescue and evacuation.

Community members are also taught about first aid and medical support, sanitation, relief operations, carcass disposal, and are given counselling. They are trained to draw up village contingency plans and to develop procedures for assessing damage. A key element of the DMTF's role is to create a disaster fund. They agree how much community members will regularly contribute, manage the bank account and purchase emergency stocks and equipment as appropriate.

Another responsibility of the DMTF is to maintain cyclone shelters constructed by CASA with combined government and international donor funding. These are usually reinforced concrete buildings constructed on two floors and raised on stilts to withstand the powerful tidal surges that accompany cyclones. They are capable of sheltering about 1,000 to 1,500 people and have safe drinking water and toilet facilities. CASA's work builds on the experiences of the Bangladesh Red Crescent Society among similarly cyclone-prone communities around the Bay of Bengal (see *World Disasters Report 2002*).

From the outset, CASA engages the community in extensive discussion about the shelters' locations, round-the-year usage and maintenance. The DMTF then ensures that maintenance of the shelter is effectively managed and that the community makes the widest possible use of it. Shelters are often used for women's and youth groups, crèches, primary health care services, space for additional school classes, community events and celebrations such as weddings.

In 2002, CASA's centre at Banamalipur provided training to 180 DMTF members, covering 30 villages across three districts.

International Federation
of Red Cross and Red Crescent Societies

The second batch to undergo training included 200 trainees from 40 villages in four districts. Community commitment to the DMTFs is strong, as villagers already recognize the value of their existing village development committees. Moreover, memories of 1999's devastating cyclone are still fresh.

During the floods of 2003, task force members were key to ensuring that possible embankment breach points were sandbagged, stranded people were rescued, first aid was administered and the shelters, which were constructed following the 1999 disaster, were effectively managed. As Birabar Mohapatra of Khursia village in Kendrapara district says: "Children of my village have saved me and my family, otherwise in the last flood we wouldn't even have got the dry food."

Building on the success of the task forces in Orissa, CASA, with support from Britain's Department for International Development, promoted DMTFs as an integral part of their flood rehabilitation programme in the neighbouring state of West Bengal. As a result, DMTFs now play a key role in 110 villages across the 22 catchment areas of the programme.

From the success at village level demonstrated by CASA, the value of DMTFs has been widely recognized. They now form an important part of community-based disaster management initiatives implemented by the United Nations Development Programme (UNDP), notably in its recently completed Orissa pilot project working with 1,603 villages in ten blocks to create community contingency plans and mitigation solutions through participatory risk assessment and mapping.

UNDP's aim was "to reduce social, economic and physical vulnerabilities" by promoting "disaster preparedness as a socio-economic development process to prevent loss of development gains and to empower the community with appropriate skills and access to all development institutions". In order to organize and systematize disaster response at the local level, UNDP trained disaster management committees and task forces not only within communities but also at higher administrative levels.

According to a recent impact assessment study: "The [UNDP] project has been successful in putting disaster preparedness on the agenda of local government and the Panchayati Raj Institutions (PRIs)... [it] has built capacity in disaster preparedness and in the integration of disaster management into the development programming process at the Block and Gram Panchayat levels to support disaster preparedness and mitigation at the community level." ■

Many farmers, who took out loans to cover the high costs of inputs necessary for cash crops, have become bankrupt as their crops fail to grow or sell well. Suicides among Andhra Pradesh's 12 million farmers have been rising. Trapped by debt and driven by despair, an estimated 4,000 to 5,000 farmers have killed themselves across the state in the last six years, according to P. Chengala Reddy, honorary chairperson of Andhra Pradesh's Federation of Farmers Associations. "While the suicides in the past were confined to a few districts and regions, this year every district is witnessing the deaths," said Reddy during an interview in May 2004.

Community grain fund

The Deccan Development Society (DDS) is a local NGO which began working in rural communities of Andhra Pradesh 20 years ago. DDS now works actively in 65 villages, focusing on building up the livelihood base and food security of local farming families. Securing better food supplies in the face of drought and debt has proved the key issue around which communities agree to cooperate. DDS employs various strategies to help increase local resilience:

- Forming women's *sanghams* (collectives) and encouraging collective farming by women.
- Initiating programmes to restore arid land back into a productive asset.
- Promoting afforestation and mini-watershed management.
- Creating community gene and grain funds.

Rural communities once held stores of grain to sustain themselves during times of need, but the practice has largely died out. However, DDS has revived the idea in the form of the community grain fund, promoted as an alternative and very effective system of distributing food to the poor. The official public distribution system (PDS) managed by the Indian government makes five key staples (wheat, rice, kerosene, cooking oil and sugar) available to poor people at subsidized rates. The significant impact of this welfare measure on rural poverty has long been recognized. However, by building the PDS on rice and wheat, grown primarily in irrigated areas, it has discouraged the cultivation of other food grains on which families in semi-arid regions used to subsist. This in turn has undermined whatever limited food security poorer households once had, leaving them dependent on government welfare.

DDS works with local communities to develop an alternative system – the community grain fund – based on two key elements: cultivating idle land and reintroducing customary farming practices. First, DDS helps each village to identify land that lies uncultivated. Landowners are given a loan to bring this fallow land back under cultivation and become project partners. They are encouraged to grow local food grains – which are more drought-resistant and less dependent on expensive, external inputs than the cash crops encouraged by the government. Secondly, DDS encourages the use of cultivation methods that rely on customary wisdom and practices. The result has been a return to cropping patterns and food production systems that are more sustainable.

Formal agreements are drawn up so that the partner-landowners can repay their loans in kind by giving back to the community an annual quantity of food grains for four years. This grain is stored in each village and becomes the community grain fund (CGF). Each community identifies the poorest households using participatory methods, grades each family's poverty on a scale from one to five, and decides on how much grain they are eligible to receive from the CGF. No one receives free food, but the poorest families are entitled to buy their allocation at a subsidized rate (in 2004

International Federation of Red Cross and Red Crescent Societies

this was Rs 3 per kilo of sorghum, compared to Rs 5.50 on the open market). The money earned through sales goes into a village bank account that becomes a revolving fund. Interest earned on the fund pays to subsidize grain for the poor, ensuring the programme becomes sustainable within three to four years.

Three principles distinguish DDS's strategy from the government-managed PDS: local production, local storage and local consumption. Through the alternative public distribution system built on the CGF, farmers are once again able to produce local, drought-resistant food grains – giving them control over their own food culture and nutrition. And the system promotes grain diversity, as it encourages the production of numerous varieties of sorghum and millet in areas where these grains are indigenous.

Rediscovering local biodiversity

To further boost the capacity of farming families to withstand drought, DDS promoted the innovative idea of a seed bank to rescue traditional crop varieties that thrive in arid conditions. Within five years, the seed bank – known as the community gene fund – had attracted 500 local women members.

DDS achieved this by inviting people from 60 villages to collect as many different kinds of seeds as possible – through organizing competitions or exhibitions. Many of these forgotten seeds were known only to the older generation, as the government's 'green revolution' had led to the disappearance of varieties such as foxtail millet, pearl millet, little millet and kodo millet. Since 2000, the community gene fund has grown into a movement across the region. Every February, DDS organizes the Biodiversity Festival, a mobile exhibition of 'treasured seeds' collected from various villages in the region and preserved in the gene fund. The seeds are ceremoniously carried in a convoy of 30 or 40 decorated bullock carts, moving from village to village, where public meetings and awareness-raising events about sustainable agriculture are held (see Box 3.2).

Through their involvement with the gene fund, women have regained control of family farming. Seed keeping is not just a physical activity, but also an intellectual activity and a vital defence against drought. For *dalit* women, it has enabled them to struggle out of the triple jeopardy of being social outcasts, poor and female. Now, they are managers of a scheme to revive traditional seed diversity for the community. Upper-caste rich men are even coming to them seeking seeds – a measure of the social revolution caused by a simple seed bank.

A study carried out in 2003 by the National Institute of Rural Development in Hyderabad shows that the impact of DDS's food security programme has been very significant. Areas cultivated have increased, producing more food and fodder crops. More jobs have been generated, which means more marginal households have returned to farming rather than migrating in search of wage labour to survive.

Mobile Biodiversity Festival

The Patha Pantala Panduga (festival of traditional crops) is a colourful annual event, organized by the Deccan Development Society since 1999. Over a period of 28 days in January/February each year, 20 specially decorated bullock carts carry the seed wealth of the region around more than 50 villages to renew people's faith and confidence in their own agriculture and the amazing biodiversity that it harbours.

The event includes food festivals under the theme of "Millet: God's own food". Folk dances, *kolatams* (mythological dramas performed by women dancing with sticks), songs and a variety of rituals add to the festival's colour and enjoyment. The 2003 festival was particularly significant:

■ The principles and issues that have been expressed by farmers in the Zaheerabad region for the last four years, during previous biodiversity festivals, have now become a national plan, included in the Indian government's National Biodiversity Strategy and Action Plan. This is probably the first time in the country's history that

farmers from a very poor and backward region have proved that they not only have the capacity to contribute to a national plan but are also able to draft a plan.

■ The 2003 festival has been making some very significant contributions towards ways in which agricultural concerns can be addressed by the Andhra Pradesh state government.

■ In a sign of the strength of their biodiversity-based agriculture, the farmers of the Zaheerabad region, particularly *dalit* women, have achieved total food self-sufficiency. It is exhilarating to note that, when the rest of Andhra Pradesh is struggling to meet its food needs by depending upon the rice supply of the central government, the women farmers of Zaheerabad say that their own agriculture can feed them and they do not need to depend on anyone.

■ At the local government's headquarters, special celebratory *sadassus* (farmers' forums) were held in which the farmers who have led their communities in enhancing the biodiversity of their crops were specially honoured. ■

As the changes brought about in these villages are based on knowledge, skills and resources largely internal to the community, rather than being dependent on large investments of external money or technology, this is a path that other communities in semi-arid regions can follow to create a more resilient future. Already, campaigning on the issues of biodiversity and genetically modified crops – inspired by DDS and partner agencies – has reached more than 300 villages in the area. However, the success of DDS's approach rests on enhancing the solidarity and community consensus needed to convert awareness into concrete actions. In this respect, the catalytic role of aid organizations is crucial.

Patanka case study

Our third case study is from Patanka in Patan district, Gujarat – a village of 250 families hit by 2001's devastating earthquake. It shows how the recovery phase

International Federation of Red Cross and Red Crescent Societies

after disaster can provide an opportunity to rebuild community infrastructure and livelihoods stronger than before – thereby boosting resilience to future risks.

On the morning of 26 January 2001, a massive tremor (7.6 magnitude) shook the state of Gujarat. It proved to be one of the two most deadly earthquakes to hit India in its recorded history. According to figures released by the Indian government one month after the quake, 20,000 people were killed and 166,000 injured.

The quake completely destroyed around 350,000 houses and damaged nearly 900,000 more (both temporary and permanent). Out of a population of 38 million people, 16 million were affected by the disaster. The impact on livelihoods was equally devastating. More than 20,000 cattle were reported lost. The government estimated direct economic losses at US$ 1.3 billion – but other estimates put the figure nearer US$ 5 billion.

Patanka was one of 7,904 villages affected across 21 districts. However, being outside Kutch district (the earthquake's epicentre), Patanka received minimal external aid – just some food aid and tents. Worse still, three years of severe drought and crop failure had eroded the community's capacity to cope.

The villagers retrieved a few assets from their collapsed houses, such as dried food, cooking utensils and clothes, and set up home in tents or under makeshift roofs amidst the rubble. They wanted to access government compensation schemes to help them rebuild their homes, but needed clarification on how to apply.

In the meantime, Patanka's villagers took the initiative and approached SEEDS (Sustainable Environmental and Ecological Development Society), an NGO started in New Delhi by a group of architects, which was itself looking for suitable villages in which to begin rehabilitation. The villagers told SEEDS they were trying to recover on their own, but needed assistance. Their motivation appealed to the architects, so both sides agreed to cooperate.

The SEEDS team joined forces with some partner NGOs from India and Japan, plus the United Nations Centre for Regional Development (UNCRD), to establish a project called Patanka Navjeevan Yojana (Patanka New Life, or PNY). Their aim was to develop a model of building stronger houses and community infrastructure, which could be replicated across the region.

Building consensus first

Unlike Samiapalli, Patanka is a mixed caste village, which presented particular challenges for SEEDS. The village is split into two political factions, although there is relative harmony between the groups. However, difficulties arose as the initial agreement to work in the village had been negotiated with the village head, who belonged to one of the factions. So SEEDS had to ensure constant transparency over the even-handedness of its approach.

First of all, SEEDS organized a series of community planning exercises, with groups of men, women and local government officials, to assess local needs and capacities. Different reconstruction plans were presented and debated until there was consensus on the need to rebuild the village's collapsed houses stronger than before. A series of discussions followed, focusing on the most appropriate earthquake-safe construction methods. Participants experimented with different cardboard and clay models, which were subjected to the 'shake table test'. Three different model houses were shaken. The first, traditional-style house completely collapsed; the second, slightly sturdier house partially collapsed; and the third, earthquake-proof design remained undamaged. This visual demonstration proved a highly effective form of communication.

The SEEDS team then built a model house to demonstrate earthquake-safe technology. Having tested a number of variations on the traditional housing construction of boulders and mud, they concluded that safer construction need not depend exclusively on cement and steel. But considerable care was needed to find the right ways of combining elements of modern and traditional materials and techniques to bring out the best features of both:
- Rubble was re-used from collapsed buildings to save resources.
- Stone masonry was employed, rather than brick or cement concrete blocks, as it was both vernacular and provided better thermal insulation.
- Traditional tile roofs were used rather than slab roofs, as tiles 'breathe', keeping inside temperatures during the hot summers up to 5 degrees Celsius lower than in buildings with slab roofs.
- Key seismic safety elements were integrated into the design, such as reinforced concrete plinths and lintels, and steel reinforcing gable bands and corner 'stitches'.
- Houses were set in traditional rural configurations, surrounded by open spaces, rather than in city-style terraces, which are unsuitable for rural lifestyles and more susceptible to earthquake damage.

Once the model house was built – and donated to the poorest person in the village, by group decision – building across the rest of the village began. Entire families got involved, with women carrying building materials and children fetching water for curing the concrete, while the men got on with construction. Villagers were free to decide on the location, design and size of their new homes, within the overall principles of seismically safer building. The average cost per house was Rs 40,000 (around US$ 1,000), of which Rs 10,000 was provided by SEEDS in the form of cement and steel reinforcements. Although in theory the government offered compensation to families whose homes had been completely destroyed, very few families in the region received their full entitlement, because the government insisted on seismic safety measures with which many villagers were not familiar. A key aspect

Photo opposite page: For recovery after disaster to be safe and sustainable, building community consensus is as important as building disaster-resistant infrastructure.

Patrick Fuller/ International Federation.

International Federation of Red Cross and Red Crescent Societies

of SEEDS strategy was to help Patanka's inhabitants receive the maximum government compensation possible.

The project's strategy was to build on local skills by training village masons in earthquake-resistant construction and employing them to supervise rebuilding Patanka's houses. Some local farmers, unemployed due to the drought, were also trained as masons. This not only met the high demand for masons, but also provided vital alternative livelihoods for drought-affected families. SEEDS trained the masons to work with wood and steel, as well as stone. Masons were trained two or three at a time, while working onsite with tools and materials. This 'show and tell' technique proved far more effective than classroom sessions. SEEDS organized an exchange with Nepali masons, trained by the Nepal Society for Earthquake Technology, which proved both instructive and inspiring for Patanka's trainee masons.

Potential tensions were avoided by SEEDS's decision to work with every family willing to rebuild its own house – and almost all families were willing. The common interests of families involved in housing construction, together with their agreement on the evolving community-wide plan for rehabilitation, gradually helped to build greater community consensus across factional divides. This led to villagers building some shared community infrastructure and facilities.

Nevertheless, the overall process was very slow. Houses were worked on in batches of 20, decided through a lottery system, and convincing people to be patient was very difficult. Meanwhile, the project's early successes raised expectations and demands – especially from neighbouring villages, which pressed SEEDS to include them.

From safer homes to better lives

The initial aim of SEEDS was to solve the immediate problem of new, safer housing. But having established credibility and rapport through their reconstruction programme, they began to discuss other common concerns with the community and how these could be addressed through developmental means. Senior citizens, the disabled and children were all involved in the discussions. Villagers were determined to improve their overall quality of life. This would mean working across the full range of critical needs – not just housing, but health, education, environment and livelihoods.

The first priority was water – a major problem for Patanka as well as for adjoining areas. SEEDS formulated a programme to access government funds to build a rainwater-harvesting system. The programme involved the community undertaking watershed development and water conservation work to ensure their use of rainwater became more efficient. Their work included deepening village water tanks, building dykes and plugging the gullies down which rainwater ran.

Local livelihoods have also benefited from SEEDS's involvement. Many of the masons trained by the project have continued in that trade. According to Ramesh Dharsi, one of the newly trained masons: "After the earthquake, masons were in short supply. People started building their houses without any technical skills. Through the project many people got trained as masons and are now working. Patanka used to have four or five masons. Now it has about 30."

SEEDS built a good relationship with local government and assisted the district administration in getting compensation forms completed by each household, to release resources for reconstruction. The local government was so impressed with the strengthening work carried out in Patanka that they asked SEEDS to retrofit about 50 more buildings in the region and to implement a disaster mitigation and preparedness programme in over 30 villages, both under contract to the government. This provided more work for Patanka's masons, trained under the PNY project. The masons are now working to establish a guild, to expand the scope of their seismic-resistant building skills from the village to the region.

However, with well over a million houses across Gujarat needing to be rebuilt or repaired, scaling-up is a major issue. The reconstruction and recovery programme is one of the largest of its kind in the world, attracting nearly US$ 1.2 billion of resources from the World Bank and a further US$ 650 million from the state and federal governments.

According to the Gujarat State Disaster Management Authority, almost 847,000 houses have been repaired and 239,000 houses reconstructed, while 15,000 masons and 3,000 engineers have been traied. Meanwhile over 80 NGOs are involved in rebuilding around 50,000 houses across 473 villages. There is clearly a danger that consistent standards of construction and coordination may not be maintained.

SEEDS's approach towards scaling-up is to concentrate less on physical building and more on sharing knowledge and lessons learned. They have developed publications and materials based on the experience of Patanka, for use in training workshops and awareness campaigns in Gujarat – as well as in the hill states of northern India that are vulnerable to earthquakes. According to SEEDS's director, Anshu Sharma: "We are currently trying to lay greater stress on developing and delivering knowledge resources as a strategic up-scaling measure rather than simply replicating the physical process in a number of locations."

Challenges and success factors

While each of the three case studies outlined above addressed different kinds of disasters, and external agencies became involved at different stages in the disaster cycle, some common challenges and success factors in creating community resilience emerge.

In each of the communities we have studied, aid organizations had to overcome the initial scepticism of some villagers that it was possible to work together to improve their common infrastructure. A balance had to be struck between building on existing knowledge and finding acceptance for the benefits of new ideas and practices. Low levels of literacy and lack of exposure to alternative practices made this harder. Many of the villagers with most initiative had already left their communities to seek a better life elsewhere. Addressing the powerlessness of marginalized villagers – without alienating those in positions of power – proved a key challenge.

Meanwhile within every community there were conflicting perspectives – particularly around the tension between today's immediate needs (enough to eat, saving money) and longer-term issues of protection from risk (clean water, safer homes). Reaching consensus over joint community action often took many months. Having achieved agreement on the way ahead, meeting the rising expectations of villagers (and their neighbours) then became a major challenge. However, ten principles are common to the success of the case studies we have presented:

1. Find the right entry point into the community
- Samiapalli: Gram Vikas recognized how delicate their work was, given the problems with alcoholism and landlessness. By encouraging a women's savings group, they enabled women to take responsibility for challenging the root causes of vulnerability.

- Zaheerabad: DDS's entry point into each community was based on meeting their most immediate and urgent needs – working towards food security.
- Patanka: SEEDS started by meeting the community's most pressing need – earthquake-safe homes

2. Create community consensus
- Samiapalli: Gram Vikas' core principle is to work with everyone in the village or no one. After months of raising awareness and building consensus, the NGO helped villagers agree on their greatest needs and how to meet them. Gram Vikas believes that only if people stand together can they address their vulnerabilities, whether social, economic, political or physical.
- Zaheerabad: DDS enhanced village cohesion through community grain and gene funds. Communities decided which of the poorest families should receive grain. The Biodiversity Festival expanded consensus around traditional solutions to food insecurity.
- Patanka: Despite being a divided community, SEEDS worked with individual families to generate debate and build community consensus on the best ways to reconstruct their homes. Transparency was key to building trust across factional divides.

3. Build on local skills and knowledge
- Samiapalli: Gram Vikas built on the villagers' desire to improve their situation – starting with the women's determination to root out alcoholism in their community. Later, community masons were employed to build the watsan and housing projects.
- Zaheerabad: As an alternative to the government's top-down distribution of inappropriate handouts, DDS championed self-reliance through local production, local storage and local consumption – using traditional sustainable farming techniques that do not depend on external inputs.
- Patanka: SEEDS seized on the motivation of Patanka villagers to recover. They incorporated locally available materials to reconstruct houses, but adapted the design to improve its strength. They trained local masons in new techniques – but in a low-tech way.

4. Empower women
- Samiapalli: Key to building community consensus and sustaining development is creating the space for women to take on responsibility in a patriarchal society. Samiapalli's savings groups gave women the courage to confront alcoholism, reduced their dependence on extortionate local moneylenders, and provided them with a forum for learning about and monitoring family nutrition, health and education.
- Zaheerabad: The collectives initiated by DDS enabled women to play a central role in producing their families' food. Ownership of the traditional seed banks has

International Federation
of Red Cross and Red Crescent Societies

given women a new-found status in society, but through a practical rather than an overtly political way.

- Patanka: Women and children played a full part in helping rebuild their homes.

5. Facilitate rather than fund – external agencies as catalysts

- Samiapalli: Gram Vikas acted as facilitator rather than funder, enabling villagers to access government loans, guaranteeing those loans and encouraging villagers to save money themselves. Villagers provided their own labour and many raw materials for building disaster-resistant homes.
- Zaheerabad: Rather than operating a welfare system, DDS chose to make loans – repayable in food grants to the poor. More important than any financial contribution was DDS's role as catalyst in creating the community consensus needed for the project to succeed and sustain itself.
- Patanka: Whole families had to contribute towards rebuilding their homes using local materials. SEEDS helped villagers access government compensation funds.

6. Provide tangible results to establish authority for future projects

- Samiapalli: The watsan system significantly improved villagers' health and nutrition. This success won Gram Vikas the trust of the community for implementing future risk reduction initiatives.
- Patanka: After achieving rapport and respect through rebuilding homes, SEEDS helped villagers identify other developmental needs, such as rainwater harvesting.

7. Strengthen local livelihoods

- Samiapalli: Enabling the village to negotiate funds from the state helped villagers to strengthen and diversify their livelihoods, through buying more livestock (sheep, goats and cows), learning about veterinary care, learning new masonry skills, turning the pond into a fish farm and planting a community forest to harvest cash crops. As a result, migration away from the village in search of work was reduced.
- Zaheerabad: Through introducing the community gene fund, dozens of diverse traditional crop varieties were rescued from obscurity, providing local farmers with more nutritious, disaster-resistant food grains than the monoculture offered by the 'green revolution'.
- Patanka: the organization provided drought-affected, unemployed farmers with new training and employment as masons – offering them a vital alternative livelihood.

8. Find ways of replicating resilience beyond single communities

- Samiapalli: Gram Vikas engaged local government as partners and enhanced their capacities as well as those of the villagers. The demonstration effect of early projects has led to 12,000 families in over 150 villages benefiting from improved watsan and stronger homes.

- Zaheerabad: DDS's approach builds on local knowledge and is locally led, requiring very little external input or investment. It has replicated its programme in 65 villages.
- Patanka: SEEDS built up a good relationship with local government, which contracted the organization to retrofit 50 more buildings in the area. SEEDS's programme of training and awareness is spreading across Gujarat to India's northern hill states.

9. Software as important as hardware

- Samiapalli: During the 2003 floods, villagers were protected by their safer homes. They were able to respond and recover swiftly, thanks to their efficient village organization and strong contacts with local government officials. Transforming Samiapalli's social fabric and creating community unity proved as important as building physical infrastructure.
- Zaheerabad: As well as encouraging physical mitigation measures such as restoring farmland and planting more trees, DDS promoted greater awareness of agricultural issues through its annual Biodiversity Festival.
- Patanka: Building the disaster awareness of villagers through the 'shake table test' proved a graphic form of communication. Training masons and building awareness is seen as more important than one-off reconstruction projects.

10. Integrate risk reduction with development

- Samiapalli: Gram Vikas believes development is the best way to boost resilience to disasters. Helping villagers build new, disaster-resistant homes was an integral part of a wider development programme.
- Zaheerabad: When vulnerability is the result of low rainfall, eroded soil, unemployment and indebtedness, a long-term developmental approach to building community resilience is the only option likely to succeed.
- Patanka: Reducing disaster risk was never an explicit aim of the community, despite its recent experiences. But for SEEDS, it was essential to ensure that local awareness of risks became an integral part of their programme.

Above all, these case studies illustrate that success is based on a people-centred approach, building on existing knowledge and resourcefulness, and upgrading the skills and status of those at risk, so they can cope with and recover from the full range of hazards which confront them.

Principal contributors to this chapter and boxes were Tom Palakudiyil, Mary Todd and Jonathan Walter, editor of the World Disasters Report. *Todd is an independent consultant on disaster risk reduction and management. Palakudiyil is Christian Aid's regional manager for south Asia. Box 3.2 was compiled with information from the Deccan Development Society, India.*

Sources and further information

Blaikie, Piers; Cannon, Terry; Davis, Ian; and Wisner, Ben. *At Risk: Natural Hazards, People's Vulnerability and Disasters.* London: Routledge, 2004 (second edition).

Department for International Development (DFID) (UK). *Sustainable livelihoods guidance sheets.* London: DFID, 1999/2000.

Disasters Emergency Committee (DEC). *Independent evaluation of expenditure of DEC Mozambique floods appeal funds.* London: DEC, 2001.

DEC. *A stitch in time? Independent evaluation of southern Africa crisis appeal.* London: DEC, 2003.

DEC. *Independent evaluation: the DEC response to the earthquake in Gujarat.* London: DEC, 2001.

International Federation of Red Cross and Red Crescent Societies. *World Disasters Report 2003: focus on ethics in aid.* Geneva: International Federation, 2003.

International Federation of Red Cross and Red Crescent Societies. *World Disasters Report 2002: focus on reducing risk.* Geneva: International Federation, 2002.

Palakudiyil, Tom and Todd, Mary. *Facing up to the storm, how local communities can cope with disasters: lessons from Orissa and Gujarat.* London, Christian Aid, 2003. Available at: http://www.christianaid.org.uk/storm

Pelling, M. *The vulnerability of cities, natural disasters and social resilience.* London, Earthscan, 2003.

Sanderson, D. 'Cities, disasters and livelihoods' in *Environment and Urbanisation,* Vol. 12, No. 2, October 2000.

Tearfund. *Before disaster strikes: why thousands are dying needlessly each year in preventable disasters.* London: Tearfund, 2004.

Twigg, John. 'The human factor in early warnings: risk perception and appropriate communications' in Zschau, J. and Kueppers, A. (eds), *Early Warning Systems for National Disaster Reduction.* Berlin: Springer Verlag, 2002.

Web sites

AlertNet **http://www.alertnet.org**

Code of Conduct for the International Red Cross and Red Crescent Movement and NGOs in Disaster Relief **http://www.ifrc.org/publicat/conduct/**

Deccan Development Society **http://www.ddsindia.org**

Disasters Emergency Committee **http://www.dec.org.uk**

Gram Vikas **http://www.gramvikas.org**

International Federation **http://www.ifrc.org**

Resilience Alliance **http://www.resalliance.org**

Sphere Project **http://www.sphereproject.org**

Sustainable Environment and Ecological Development Society (SEEDS) **http://www.seedsindia.org**

Voluntary Health Association of India **http://www.vhai.org**

Bam sends warning to reduce future earthquake risks

A mound of bare earth. An old lady gently pats it, her fingers moving up and down, up and down. Rhythmically. Endlessly repeating the same name in a high-pitched voice. Motionless, her husband stands hunched at the foot of the grave. Nearby, a bulldozer claws holes in the ground. But the noise fails to drown out her lament.

The cemetery of Bam is divided into two parts. In the first are orderly rows of well-constructed tombs, bearing photos of the deceased. The second section is no more than freshly turned soil, improvised graves bearing a jumble of names, some traced by hand in wet cement. Others are marked simply with some humble object – a blue plastic bowl or a piece of cloth tied round a stick in the ground. Dirty, broken stretchers have been thrown into a corner. This is the earthquake section.

It took a mere 12 seconds, at dawn on 26 December 2003, to annihilate a city. Of the 120,000 inhabitants of Bam and nearby villages, between 30,000 and 40,000 people were killed. The government's February estimate of 43,200 deaths was revised down to 26,271 the following month. The difference in death toll was put down to double counting of bodies during the chaotic aftermath of the disaster, although many aid workers and Bam survivors expressed disbelief at the new figures. Meanwhile, another 30,000 were injured. Practically all the survivors, some 75,000 people, were left homeless, as 85 per cent of the city's buildings had been destroyed. According to the World Bank, total economic damage was estimated at around US$ 1.5 billion.

Was this an unpredictable 'natural' disaster or a man-made tragedy that could have been avoided? Was Bam an isolated incident, or are the same factors at work elsewhere in Iran, secretly conspiring to create more catastrophes in the future? How did the survivors of Bam cope and what lessons can be drawn? Experts warn that millions more lives are threatened by fault lines beneath other Iranian cities, including the capital Tehran. What should be done to protect ordinary people and increase their resilience in the face of such risks?

Rich and poor suffer together

A number of factors combined to crush the city of Bam and its inhabitants. Firstly, the earthquake itself had an enormous impact – not because of its intensity (a 'moderate' 6.5 on the Richter scale) – but because its epicentre was located just beneath the city at a depth of barely ten kilometres. This was the shallowest earthquake Iran had ever known. The quake's timing also had tragic consequences:

Photo opposite page: Hundreds of lives were saved by neighbours using their bare hands. The resilience of local people provides the foundation on which to build disaster preparedness and response.

Farooq Burney/ International Federation.

05:28 on Friday morning, a holiday, when almost everyone was asleep in bed. A third key factor was Bam's traditional architecture: houses with over-heavy roofs and over-thick walls, built of mud bricks, which crumbled as they collapsed, leaving no air pockets and suffocating those inside.

"What can you expect? It was an old city," say the Iranians. They mention the citadel which had made Bam world famous, some parts of which were 2,000 years old. This jewel in the tourism crown, a legacy of the Silk Route, collapsed like a sandcastle at high tide. But while it may be understandable for a building several hundred years old to succumb, can the same be said of modern concrete and steel constructions? The offices of the governor and the municipality, Bam's three hospitals, its schools, the central bank building: all were less than 30 years old, yet were badly damaged, if not completely destroyed. Expensive residences suffered the same fate as the hovels of illegal Afghan workers. For once, rich and poor found themselves in the same boat. Bam's governor, who lost his sister and two nephews in the quake, was among the homeless.

And yet, some buildings remain standing. Very close to the epicentre, the youth centre of the Iranian Red Crescent Society (IRCS) is intact, apart from some plaster coming away from the walls. The IRCS closely supervised its construction in 2002 – it was built to resist an earthquake of 8 on the Richter scale. Not far away, virtually alone in a street resembling the aftermath of a bomb blast, stands a fine mosque. Not a single brick dislodged. Behind it, the scaffolding for an extension project remains intact. A smartly dressed, bearded man introduces himself: "Hossein Zakeri. I'm the person who built this mosque in 1994, using earthquake-resistant standards." Not a single one of Bam's mosques, whether new or old, collapsed.

Poorly prepared

Surrounded by her three children, Farzane shivers in front of the tent which is now her only shelter. Small and slim, she makes a visible effort to master her shattered nerves. Farzane is one of the lucky ones: she panicked when the earth shook, nearly an hour before disaster struck. She dragged her family into the street and refused to return. She watched her home collapse onto all her possessions. She lists what she lost: refrigerator; television; the wages her husband – a building worker – had just brought home. But at least Farzane and her family are alive.

Earthquakes cannot be predicted and, according to most experts, the three small tremors which preceded the disaster did not justify launching an evacuation. Mahmud Ranjbar would not have agreed. When the earth shook at about 04:45 on the morning of 26 December, he decided it was time to raise the alarm. Two minor tremors had already taken place the previous afternoon and evening. Mahmud, an IRCS volunteer, started phoning people he knew. "Get out of your house, and, if possible, gather in front of the Red Crescent building," he told them. He managed to

International Federation
of Red Cross and Red Crescent Societies

reach at least 25 families – about 100 people – before the fatal quake at 05:28. His body, along with those of his wife and two children, was found under the rubble of his house. He was still clutching the phone in his hand.

So could more have been done by local authorities to prepare and warn residents about the impending disaster? One Tehran-based earthquake scientist revealed that Iran has a large stock of 'accelerograms', sensitive seismic instruments which are triggered by tremors. If such a device had been operational in Bam – and crucially, if it had been connected via a computer and human operator to an efficient siren system – then an alarm to evacuate could have been raised. The problem is: what level of tremor is strong enough to justify evacuation? Then of course, an efficient evacuation system would be needed. But Akbar Alavi, the representative in Bam of the governor of Kerman (the provincial capital) said that no such system was in place in Bam.

What was well known, however, was the existence of an active fault, 120 kilometres long, right on the outskirts of Bam (see map). "Why were the hospitals in this city not reinforced?" asks Manuel Berberian, the geophysicist who identified the fault in 1976. It was shown on all the maps. Four years before the tragedy another seismologist, Mehdi Zare of Tehran's International Institute of Earthquake Engineering and Seismology (IIEES), had announced publicly that Bam would be the victim of a major disaster one day. "People laughed in my face," he recalls.

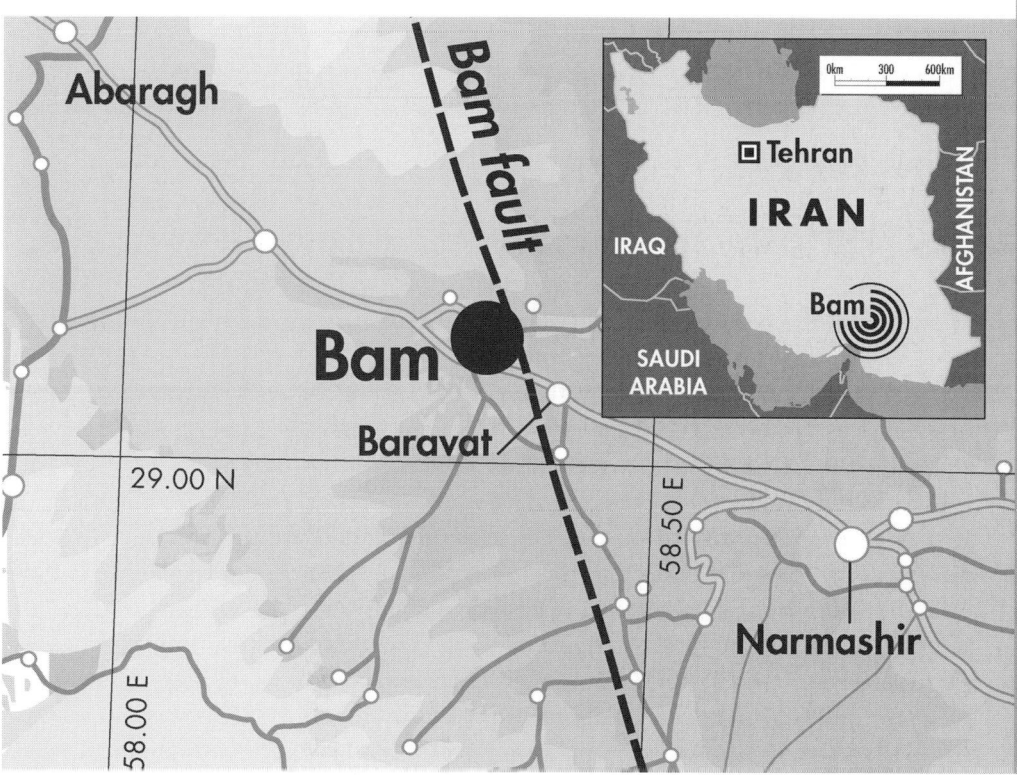

Why was nothing done to protect the city? Dr Alavi, the governor's envoy, sighs, summing up what most people in the area thought before 26 December. "Because the citadel, which is built of mud bricks, had been here for 2,000 years, we knew that there had never been a major earthquake in the region. Everyone thought there never would be."

Yet a cursory glance at Iran's earthquake record over the last century reveals that between 143,000 and 178,000 Iranians have lost their lives in 19 major earthquakes since 1909 (see Figure 4.1). With such a history and such an array of national and international experts issuing constant warnings, how could the country fail to be better prepared? How can such a gap between the experts and the policy-makers be explained?

Fatalism and greed

"Look at this!" says Sassan Eshghi of the IIEES in Tehran, "*Kimia* was the most modern building in Bam, brand-new and expensive." He points to a photo of a black and red building, all steel and glass, which seems to have fallen to its knees. "But the welding was really bad – workers from the villages, no proper training. When the earth shook, the welding gave way and everything collapsed like a pack of cards." Of

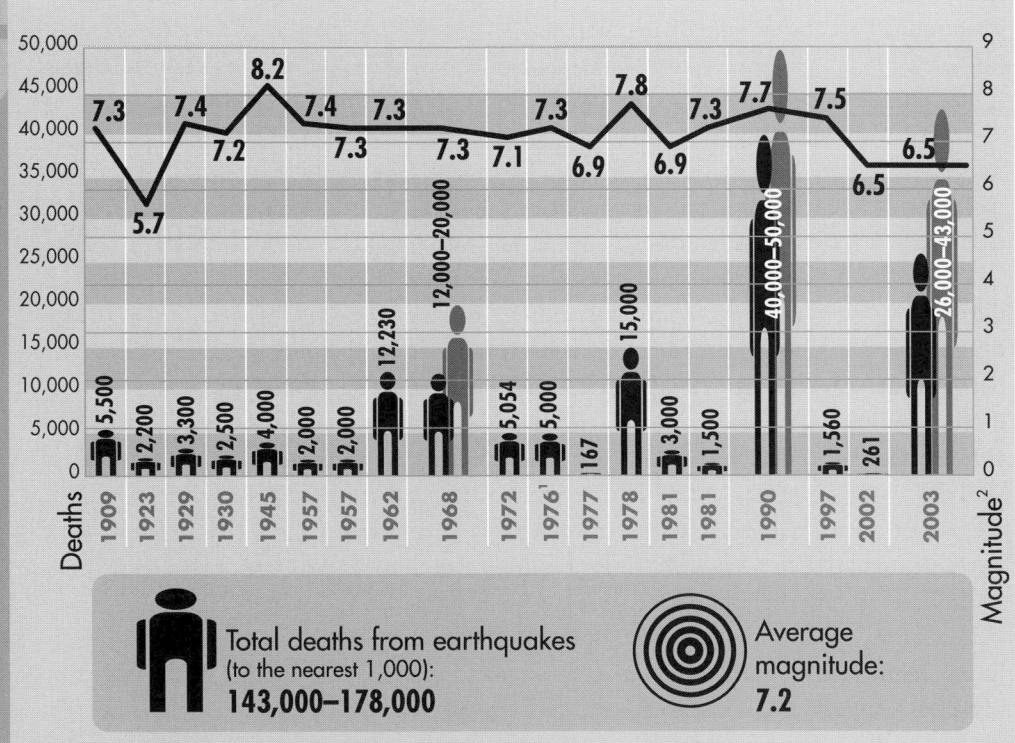

Figure 4.1
Iran: shaken by a
century of quakes.

Source: US Geological
Survey, 2004.

[1] Iran/USSR border.
[2] NB. The impact of an earthquake is a function of both its magnitude and its depth.

the five original floors, only two remain, the three lower floors crushed under the weight of the upper ones. The Ministry of Housing fared no better – 120 of its brand-new housing units, destined for underprivileged families, were badly damaged. They were yet to be occupied. Incredibly, points out Dr Eshghi, even the building housing Tehran's earthquake institute would not itself survive a strong tremor – its pillars are too weak, he says.

Building well costs more, obviously. But spending money is no guarantee of safety. "There are plenty of grand buildings around, with a beautiful façade, but which are just like a sword of Damocles hanging over their inhabitants," says Dr Eshghi. Bam was far from poor: the city thrived thanks to its date palms (famous throughout the country), the tourism its citadel attracted and its light industry, which drew in workers from far and wide, including Afghanistan. "You often see the ruins of beautiful houses," remarks Jamie Richardson, an engineer with the International Federation of Red Cross and Red Crescent Societies. "So, if you go to all that expense, why not do it properly? There is both poor workmanship and tolerance of it."

Legislation is simply not applied. Iran adopted a seismic building code in 1989, but all too often it remains theoretical. To house a population that has more than doubled in 25 years – from 27 million in 1979 to 68 million in 2003 – Iran has been gripped by building fever. It's a lucrative market. "Construction brings a profit of between 50 and 100 per cent. There are even investors from neighbouring countries who come here. This is a hot business, you cannot interrupt it," warns Dr Eshghi, adding: "There is some corruption, and enormous ignorance." Iranian sources claim that the inspectors sent to examine new public and commercial buildings are often paid off by developers to certify their constructions as conforming to earthquake norms, without carrying out a thorough inspection.

Ultimately, there are no credible sanctions. "In the United Kingdom, I am legally responsible if there is a structural fault in a building I constructed," points out Richardson. Iran's seismic building code theoretically holds the engineer responsible, if the building was constructed after the code's introduction in 1989. But prosecutions of individuals are almost non-existent, and there are no laws against negligent municipalities which fail to protect their infrastructure through retrofitting. That said, blame for weak construction may be often shared. People who occupy well-constructed buildings may add floors or remove supporting columns and internal walls without first seeking permission or expert advice.

In the aftermath of the Bam tragedy, there were vague mutterings about an enquiry – but it never actually happened. Public protests in Bam turned into riots on 4 March 2004. But they were prompted by the slow pace of relief, rather than by anger at the government or at building contractors for failing to ensure that houses

CHAPTER 4

were earthquake-proof in the first place. This reveals a lack of awareness among many Bam inhabitants of the systemic weaknesses that caused the disaster.

Lack of disaster awareness may in turn fuel or feed off a wider sense of fatalism. According to Dr Eshghi: "Nobody thinks this is an earthquake country! We live outwardly in a modern style, but we think in a fatalistic way. Maybe it [fatalism] is linked to religion, but it is wrong: God is merciful! Our religious people should remind the population of this."

It should be said that fatalism is common in many other countries – including the West. Psychologically, it is an attitude that helps at-risk or traumatized populations to accept the status quo, rather than taking responsibility (to mitigate the risk) or blame (for not doing more to mitigate the risk) upon their own shoulders. Fatalism may also help people, who are unaware of the technical reasons for structural failure, to explain why some buildings survive a quake while other apparently similar buildings nearby collapse.

In a highly centralized country like Iran, a strong government has, in principle, the capability to enforce building codes, fight corruption and spread disaster awareness, if it so chooses. Given Iran's history of devastating earthquakes, why weren't more measures taken to reduce the risk? Dr Eshghi suggests that perhaps part of the fault lies with people like himself: "We have failed to communicate to the public in a proper way," he says. Wherever the blame lies, a lethal combination of ignorance, fatalism and greed conspired with the forces of nature beneath Bam to create a massive disaster.

Iranians lead disaster response

On the morning of 26 December 2003, Bam found itself deprived of water, electricity and all means of communication with the outside world. Its government structures were destroyed, its streets littered with corpses. Nearly half the doctors and nurses were dead and not a single medical centre was left to take in the injured. At night, temperatures fell to freezing.

Barely two hours after the quake, the first Iranian Red Crescent teams arrived by road from Kerman, 190 km away. The army followed. By the afternoon, the airport was again operational, thanks to three mobile control towers. Around 10,000 seriously injured people were evacuated – by air or overland – to 72 hospitals throughout the country. Enormous traffic jams built up, as thousands of citizens from outside Bam responded to the appeal of Kerman's governor and rushed in to help.

Around 8,500 Red Crescent staff and volunteers – trained and experienced in disaster response – were deployed. Survivors' most pressing needs were met by IRCS

International Federation
of Red Cross and Red Crescent Societies

emergency supplies, stocked both in Bam and across the country. "After four days, everybody had a tent and a blanket, which is quite remarkable under the circumstances," says Steve McAndrew of the American Red Cross.

In the afternoon of 26 December, the Iranian authorities launched an appeal for international aid and even waived visa requirements for foreign aid workers – both unprecedented decisions in a country normally very protective of its borders.

A few foreign teams arrived within 24 hours, most within 48 hours. Strikingly, a major international effort in search and rescue yielded meagre results: 34 teams from 27 countries found just 22 people alive. Meanwhile, local IRCS search-and-rescue teams deployed within minutes, despite losing four team members and their headquarters in the disaster: they saved 157 lives with just ten sniffer dogs (see Box 4.1). Neighbours saved hundreds more people using their bare hands. As Mostafa Mohaghegh, the Red Crescent's director of international affairs at the time, points out: "Undoubtedly, training and preparing local search-and-rescue teams is far more effective than bringing external teams into the operation. It is not only cost-effective, but rather more importantly it is time-effective. In search and rescue, the first minutes, hours and days are vital."

The international response was massive and not limited to search and rescue: 1,800 aid workers arrived from 44 countries, but the Iranian Red Crescent took the lead role in coordination. Some things went wrong – inevitable perhaps, given the overwhelming scale of the catastrophe. Thousands of victims were buried too hastily in communal pits without being recorded, through a mistaken fear that dead bodies spread disease. Apart from the consequent psychological trauma for relatives, the lack of burial records will cause them administrative problems when claiming inheritance or pension rights.

The crisis also exposed serious failures in the country's disaster management, including competition between the army and the Red Crescent during the first few days of response. According to a legislative code passed in May 2003, the IRCS should play the lead role in disaster response, acting like civil defence bodies in other countries. However, tensions arose between the army, which wanted to restrict aircraft to evacuating the injured, and the Red Crescent, which requested that aircraft bring back emergency equipment on their return. "There had not been enough time for the new code to be absorbed, and for everyone to know their responsibilities," says Mohaghegh.

At the root of the problem is the lack of a clear chain of command going right to the head of state. The director of the national disaster response committee lacked the authority to resolve the conflict. "In the light of the evaluation of the operation at Bam, there is talk that in the future it will be the first deputy president of the republic

Box 4.1 Iranian sniffer dogs save more lives

In 1990, during the deadly Gilan earthquake in north-west Iran, the use of dogs by foreign search-and-rescue teams trying to save people buried under the rubble was a sticking point: in Islam, dogs are considered impure. But, 13 years later, in Bam, Iranian Red Crescent Society teams with Iranian sniffer dogs were at work less than five hours after disaster struck, and hardly anyone objected. They saved around 157 lives – seven times the number saved by 34 international teams combined.

In between Gilan and Bam is the story of a remarkable change in attitudes. It all started by chance: "In 2000, one of our chairpersons donated eight German shepherd dogs to us," recalls Farshid Towfighi, deputy head of planning and training at the IRCS. "We immediately thought it would be an excellent opportunity to reinforce our own capacity in search-and-rescue operations. In a country that is as vulnerable to disasters as Iran, this makes much more sense than relying on outside help."

The German Red Cross, which has considerable experience in this field, was asked to train the Iranian teams. But the German experts came back from Tehran with a negative assessment. The dogs could not live with the handler's family, they could not search 'off-lead', and they would never reach the (very high) German testing and performance standards. Applying German standards to Iran resulted in the project being frozen.

But two years later, the idea was resurrected during a German Red Cross disaster management training session in Tehran. There was a new assessment and a more realistic programme was designed, to raise the dogs' performance to the highest possible standards taking account of local circumstances. In parallel, the IRCS advocated the idea with the Supreme Islamic Council, which declared that working with dogs was acceptable in the interests of saving human lives. From then on, the IRCS kept on promoting the dog as a rescuer and frequently, the Red Crescent's president would be seen alongside a sniffer dog when attending public events.

With compromises on both sides, the two-year programme started in January 2003. Costs were kept to an absolute minimum, by limiting training to a series of learning steps. The German trainer spends no more than 14 days at a time in Iran. After each visit, the IRCS dog handlers have two or three months to reach an intermediate goal. At the end of 2004, the dogs will be tested according to slightly adapted German standards.

"We now have 20 teams and would like to further strengthen our capacity in the future," says Dr Towfighi proudly. A six-day search-and-rescue mission from Europe to Iran (six people with five dogs) costs a minimum of US$ 50,000. The same amount of money provides a two-year training programme for three Iranian dogs and their handlers (US$ 15,000 per dog). They can intervene hours rather than days after a disaster. And they are in the country to stay. ∎

who will be in charge," notes Mohaghegh. Another problem is that high staff turnover in the ministries and IRCS since 1990, when the last major earthquake hit Iran, means that valuable lessons learned about disaster management were forgotten.

Provinces 'sponsor' relief and recovery

When Hossein Ashrafi arrives, he is besieged with requests – for extra blankets, for toilets and showers to be erected as quickly as possible, for a sick child to be treated, for a hot meal after three weeks of baked beans. Ashrafi, who has 23 years of disaster experience with the IRCS, comes from Hamadan province in north-west Iran, which was struck by an earthquake in 2002. He embodies the system, introduced to Bam by the IRCS, of dividing the city into 13 sectors, each 'sponsored' by an Iranian province. In the 'Hamadan camp', with its neat rows of tents reserved for the families of the seriously injured, Hossein Ashrafi has undeniable authority.

Members of the Red Crescent, ministry representatives, medical staff, engineers and even imams arrived from across Iran to take over local positions of responsibility from those who were dead, injured or simply burnt out (see Box 4.2). Hamadan province sent 100 IRCS members, four civil servants and 80 volunteers to its sector of Bam – plus practical relief aid such as food, clothing and logistical support. They were helped by the recovery efforts of traditional neighbourhood networks: the 'notables' or 'white beards', five or six men of influence who, based around the local mosque, would organize the local community.

"This is the first time I've seen something like that. The largest sector has a maximum of 3,000 to 4,000 families, and they get help from a whole Iranian province!" says the American Red Cross's McAndrew enthusiastically. "The sheer volume of response outweighs the disadvantages."

For there are undeniable disadvantages. Coordination is one. Equality between sectors another. There are 'five-star' sectors, such as the one sponsored by East Azerbaijan province, which features a network of 160 clean water standpipes, while elsewhere water is delivered in tankers. Another problem is that the provincial authorities and the IRCS initially rotated key workers every two to three weeks. According to the International Federation's senior health officer, Hakan Sandbladh, this practice "put extraordinary strain on the expatriate health professionals" in the emergency referral hospital, since they had "to train and introduce new people all the time, leaving less time for essential patient work". The situation later improved.

Meanwhile, as Iran has 28 provinces and Bam 13 sectors, the 'sponsorships' change frequently. This exacerbates the already chronic loss of 'municipal memory', in a city where it is very difficult to find senior figures who understand what is going on or who is responsible. When talking to these troubleshooters from as far away as Tehran, Hamadan and Yazd, it is hard to avoid the conclusion that it will take a long time for the inhabitants of Bam to take control of their own destiny again.

Box 4.2 Hope amid the dust and destruction

In Bam, at the welfare organization (the government agency dealing with social affairs), Mojtaba Babaey is at a loss to find the number of people on welfare before the disaster. Like many of those in charge these days, he comes from Tehran. His only records are a few figures, neatly handwritten on one single sheet of paper. His predecessor, says Babaey, knew many things by heart. But, after working for ten days after the earthquake, he couldn't carry on any more. He had lost his whole family.

Dr Babaey's 'office' – a prefab container – consists of a few rugs, a kerosene stove and a large samovar of hot tea. He almost has to shout to make himself heard over the sound of the bulldozer clearing rubble just outside. Orange dust rises in the air, infiltrates his office, settles on his sheet of paper. There is dust everywhere. On the palm trees, which have all withstood the quake, on the cars, on people's clothes, in their nostrils, in their throats. Everyone in Bam keeps choking and sneezing. Some wear a surgical mask, in the hope of protecting their lungs.

It is a sunny day, but the bitter January wind brings tears to the eyes of the little boy who is selling apples and oranges at a large crossroads, just in front of the stadium. His thin sweater is no match for the biting cold. His young uncle explains that the boy's parents died when their house collapsed. The vegetable shop they owned together, on the ground floor, was lost along with everything else. When asked, he lists his dead relatives: brother, sister, father, uncles. He complains he cannot sleep at night under his nearby tent: "I have to keep an eye on the fruit, otherwise it will get stolen." Does he have any close relatives left? "There was my wife and my 1-year-old son. He is dead." Why didn't he mention the baby before? He looks away: "It bothers me."

There is a small queue in front of a shipping container. Bank Keshavarzi, the agricultural bank, has reopened three weeks after the disaster. Some civil servants and businessmen are drawing money. A man in his thirties, with a thin moustache, has lost his brand-new house: "I knew it was not really well built." The money in his account will last for just two weeks, he says. Customers of his spare-parts shop had paid him with cheques, "but now they are dead, no one will reimburse me". Does he believe the government will help him? He gives an empty stare. "My mind doesn't work."

As the sun sets, groups are huddling around small fires on the street. It is freezing.

A car with a damaged bonnet drives by. A sign on its back windscreen says, in Farsi and English: "Our dear city is alive and will be alive." ∎

As with the influx of international aid agencies, there is a danger that too much external assistance could undermine local resilience. Knowing how and when to hand back responsibility for recovery to local people is crucial. During March and April 2004, the provinces began a gradual withdrawal, prompting one humanitarian worker to predict "a challenging transition period".

International Federation
of Red Cross and Red Crescent Societies

Helping survivors to help themselves

"What is unique in Bam is the fact that a whole town has been destroyed," says Rikke Gormsen, a psychosocial delegate with the International Federation. "The structures and people one can link with – leaders, hospitals, shops – everything has been lost. There is no experience as to how to re-establish such a place." Gormsen can find nothing to compare with Bam, despite a long and varied career. Others on the spot stress that it took over two weeks for inhabitants to take tentative steps towards recovery, such as selling fruit, vegetables or cigarettes – steps which, following 'lesser' disasters, can emerge overnight.

The Ministry of Health estimates that 25,000 people will need long-term psychological support. The Iranian Red Crescent, which has a very strong psychosocial department – a legacy of the war against Iraq and a long series of disasters – dispatched 85 well-trained volunteers the day after the quake. Moving from tent to tent, they play with the children and listen to the women, giving them a few basic toiletries and some simple advice. "We have to listen, to sympathize, to accept anger too," says Aghdas Kafi, head of psychosocial support for the IRCS. The team has just recruited a bereaved young woman, previously consumed by her rage and resentment. "If people are busy, it separates them from their pain," she says. "We want to give them responsibilities. And the people of Bam can help themselves better."

Social links (between families, friends and neighbours) are particularly strong and justify a community-based approach. In late January, only 200 of the 1,850 children left unaccompanied by the disaster were in orphanages – all the others had been taken in by their extended families. The Red Crescent and other non-governmental organizations (NGOs) are helping women to practise skills they used before the disaster, by providing sewing-machines, material or bread-baking ovens. This helps survivors to recover their self-esteem and may eventually provide them with an income.

Psychosocial support programming (PSP) includes a major religious dimension, fundamental in this society. "One of our biggest problems is that people could not bury and mourn their dead properly," says Aghdas Kafi. In addition to hasty burials, the scale of the devastation prevented the ritual slaughter of a lamb, the sharing of dates around the tomb and the giving of alms to the poor. The IRCS, helped by clerics, was careful to organize joint ceremonies on 4 February, 40 days after the tragedy, in accordance with Muslim tradition. "People need to be able to cry," says Kafi.

"PSP is a long-term commitment," warns Rikke Gormsen, "otherwise, it makes no sense." If Bam's torn social fabric is not repaired, family violence, adolescent delinquency and drug addiction could soon follow. There is no shortage of drugs in Bam, which straddles the opium route from Afghanistan. And there are already signs of an increase in drug abuse. However, argues Gormsen, the IRCS can manage on its own: "It is important we don't interfere. There is no need for expatriates, we should simply provide financial support and technical feedback." Gormsen herself left Bam at the end of January, confident that donors would provide long-term funding for psychosocial recovery.

Reconstruction to boost local livelihoods

Iran is watchful of its independence. The sudden invasion of 1,800 foreigners into a small city like Bam was an unprecedented influx which Tehran rapidly wanted to reverse. The authorities announced restrictions on the number of expatriates allowed to continue working in Bam from April 2004 onwards. Given that Iran has qualified professionals in many fields, this decision is understandable. Most aid programmes are being implemented through Iranian (usually governmental) organizations. In theory this should help avoid dependence on external aid and ensure that local capacities are boosted.

The reconstruction task ahead is daunting. The irrigation system has been seriously damaged, jeopardizing valuable date and citrus fruit plantations. Provided repairs proceed well, a harvest should be possible this year, although quality and quantity will be less than normal. Only the rebuilding of the citadel itself can resurrect tourism. The surrounding countryside has been seriously affected: the city was its market, its pool of doctors and the provider of jobs for 250 villages. Many schools have had to close because their teachers, originally from Bam, have been killed.

Two months after the quake, inhabitants started to leave the tents erected near their homes for the temporary camps on the outskirts of the city, to make way for clearance work. Before rebuilding permanently, prefabricated shelters are set up, as only these offer protection against sandstorms and the intense desert heat. If a mass exodus of survivors is to be avoided, not only do they need decent shelters, but they must restore their livelihoods, too.

Although the Iranian Red Crescent promised to provide subsistence supplies for six months, by late January, survivors were already demanding "the opportunity to work", not only to maintain their dignity but to enable them to buy more than the very basic relief goods handed out. They should get the chance to work on government construction sites. In April, the IRCS introduced a cash voucher system, replacing the distribution of all relief items except for hygiene kits. This has enabled disaster-affected people to choose what they most want and need, which in turn has prompted traders to set up stalls selling shoes, clothes and fresh fruit.

International Federation
of Red Cross and Red Crescent Societies

Some international NGOs, including World Vision and Medair, are providing locals with 'cash for work' to clean and repair the traditional irrigation channels blocked by debris. This builds resilience in two ways: in restoring the lifelines for agriculture, Bam's most essential economic sector, and in providing employment for survivors who would otherwise be out of work.

The International Labour Organization has started a US$ 200,000 community-based project to provide socio-economic support for 5,000 vulnerable women (widows, displaced women and household heads). The aim is to encourage them to form self-help groups, and then to provide training in generating income (through agriculture, food processing, handicrafts), building savings, raising credit and accessing available financial resources.

Meanwhile, in May 2004, the World Bank proposed a loan of US$ 300 million to help the Iranian government rebuild Bam's shattered infrastructure. Of this loan, US$ 42 million is earmarked for economic recovery, by restoring irrigation systems, replenishing livestock losses, building cattle breeding centres, re-establishing facilities to store, wash and package dates, reforestation and protecting watersheds.

Will recovery improve resilience?

The authorities have estimated that reconstruction will take two years; observers believe that five years is nearer the mark. Despite the huge sums required – around US$ 1 billion according to the United Nations (UN) – funding is not the main problem. The money will come from the Iranian government, with help from the private sector and international donors. As after other disasters, the authorities will provide loans, partly non-reimbursable, for the reconstruction of private houses. The real question is: will Bam rise from the ashes more resilient than before?

The early signs allow cautious optimism. Foreign stakeholders, such as Dr Unnikrishnan of the NGO ActionAid, point out that the "active involvement of the affected people will make or break a rehabilitation programme". At the suggestion of the UN, a series of consultations with affected communities, local NGOs and the private sector took place in March and April, entitled "The Bam we want". Their suggestions should be taken into account in reconstruction policy.
Two key areas are being addressed:
- Training in sound building practices.
- Promoting public awareness of disasters.

The Iranian Red Crescent, which has an excellent construction department, will highlight the importance of safe building by showcasing the reconstruction of two of its destroyed offices. The Swiss Agency for Development and Cooperation has a construction training project which aims to "restore the links between theory and practice". Its representative in Bam, Tom Schacher, insists on "using local technology, i.e. bricks and concrete, so that people can carry on the day we're no longer here". The Swiss aim to publish an easily understandable, illustrated building manual for Iranians.

Meanwhile, the World Bank aims at targeting US$ 140 million of its US$ 300 million loan at reconstructing domestic housing and commercial buildings "with improved standards and less vulnerability to future earthquakes". The Bank points out that one of the major benefits of its proposed loan will be to provide "training on self-construction and quality assurance [which] will enhance the confidence of the population to deal with natural disasters".

The Bank has also set aside US$ 15 million of its loan for disaster preparedness in Kerman province. This would finance the retrofitting of essential infrastructure such as hospitals, local administration buildings and emergency stores to resist earthquakes, as well as to buy emergency search-and-rescue equipment for the province.

The IRCS has had an ambitious programme of awareness-raising and disaster preparedness for several years (see Box 4.3). They conduct emergency drills three times a year in public places such as town squares and parks. Through its provincial branches, the Red Crescent is able to provide children and young adults in almost every school and university across the country with courses in disaster awareness and preparedness. The courses include training on first aid, how to evacuate the injured, and immediate actions in the event of fire or earthquake. The IRCS also uses television and radio media to get its messages across. The programme has already reached 3 million Iranians. Ultimately the aim is to train one person per family. "We can and should do more," asserts Farshid Towfighi, the deputy head of planning and training at the IRCS. "After all, it is our mandate. Disasters like this one will happen again."

The IRCS had conducted community-based disaster preparedness (CBDP) training at their youth centre in Bam before the earthquake struck. When asked how those who were trained had fared in the earthquake, the Red Crescent's Hassan Esfandira said: "The situation was very chaotic and many people that had been trained for an emergency had actually been killed. But yes, those who had been trained for rescue performed better than others, especially for rescuing their families." Clearly, in the event of a quake as massive as Bam's, CBDP alone is not enough to protect lives. A complete transformation of building practices is required. Nevertheless, the role of CBDP in spreading disaster awareness is a very valuable start.

International Federation
of Red Cross and Red Crescent Societies

Box 4.3 Iranian Red Crescent helps prepare public for disasters

Since the devastating Gilan earthquake in north-west Iran in 1990, which killed 40,000–50,000 people, the Iranian Red Crescent Society has invested considerable resources to train the public in disaster awareness and preparedness. One of its key aims is to create an atmosphere in which young Iranians can acquire the skills and resources to plan and implement their own humanitarian programmes.

In close cooperation with the Ministry of Education, the IRCS has encouraged the formation of Red Crescent student committees in 15,000 high schools across the country. The students establish the committees themselves and select one contact person to liaise with the Red Crescent. The committees plan their activities based on the humanitarian principles of the International Red Cross and Red Crescent Movement, and propose their programmes to the IRCS for support with implementation. Activities usually consist of first-aid and disaster preparedness (DP) training, including earthquake awareness, charity services and the dissemination of humanitar-ian principles. The committees also organize sports competitions and other social events. The IRCS holds meetings during the year when the committees' contact persons can coordinate their activities.

At tertiary level, the IRCS, in cooperation with the Ministry of Science, Research and Technology, has helped establish similar committees in 300 universities. The activities of these committees are more specialized and focus on: disaster management training; dissemination of and training in international humanitarian law; promotion of peace, tolerance and friendship; and voluntary services in the community. The IRCS also runs a higher institute for applied sciences, authorized by the government, which offers an undergraduate degree in disaster management and rehabilitation.

Training in disaster preparedness is not limited to students. The IRCS provides DP training at national, provincial and local levels to three groups: its relief workers; its youth and volunteers; and the general public. The training is graded from level 1 to 3, where level 1 is for very experienced relief managers who will become DP trainers. Red Crescent volunteers are sent on training courses throughout the year, while any member of the public can register on one of the society's first-aid and DP training courses. In addition, the IRCS runs special training courses for workers in government offices, factories and companies.

The IRCS's long-term objective is to ensure that at least one member of every Iranian family has been trained in first aid and DP. Although the society is one of Iran's largest volunteer organizations, it is making increasing use of mass media, particularly television and radio, to reach more people.

The devastating earthquake in Bam taught the IRCS several important lessons in terms of disaster awareness and DP training. First, the rapid response by Red Crescent volunteers and local people in the aftermath of the earthquake has shown that the society's community-based approach to awareness-raising and preparedness training was correct and should be continued. A second lesson is that organizing good training courses is not enough to prevent disaster. There should be more public advocacy by the Red Crescent to promote standardized techniques for earthquake-resistant house construction. ■

Creating a culture of prevention

The shock of Bam has been enormous, but the window of opportunity which it has opened will nevertheless close fast. The policy responses to earthquakes are familiar the world over: countless studies and international conferences on the 'lessons learned'. In the wake of Bam, a whole series of similar initiatives has been announced. But as the IIEES's Sassan Eshghi puts it: "Earthquakes in Iran are not a technical matter. They are a sociological, an economic, a political matter." Money alone cannot buy protection: Bam has shown that being rich and powerful does not shield you from a catastrophe which could have been largely avoided. Nevertheless, the richer and more powerful you are, the quicker you are likely to recover.

There will probably be sufficiently strong pressure for Bam to be rebuilt, as promised by President Khatami, "stronger than before". But what about the rest of Iran? Bam will not be Iran's last major earthquake – the country is criss-crossed with fault lines, many of them near large population centres. According to Mehdi Zare of the IIEES: "There is an important seismological risk in most of the country." A 1994 study by his centre determined that there are "24 large Iranian cities", including the capital, which are exposed to "immediate" or "important" risk. Earthquakes expert Manuel Berberian adds that the vulnerability of Tehran, Mashhad and Tabriz is "scary", because these cities are located next to fault lines with a documented history of large-

Building codes have not been sufficiently enforced in Iran, putting many of the country's major cities at risk of disaster.

Iranian Red Crescent.

International Federation of Red Cross and Red Crescent Societies

magnitude earthquakes. A major quake in Tehran could kill 700,000 people. Some analysts have even suggested moving the capital, but there is hardly anywhere in Iran that is not earthquake-prone (see Box 4.4).

Box 4.4 Tehran time bomb

Mehdi Zare points out the elegant buildings sprawling across the snow-capped slopes of northern Tehran. With its beautiful views, no wonder this district is where the wealthy choose to build their homes. But living here carries a high risk – just under their expensive residences runs a major fault line. "Building on the slope should simply be forbidden," says Zare, a seismologist at Tehran's International Institute of Earthquake Engineering and Seismology. "But in spite of repeated statements on the issue, nothing is being done." The price for one square metre of land here is US$ 2,000. "With such money to be made, investors are of course rushing in," he adds.

Tehran was hit by a major earthquake in 1830. The fault line running beneath the city's northern district generated earthquakes to the west of Tehran in 1962 and 2002. Along with other seismologists, Zare is concerned that "there is a great risk that this fault will move one day". After disaster struck Bam, experts made some chilling predictions. Bahram Akasheh, a professor of geophysics at Tehran University, wrote to President Khatami to say that if an earthquake similar in magnitude to Bam's were to strike Tehran, it would kill over 700,000 people, destroy government buildings and paralyse the country. According to the New York Times, the head of Iran's union for construction engineers, Alireza Sarhadi, said such a quake would destroy 70 per cent of Tehran's buildings.

Professor Akasheh proposed moving the capital back to Isfahan, which was supplanted by Tehran in the 18th century. 'Moving the cap-

ital' is an issue that is raised in government circles after any earthquake strikes. Bam's tragedy sharpened the debate again: in January 2004, Hassan Rohani, the head of the country's Supreme National Security Council, announced that the issue would be discussed and a conclusion reached later in the year.

But most experts don't treat it as a serious possibility, arguing that there is no earthquake-safe place in Iran. "Moving the capital? What about the other cities, towns and villages? What about moving the whole country?" asks geophysicist Manuel Berberian ironically. Fatemi Aghda, who directs Iran's Research Institute for Natural Disasters (affiliated to the government's powerful Housing Foundation) agrees. "Running away from danger makes no sense – Tehran is too big an economic centre for that," he argues. "What we suggest instead is strengthening lifelines, rebuilding certain areas which are too dilapidated, and training both the managers and the public in disaster-related issues."

The government has allocated US$ 300 million for retrofitting key infrastructure in Tehran and six other cities, such as government offices, schools, hospitals, telecoms installations, gas and oil pipelines, and some large hotels and housing complexes. Since early 2003, Dr Aghda and his staff have supervised vulnerability assessments and reinforcement of buildings in Tehran. They also train city councils and mayors in disaster management. Ironically, the training in Bam's home province of Kerman was planned for March 2004. ■

Preventing catastrophes on the scale of December 2003 requires action on many levels. Key measures at a national level to reduce the risk of future disasters include:

- **Reinforce existing public infrastructure,** especially hospitals, health clinics, schools, government offices, power utilities and emergency services ('lifeline infrastructure').
- **Reform the construction industry:** introduce earthquake classes into university curricula, enforce a strict inspection system, and impose heavy penalties on those who fail to comply with the law.
- **Implement a disaster insurance scheme** to include research into probable losses and pricing of insurance, preparation of a natural disasters insurance law, and training Iranian insurance professionals in assessing property damage.
- **Strengthen Iran's national disaster management system** by anchoring it to a single, indisputable source of authority at cabinet level, and ensuring it addresses not only earthquakes but also droughts and flash floods.

According to an official Iranian report, between 1993 and 2001, 600,000 dwellings (5 per cent of the country's total housing stock) were severely damaged or destroyed by disasters, causing over US$ 10 billion in damage. From 1999 to 2001, government subsidies to homeowners affected by disasters exceeded US$ 1 billion or about 1.3 per cent of gross domestic product (GDP).

Against this background of mounting disaster damage, investing in risk reduction will pay dividends. And the money is there. Iran is home to 7 per cent of the world's proven oil reserves and huge supplies of natural gas. In 2002, it exported US$ 19.2 billion worth of petroleum products. In 2003, its GDP (real prices) was US$ 135 billion, according to the International Monetary Fund. Disasters will continue to inflict unnecessary suffering and damage, unless policy-makers and donors insist on integrating disaster risk within development plans (see Box 4.5).

Harnessing community resilience

However, reducing risk cannot be left to the government alone. Much can be done at a local level too, whether through municipalities, communities, schools or households. Amid the devastation of Bam, it may seem unrealistic to speak of 'community resilience' to disaster. What could any Iranian community do in the face of such a colossal threat? However, creating resilient communities means seeking out whatever local capacities are already there and building on them.

In Bam, we have seen the selfless devotion of Red Crescent volunteers, such as Mahmud Ranjbar, who lost his own life while warning others to save theirs. We have seen the solidarity shown by thousands of Iranians across the country as they descended, province by province, on Bam to offer their aid and administrative

International Federation
of Red Cross and Red Crescent Societies

Box 4.5 Sticks and carrots: developmental solutions to disaster

Several radical suggestions to get risk reduction on the development agenda are currently circulating. Geophysicist Manuel Berberian argues that the "unacceptable death toll" of the Bam earthquake "resembles a nuclear explosion". He says new ways must be found to break the disaster cycle and advocates that: "There should be specific criteria for granting financial aid to the governments who comply with hazard minimization and serious consequences for those that do not."

So, is a five-year disaster reduction plan – complete with carrots and sticks – a realistic way of cajoling reluctant governments into taking disaster risks more seriously? Ideas like this are in danger of stalling in the face of political hurdles. At the World Bank's Hazard Management Unit, Margaret Arnold observes: "It would be difficult for donors not to respond to disasters. But yes, we do sometimes try sticks. In at least one case, when support started for disaster recovery, there was a clause saying there would be no help if nothing was done for prevention."

Why not make this normal practice? To begin with, more donors would need, in the words of Margaret Arnold, to start seeing "disaster risk as a development issue and not as a humanitarian one". The realization that poorly planned development can turn recurring natural phenomena such as floods and earthquakes into human and economic disasters is slowly dawning. But reducing the risk of disasters must become a higher priority for development programmers in the years ahead, if unacceptable losses are to be avoided.

Meanwhile, Ilan Kelman, deputy director of the Cambridge University Centre for Risk in the Built Environment, has been lobbying for a long time to "build a culture of prevention". One of his many suggestions is that donors to an earthquake relief operation should commit themselves to allocate 10 per cent of the value of their aid to earthquake mitigation for schools and hospitals. The mitigation projects would be in another earthquake-prone part of the same country, to be chosen by consensus with the national authorities. Spending the money on mitigation measures in other at-risk areas outside the immediate disaster zone would, according to Kelman, "make a political point that mitigation should happen before (not after) we see the dead bodies".

One obstacle would be charity laws, which often state that money raised for an emergency has to be spent on that particular emergency. "Change the rules," answers Dr Kelman, "by defining the 'emergency' as including the long-term sustainability of the society." He insists operational and legal definitions should take into account the more and more widely accepted link between emergency on one hand and mitigation, disaster reduction and sustainability on the other. ∎

support. We have seen the power of religion, which inspired the people of Bam to build mosques that survived one of the most devastating earthquakes in Iran's history.

The challenge now is to transform these humanitarian urges and religious values into a force for disaster prevention. Bam has created a tremendous opportunity for change: it has raised the awareness of earthquake risk across the country. It is clear that the knowledge, expertise and resources exist to make Iran far more earthquake-safe than it is now. What has been missing is the sense of urgency and awareness needed to overturn the complacent 'business as usual' model of development. Key measures to build disaster resilience at the local level include:

- **Invest in the public's awareness of disaster risks** and of what they can do to mitigate these risks. More support for the awareness-raising work of the Red Crescent and other NGOs, through mass media as well as in schools and universities across the country, is urgently needed.

- **Promote community values of safety and responsibility** among local construction companies and political leaders. Those who construct substandard buildings, or fail to inspect them rigorously enough, are at as great a risk as everyone else in the community. Encouraging public debate of such values could help outlaw unsafe planning and building practices.

- **Engage traditional neighbourhood networks,** such as the 'notables' or 'white beards', in disaster preparedness and mitigation. This includes capturing the positive role religion could play in reducing disaster risks. Why did Bam's mosques survive the earthquake? Are there lessons about the design of mosques or the ways in which communities build them which can be applied to secular contexts?

- **Invest in local search and rescue.** The Red Crescent's sniffer-dog teams have proved that they are far more effective in saving lives than costly international teams. More local dog teams are needed – as well as search-and-rescue equipment, to be stored at provincial level.

- **Strengthen local disaster preparedness and response** within at-risk neighbourhoods, through emergency drills, training and equipping local response teams and first-aid training. This should extend beyond the Red Crescent and include other community-based networks. Psychosocial support, in particular, is a long-term need and should be conducted by local people, with international intervention limited to funding.

- **Support local livelihoods.** A deluge of international relief can undermine local resilience. Linking rehabilitation to 'cash for work' schemes and issuing cash vouchers rather than distributing relief items can help stimulate local traders back into business as well as giving those affected by disaster more choice and dignity.

- **Develop long-term partnerships** between domestic and international aid agencies, especially given the high level of knowledge and preparation among aid groups such as the 120,000-strong Iran Nursing Organization or the Iranian Red Crescent.

Iolanda Jaquemet, an independent journalist presently based in Jakarta, Indonesia, was principal contributor to this chapter and Boxes 4.2, 4.4 and 4.5. She collaborated with Gert Venghaus, the German Red Cross's head of international disaster relief, on Box 4.1. Box 4.3 was contributed by Mostafa Mohaghegh, the Iranian Red Crescent Society's director of international affairs at the time of the Bam earthquake. Figure 4.1 was compiled by Jonathan Walter, editor of the World Disasters Report.

International Federation
of Red Cross and Red Crescent Societies

Sources and further information

Blaikie, Piers; Cannon, Terry; Davis, Ian; and Wisner, Ben. *At Risk: Natural Hazards, People's Vulnerability and Disasters.* London: Routledge, 2004 (second edition).

Fathi, Nazila. 'With Capital at High Risk of Quakes, Iran Weighs Moving It to a Safer Place' in *New York Times,* 6 January 2004. Available at http://www.nytimes.com/2004/01/06/international/middleeast/06IRAN.html

International Federation of Red Cross and Red Crescent Societies. *Psychosocial Support Assessment Mission to Bam. 7–26 January 2004.* Geneva: International Federation, 2004.

International Federation. *Recovery Advisory Team. Recommendations. 3 February 2004.* Geneva: International Federation, 2004.

United Nations (UN). *From Emergency Humanitarian Assistance to Reconstruction and Risk Management: A United Nations Strategy for Support to the Government of the Islamic Republic of Iran following the Bam Earthquake of 26 December 2003.* Geneva: United Nations, 2004.

UN Development Programme (UNDP) Bureau for Crisis Prevention and Recovery. *Reducing Disaster Risk. A Challenge for Development.* New York: UNDP, 2004.

UN Office for the Coordination of Humanitarian Affairs (OCHA). *United Nations Disaster Assessment Coordination (UNDAC) Mission following the Bam Earthquake of 26 December 2003. 26 December 2003–9 January 2004.* Geneva: OCHA, 2004.

World Bank. *Technical Annex for a Proposed Loan of US$ 180 million to the Islamic Republic of Iran for an Earthquake Emergency Recovery Project.* Washington DC: World Bank, 2004.

Web sites

AlertNet **http://www.alertnet.org**

Earthquakes and Megacities Initiative
http://www-megacities.physik.uni-karlsruhe.de/

International Federation **http://www.ifrc.org**

International Institute of Earthquake Engineering and Seismology (IIEES)
http://www.iiees.ac.ir

Iranian Red Crescent Society **http://www.rcs.ir**

Provention Consortium **http://www.proventionconsortium.org**

Radix, Radical Interpretation on Disasters
http://online.northumbria.ac.uk/geography_research/radix/

United Nations Inter-Agency Secretariat for the International Strategy for Disaster Reduction (UN/ISDR) **http://www.unisdr.org**

World Bank **http://www.worldbank.org**

Focus on community resilience

SOUTH
CHINA
SEA

PHILIPPINE SEA

San Fernando
Polillo
Malolos Valenzuela Polillo Islands
Balanga Quezon City
MANILA
Pasig
Trece Martires Santa Cruz Daet Catanduanes
Lubang Lucena
Batangas Naga Virac
Mamburao Calapan Boac Pili
Naujan Marinduque Legazpi
Mindoro Pinamalayan Burias Sorsogon
Sablayan Roxas
San Romblon Sibuyan Masbate Ticao Catarman
José Tablas Masbate Samar Oras
Busuanga Catbalogan
Culion Kalibo Roxas Biliran Borongan
Panay Bantayan Tacloban
San José de Ormoc Burauen
Buenavista Iloilo Bacolod Baybay Leyte
Dumaran Guimaras Cebu Silago
Guimaras Cebu S. Roque Dinagat
Palawan Maasin Siargao
Negros Bohol Bucas
Puerto Princesa Tagbilaran Surigao Islands
Dumaguete Camiguin Tandag
PHILIPPINES Siquijor Butuan Prosperidad
Siquijos
Dipolog Oroquieta Cagayan de Oro
SULU Iligan Malaybalay
SEA Pagadian Marawi
Mindanao
Balabac Camiguin Tagum
Kidapawan Davao
Cagayan Maganoy Mati
Sulu Isabela Digos
Pangutaran Basilan Isulan
Jolo Koronadal
Jolo CELEBES General
Borneo Siasi SEA Santos
Tawitawi

0 km   60   120   180 km

International Federation
of Red Cross and Red Crescent Societies

Building community resilience to disaster in the Philippines

CHAPTER 5

Until last year, Punta San Francisco was a quiet seaside town of 500 people, situated on Leyte island in the southern Philippines. Then on 19 December 2003, after five days of torrential monsoon rains, disaster struck. A massive mudslide swept down the mountain behind the town, destroying all but three of the town's 90 houses and claiming 105 victims. Many who survived were left with almost nothing. Gregorio Dangoy, 27, lost his wife Maria Liza and three-month-old son, Greg Louize. His coconut plantation was destroyed. "My small plantation was all I had to build a bright future for my family," said Gregorio to a Red Cross worker, adding: "Now that it's gone, our future is shattered."

The devastating landslides that engulfed villages across the southern Philippines in December 2003 killed around 200 people and left thousands homeless. Once again, the issues of disaster prevention and preparedness hit the headlines. But, as the press and local residents were quick to point out, these events were tragically predictable, given decades of deforestation. Although the landslides were triggered by heavy rainfall, the level was not unprecedented for the time of year.

The Philippines is one of the most disaster-prone countries in the world. From 1971 to 2000, nearly 300 'natural' disasters – including typhoons, floods, landslides, earthquakes and volcanic eruptions – killed around 34,000 Filipinos, according to the United Nations Environment Programme. And from 1990 to 2000, a total of 35 million people across the country were "severely affected by natural disasters", according to The Philippine National Red Cross (PNRC). Typhoons accounted for 85 per cent of those affected.

This chapter seeks to analyse the role that community-based disaster preparedness (CBDP) can play in strengthening the resilience of vulnerable Filipinos to the range of recurrent hazards which threaten their lives and livelihoods. What are the potential pitfalls of CBDP as well as its advantages? What are the limits to community-based action – in terms of its ability to address factors underlying vulnerability? How can CBDP play its part in a broader nationwide strategy of disaster risk reduction? In the Filipino context, CBDP includes activities to mitigate as well as prepare for disasters.

Photos opposite page:
Typhoons lash
the Philippines once
a month during
the storm season.
But seawalls, built
with the participation
of coastal communities,
can help protect lives
and livelihoods.

Knud Falk/
Danish Red Cross.

Recurrent disasters arrest development

Disaster data fail to capture the full extent of the damage inflicted by smaller, recurrent hazards in the Philippines. In the majority of cases, few people lose their lives – precisely because individuals and communities are used to coping with hazards, with limited (if any) outside assistance. Even so, 'ordinary' typhoons and floods that do not hit the international headlines still have devastating consequences for many people.

On average, the country experiences one typhoon per month during the storm season. Typhoons cause considerable damage to property and infrastructure. High winds and heavy rainfall cause direct damage to crops and property, while storm surges from the sea threaten coastal communities. The flash floods that often accompany typhoons cause soil erosion and landslides, and litter agricultural land with silt and stone deposits.

In poor rural areas, estimates of the economic costs of disasters give us little idea of the relative impacts on the lives and livelihoods of those affected. For instance, relative to the destruction of large-scale commercial assets, the loss of a hectare of rice crop and a few banana trees does not amount to much in economic terms. However, for the household that depends on these assets for its survival, the loss can be devastating. The livelihood repercussions of damage to agricultural land, crops, infrastructure, livestock and property are often felt for months after the initial event.

Farmers usually suffer more than others from typhoons and floods. Retreating flood waters deposit debris which has to be cleared before the fields can be prepared and seeded. Replanting requires adjusting cropping seasons which, depending on the time of year, increases the likelihood of further damage from floods, droughts or pests. "My rice fields were flooded twice during 1998 and I had to replant twice," says Candido Bautista, a farmer from Mindoro province, adding: "Plants that survived the floods were attacked by rats after the waters receded. My entire crop was destroyed. In some areas, fields were covered in thick silt, in others the plants had been completely washed out."

Risks are increasing, not decreasing, adds Bautista: "We have always experienced flooding but not as frequently as nowadays. The floods are making us all poor. We spend so much time planting and then the floods come, and we have to start all over again. We use up all of our resources, including our food stocks, repairing the damage and replanting. Even minor floods can be hugely damaging."

Tenant farmers tend to suffer more than landowners as they often bear the brunt of costs and losses. However, worst off are the agricultural labourers who work for a share of the harvest rather than a daily rate. When harvests are small, they may not be paid their full quota. Despite the need for replanting following a flood, the demand for agricultural labour tends to drop as small farmers seek to economize. "After flooding there are always far too many workers chasing too little work… those are hard times," says Candido Macalipay, a labourer from Mayabig village in Mindoro.

Typhoons and floods have repercussions for almost all the members of agricultural communities. Plantation crops such as coconuts and bananas are prone to wind, as well as to damage from floods and landslides. This cuts the demand for labour in the copra-producing sector, among others. Experience of typhoon damage has discouraged many farmers from investing resources in maintaining or improving their plantations, for fear of wasting money. Traders in agricultural and other produce, as well as trades such as carpentry, generally experience a downturn in business in the months following a severe typhoon, particularly where harvests have been badly affected.

Meanwhile, typhoon winds and storm surges frequently damage or destroy housing constructed of light materials. The homes at greatest risk tend to belong to the poor. Those who can afford to, build their houses of robust materials in (relatively) safe locations and with features such as raised platforms for safe storage during floods.

Although most disaster damage could be repaired within a week or two, in practice there are lengthy delays in acquiring the necessary materials. Demand outstrips supply for raw materials such as nipa palm for roofing in the aftermath of typhoons. Many people cannot afford to buy the materials they need or pay for carpenters. To make matters worse, income-earning opportunities are in short supply following a disaster. So, many households delay repairing their homes until they have the necessary resources. Some economize by using materials collected from the wild and carrying out the work themselves. However, family members often cannot offer financial assistance as they have themselves suffered losses.

In addition to the destruction of homes, buildings and agricultural assets, recurrent disasters also lead to outbreaks of disease and shortages of necessities such as food and medicine, driving up prices. In the aftermath of flooding, water-borne diseases such as bilharzia and diarrhoea are common. These disaster impacts aggravate pre-existing poverty, creating a downward spiral of vulnerability. As village captain Sonny Bautista from Mayabig, Mindoro says: "The number one obstacle to development is calamities – especially floods."

Communities mitigate and prepare

Since the mid-1990s, the Philippine Red Cross has been transforming its approach to disasters, shifting the focus from post-disaster response and service-delivery towards encouraging proactive measures at community level to mitigate and prepare for the impacts of disaster.

The Red Cross strategy is to work with and through vulnerable communities, and vulnerable people within those communities. With the help of local volunteers, their stated aim is to provide a "space where people can come together to achieve solutions to community problems". The PNRC says their community disaster planning "has an ultimate goal of reducing vulnerabilities by increasing the capacity of the communities as well as the local government units to prevent, mitigate and prepare for disasters". In practice, most of the Red Cross's efforts in CBDP have been directed towards alleviating the effects of typhoons, seasonal flooding, and poor water and sanitation.

Since 1994, the PNRC, whose network extends to all of the Philippines' 76 provinces, has implemented community disaster preparedness across the country under several different programmes. Despite variations in emphasis and funding, the projects share similar objectives and approaches. This chapter is based on first-hand field research into two of these projects, one implemented in Oriental Mindoro province, the other in Southern Leyte province (see map).

The projects began by identifying villages prone to floods and storm surges, in which to train local volunteers in disaster preparedness (DP) skills. Training sessions included elements of disaster management theory and procedures, first aid and local hazard mapping. Once trained, teams of local participants were charged with implementing village-level DP activities.

Physical mitigation measures not only protect houses and land at risk – they are symbols of the priority local communities and authorities place on reducing disaster risks.

Knud Falk/
Danish Red Cross.

In Leyte, village officials and DP trainees were encouraged to produce a disaster action plan, which would be integrated with local development planning (see Box 5.1). Emphasis was placed on putting the theory taught into practice by implementing small, local mitigation measures in collaboration with local government bodies, such as:

- mangrove planting to limit coastal erosion and protect against storm-surges;
- planting trees to limit soil erosion and mark evacuation routes during floods;
- construction of seawalls;
- river dyke construction and repair;

Box 5.1 Six steps towards increasing community resilience

The approach adopted by The Philippine National Red Cross in Benguet, Southern Leyte, Surigao del Norte and Palawan is known as the Integrated Community Disaster Planning Programme (ICDPP). Six closely linked steps aim to ensure that communities (*barangays*) are encouraged to identify the risks they face and take measures to mitigate them. Integrating risk reduction measures into the development plans and budgets of local government is seen as critical to the long-term sustainability of the programme.

1. Partnership with municipal and provincial government units. It is imperative from the very beginning to ensure collaboration with local authorities in order to ground the preparedness concept firmly in local planning, gain technical and financial support for implementing mitigation measures, and ensure long-term sustainability.

2. Barangay disaster action team (BDAT) formation and training. At the heart of the programme is the group of community volunteers who receive training in hazard management, spread information and work with the whole community to prepare a *barangay* disaster action plan, which is the basis for deciding how to improve the safety of community resources.

3. Risk and resources mapping. It is necessary to map the most important local hazards, showing who and what they are jeopardizing. The maps are used to identify suitable mitigation measures to protect the community, and also as land use planning tools for the local government units (LGUs).

4. Community mitigation measures. Based on the disaster action plan, the community establishes some kind of mitigation measures to reduce the impact from potentially relevant natural hazards. Mitigation measures may be physical structures such as seawalls and evacuation centres, health-related measures such as water supply, or less tangible elements such as land-use and evacuation plans.

5. Training and education. Important both for the BDAT training and for raising awareness within the whole community, training and education is applied in all steps of the ICDPP.

6. Sustainability. The last step is linked to the first step – the long-term impact can only be ensured by fully integrating the ICDPP concept in the LGUs. This includes taking hazard preparedness into account and incorporating the main *barangay* disaster action plan recommendations into LGU land-use planning and annual budgeting. Sustainability also implies regular updating and training of the BDAT, so that the disaster action plan becomes a continuous risk reduction effort. ■

- diverting or containing river channels;
- clearing irrigation channels and other waterways of plant growth, silt deposits and debris;
- sandbagging sections of rivers prone to flooding to protect property and farmland; and
- construction of evacuation centres (used as day-care centres and health posts between disasters).

These initiatives were selected and planned with the participation of community members and local government units (LGUs). Although the PNRC supplied the financial and managerial support to get the initiatives going, they also sought contributions – in cash or in kind – from LGUs and the community. LGUs control local development funds, and for eight of the Red Cross projects they covered more than half the costs.

For example, to construct a seawall in the village of Tigbao in Southern Leyte province, community volunteers offered their labour for free, while local government provided a municipal engineer and the loan of heavy equipment. This collaborative approach is an integral part of the projects, designed to reinforce other capacity-building elements. Monitoring and evaluation of activities ensured the Red Cross maintained contact with participating communities throughout the course of the project. This also provided a mechanism for supporting the spin-off activities of local volunteers in Leyte, such as mangrove planting.

Process as important as product

Physical mitigation measures have had some positive impacts on community resilience to disasters, according to the Philippine Red Cross.

In the Southern Leyte village of Catublian, a concrete dyke was built to control the dangers posed to homes and rice fields by the erosion of a river bank. When a typhoon lashed the area with heavy rains in February 2001, the dyke prevented the river from damaging an estimated 100 hectares of agricultural land on which 200 farmers depended for their livelihoods.

In the mountainous village of Gusaran in Benguet province, typhoon rains used to contaminate drinking water in the village well every year. After the community built a small concrete wall to divert the surface runoff, they suffered far fewer cases of serious diarrhoea during the rainy season.

In the village of Tigbao in Southern Leyte, part of the area behind a new concrete seawall has been planted with trees as a public space, while crops are now being cultivated where floods had previously made this impossible.

International Federation
of Red Cross and Red Crescent Societies

However, for the PNRC, the main value of community-based disaster preparedness lies not so much in the physical products themselves as in the process by which they are implemented:

■ Concrete project outputs have symbolic value. They illustrate both the achievements of participating villagers and the recognition by disaster managers of vulnerability in the community concerned.

■ Participating in these activities increases knowledge and skills in the community.

■ Project outputs provide a focus for the introduction of new forms of local-specific planning and organization.

■ Implementing projects raises awareness of what can be done locally, both among people living in neighbouring settlements and among local officials, creating a 'ripple effect' in the area.

■ Building mitigation measures provides the Red Cross with an opportunity to consolidate links with the community concerned. This increases the ability of the PNRC to continue to influence community decisions and assert the values that underpin CBDP.

■ When implemented in collaboration with local government, the focus on project outputs provides an opportunity to improve communication between the community and government officials, as well as between the PNRC and government.

The process of building resilience to disasters is as important as the physical product. Creating local hazard and vulnerability maps boosts the disaster awareness of exposed communities.

Knud Falk/
Danish Red Cross.

Reactions of participants have been largely positive. In Mindoro, local officials who received DP training used their newly acquired organizational skills during subsequent floods, for example, community-wide monitoring, flood warning, information dissemination, stockpiling necessities and evacuation procedures. They claimed that training had "increased awareness" of disaster management issues and practices in the community and had fostered "unity of purpose" among participants.

Where previously the community in Mindoro reacted to floods as and when they occurred, since being trained by the Red Cross, village leaders have focused more on preparedness. They have sent letters encouraging the village day-care centre to prepare for flooding, and requesting the school, church and houses in elevated areas to be prepared to act as evacuation centres in an emergency.

In Leyte, local volunteers said they had "learnt the importance of community organizing activities". They found training sessions fun and informative, and enjoyed meeting others from outside their community, as well as learning disaster management and community organizing skills. Many felt empowered. Volunteer Efren Saldivar described how the training helped him become "convinced of the power that individual DP volunteers and community members have" to change their situation.

Obstacles to greater resilience

Despite the strengths and achievements of the PNRC projects, there have been various difficulties associated with the implementation of community-based disaster mitigation and preparedness.

Projects tend to focus on short-term outputs, rather than long-term outcomes. This is a common problem, caused largely by funding constraints and pressure to provide evidence of tangible project successes within short-term deadlines. Much of the responsibility lies with donors who have tended to provide funds for monitoring and evaluation only during the implementation phase of short-term projects. This increases the pressure on PNRC to declare that projects have been 'successfully' completed and move on to the next project site, before the long-term impacts on vulnerability and resilience can be seriously evaluated. Moreover, communities often feel they've 'done their bit' once the physical mitigation measure is installed. This issue has been partly addressed in Leyte, for example, where donor funding has been extended beyond the initial time frame.

CBDP's focus on the need for local people to reduce their own vulnerability can place heavy demands on their time and livelihoods. According to one villager from Mindoro: "I have no time for activities such as the organized river cleaning – however good the outcome – because I cannot afford a day without paid work." The priority of most community members is to ensure or enhance their family's livelihood security. This means a large sector of the population may not want – or be able – to participate in unpaid community activities. Persuading people to volunteer their labour for the sake of a project which may only bear fruit in months or years to come can prove challenging (see Box 5.2).

Viewed in this context, CBDP can become a burden, requiring participants to sacrifice their time, energy and opportunities of more remunerative work in the short term. This situation is compounded by the fact that communities often suffer divisions between individuals, families, political factions and socio-economic or ethnic groups. Community leaders often have to work hard to persuade groups with opposing interests to work together.

Even income-generating community initiatives can be held back by the widespread inability of people to invest their time and resources in communal projects. This can have a negative impact on any community-based initiative. It increases the pressure on village officials to find external sources of funding for repairs or development activities, from government programmes (often under-resourced) or non-governmental organizations (NGOs).

Several factors compromise project sustainability and momentum. A number of young DP volunteers in Leyte migrated in search of employment within a few months of their training. Meanwhile in Mindoro, although DP volunteers recalled the disaster

Box 5.2 Motivating local people to participate

Community-based disaster preparedness projects can make great demands on the time and resources of local community members. Democrito Hermogino, captain of the coastal village of Tigbao in Southern Leyte province, describes how he turned reluctant villagers into enthusiastic participants (paraphrased below):

"Workers were not paid for their labour to gather and haul boulders for the construction of the seawall. It was difficult to recruit workers during the early stages of the project because the need for voluntary participation was poorly understood. The seawall project began with only 15 instead of the planned 20 workers because most felt they would be losing out on other, well-paid job opportunities.

"As the project got under way, understanding of its aims and objectives spread in the community. Village officials took turns to provide snacks to the workers during their breaks. These were paid for partly from the proceeds of a benefit dance (which also raised funds to purchase shovels) and partly from officials' personal contributions. This gesture helped to inspire the workers with participatory spirit. After a few weeks of implementation, people became very coopera-tive, to the extent that they were quarrelling about who should be picked to work." ∎

management procedures they had been taught a year earlier, first-aid skills were only partially remembered and could only be applied with confidence by those with previous training, such as health workers. Volunteers in Leyte reported mixed reactions to their efforts to disseminate information on topics such as the protection offered by mangroves in coastal areas and the causes and prevention of dengue fever. Often, few community members attended their meetings and those who did tended to be people who were already supportive. Their biggest impact was through informal interaction with family and friends.

The emphasis on physical mitigation structures does not adequately address local livelihood vulnerability. In Tigbao, Southern Leyte, some of the villagers whose homes and land the seawall was intended to protect expressed doubts about its usefulness: "I don't think it brings any benefits," remarked one villager. "Its presence makes it difficult for us to take our boats out to sea."

The Philippine Red Cross's approach to CBDP tends to focus more on hazards than vulnerabilities. The process followed in Southern Leyte of hazard mapping using GPS and GIS technology built up an accurate picture of hazard risk, but did not capture all the factors that make individuals and households vulnerable to such hazards. The mitigation measures that result from hazard mapping, such as seawalls or dykes, therefore tend to be 'event-centric'. While physical structures may protect villagers from flooding, they only address one dimension of overall livelihood vulnerability.

The CBDP approach can be disempowering, as it may raise expectations that the risk of disasters will be reduced without increasing the community's capacity to address the root causes of vulnerability. CBDP does recognize local people as capable actors, rather than portraying them as victims. However, many measures to reduce vulnerability and prevent disasters fall outside the areas over which local people have influence. Patterns of urban development or upland deforestation, for example, which have a direct impact on the vulnerability of local communities, are often the result of decisions taken outside the community.

Participants may be steered away from linking the DP agenda of a project to the bigger, more politically contentious issues that drive vulnerability (e.g., land-use planning). There is a danger that politicians will use CBDP projects (whoever they are implemented by) to deflect attention away from their own responsibilities for vulnerability and disaster reduction.

The projects implemented with Red Cross support fall within the area of responsibility of local government agencies. PNRC's approach is based on the premise that local government can be motivated to act by disaster-aware communities volunteering to help themselves. In practice, however, community leaders can find themselves burdened with more responsibilities, without the resources or decision-making powers needed to address the wider political causes of vulnerability.

Causes of vulnerability

Underlying the concerns raised above about CBDP is the allegation that it addresses the symptoms of disaster rather than the cause. Of course, small-scale community DP projects cannot be expected to solve all the root causes of vulnerability. However, a clearer assessment of the factors that lie behind vulnerability (and resilience) to disaster could lead to more effective interventions – as well as to advocacy around issues that prove difficult for the community itself to influence.

Although disasters threaten to derail development, field research makes clear that unequal opportunities and misguided development are responsible for turning natural hazard events such as floods or landslides into disaster situations. As John Twigg, honorary research fellow at University College London's Benfield Greig Hazard Research Centre, made clear in a recent working paper on disaster mitigation: "To understand what makes people vulnerable, we have to move away from the hazard itself to look at a much wider, and a much more diverse, set of influences: the whole range of economic, social, cultural, institutional, political and even psychological factors that shape people's lives and create the environment that they live in."

Filipinos are vulnerable to the effects of floods and typhoons for three key reasons:

1. Their livelihoods are vulnerable. Villagers' accounts of their experiences of vulnerability share a strong emphasis on livelihood insecurity. Where local economies are dependent on agriculture, poverty is widespread – partly because of climatic variability and the cumulative impacts of recurring typhoons and floods. However, the main causes of vulnerable livelihoods are:
- shortage of employment opportunities for a fast-growing population;
- dependence on the business of a limited number of poor local customers;
- low wages;
- declining natural resources (e.g., fish stocks);
- decreasing profitability of rice farming; and
- inequitable tenancy arrangements.

In such a context, a flood (or other hazard) simply brings submerged forms of vulnerability to the surface.

2. Patterns of natural resource use are changing. Urban development and the expansion of commercial quarrying and logging activities (with or without government permits) are degrading the environment. The consequent deforestation of upland slopes and coastal mangroves is exposing people to disasters.

3. People are poor and marginalized. The poor and marginalized find it difficult to access resources such as development loans or land, reducing their ability to build resilient livelihoods. Their interests tend to be under-represented in policy-making circles.

Insecure land tenure, in particular, discourages people from investing in more disaster-resilient crops, as the following tenant farmer from Mayabig in Mindoro province makes clear: "The rice field we farm is low-lying and is flooded on a more-or-less annual basis… Flooding greatly reduces our harvest… This land would be better suited to growing plantation trees. However, as tenant farmers, we cannot plant trees. Even if we got permission, as tenants we would have no guarantee that the landowner would not reclaim the land (and trees)… We have no tenancy contract – landowners do not need to give notice or compensation to their tenants if they wish to reclaim their land."

How do local people cope?

An understanding of the factors lying behind vulnerability to disaster must be complemented by an analysis of how local people cope with and recover from disaster. When faced with disaster or crisis, those at risk often find creative ways of coping and recovering. The strength of individual and household livelihoods emerges as the most critical factor in determining both vulnerability and resilience.

An important part of this analysis will be to understand how different groups of people within the community experience different levels of vulnerability and have different options or skills available to address their situation. For example, during times of stress, women can diversify their livelihoods through working as domestic helpers, while men are more able to find work as labourers or carpenters.

Divisions in terms of needs, priorities and capacities within the community must be carefully analysed, so that different groups – whether women, men, youth, the elderly, ethnic minorities or the poor – can all be engaged in the process of building community consensus around the need to create resilience to disasters.

During difficult times, many Filipino households change their eating habits. They eat cheaper home-grown produce such as bananas and root crops, rather than more valuable crops such as rice and fish. After being trapped by flood waters in December 1998, and having to eat bananas for days on end, Florian Alba from Mayabig in Mindoro province says: "I've learnt the importance of keeping the house well-

International Federation
of Red Cross and Red Crescent Societies

stocked from these experiences. It is important to grow not only rice, but also coconuts, bananas, vegetables and root crops so that we can be self-sufficient if necessary."

Disaster-affected people often call on networks of family and friends – crossing provincial, regional and even national boundaries – for financial support or help finding work. One agricultural labourer from Mayabig says: "I have a friend in another area of the province where the land is more elevated. This friend helps me to obtain work on farms in this area during times when the rest of the province has been badly affected by flooding, and little farm work is available."

Filipinos seek to diversify their livelihoods to protect themselves during hard times, sometimes even looking for work in other countries. As Patricia Beri, also from Mayabig, points out: "My husband and I set up a business raising ducks... We are tenant farmers and this has always been our main livelihood activity but the ducks provided a supplementary cash income. We also raised pigs and had established a small store."

Unfortunately, Mindoro was struck by three severe typhoons in quick succession during 1993, bringing devastating floods and destruction. "During the floods," says Patricia, "most of our stock was drowned or swept away. Our farmland was also badly affected, and due to our lack of resources we were unable to continue to stock the store." As a result, "I left my husband and children and worked abroad as a care worker for almost two-and-a-half years."

At-risk households often get involved in local cooperatives and micro-credit initiatives, which offer members low-cost goods, savings schemes and loans for micro-enterprise. During dangerous times, local organizations adapt to provide members with financial or other aid. For instance, rice farmers' cooperatives may offer their members access to seeds and other agricultural inputs, on credit, to replant rice fields when flooding has destroyed crops.

Integrating DP with development

No single aid programme or organization can hope to address all the factors that lie behind vulnerability to disaster. However, for CBDP initiatives to have a real impact on reducing local vulnerability, they need to be positioned within wider development planning and debates. Equally, a clear understanding of the ways in which local people cope with and recover from disaster is essential, if aid interventions are to strengthen, rather than undermine, community resilience. Just as CBDP cannot address the causes of vulnerability without reference to developmental factors such as livelihoods, natural resource use or marginalization, so development cannot be fully sustainable unless it is integrated with disaster mitigation and preparedness. Disaster reduction and sustainable development go hand-in-hand.

In the Philippines, infrastructure has been a major focus of development. Yet, although flooding drains local resources through a continuous cycle of damage and repair to infrastructure, disaster preparedness is not a priority funding area for the government. However, ensuring DP measures are integrated with development goals greatly increases the likelihood of accessing funding for disaster reduction. For instance, evacuation shelters can double as community centres, while developing irrigation systems could improve agricultural efficiency as well as controlling sudden influxes of water.

The Philippine Red Cross's CBDP projects aim to promote the integration of DP in local development planning through producing detailed, electronic hazard maps. Although the focus is on village-level planning, the Red Cross hopes that elements of the CBDP approach will filter into the local government system as planning and funding applications are made. In addition, the Red Cross promotes DP through its presence on national, regional and provincial disaster coordinating councils. Their priority is to maintain a cooperative – yet politically impartial – working relationship with local government institutions, in order to influence decision-making.

However, as we have seen, the PNRC's approach to community-based disaster preparedness has focused more on hazards than on the factors underlying people's vulnerability to those hazards, such as weak livelihoods. There are several practical reasons why CBDP projects have not been more integrated with developmental concerns. In particular, the divide between disaster management and development is very real for the donors, NGOs and government agencies that provide funding and set the agenda for vulnerability reduction initiatives.

For example, the donor to a PNRC pilot project in Benguet province prematurely cut back financial support, after concluding that the project did not include adequate 'disaster mitigation' measures. However, in the eyes of local participants, officials and project staff, the project initiatives were valid because they addressed wider aspects of vulnerability. The most controversial project elements concerned income-generation, including a women's loom-weaving initiative and plans to introduce a goat-raising scheme and start up a small enterprise producing herbal medicine. Other project measures included constructing public latrines and improving mountain footpaths and bridges, to reduce the risk of accidents as well as the time taken to reach local markets.

Support for this project has since been renewed. Although the other income-generating schemes have not materialized, the loom-weaving enterprise initiated under the project has continued and is now a profitable business. In fact, the incorporation of this livelihood element is now considered a particular strength of the project. From their experience of implementing CBDP, the Philippine Red Cross has learnt the importance of engaging local participants in livelihood initiatives.

According to the PNRC's Danny Atienza, people cannot be expected to participate in DP when they do not have enough income to sustain their families or send their children to school. Unfortunately, funding to implement livelihoods-based initiatives in a CBDP context remains scarce. This is partly due to the relatively high expense of livelihoods projects compared to traditional DP measures and partly because donors (including government) want to maintain the divide between disaster management and development.

Showing the way, sharing the burden

The participatory process by which humanitarian organizations help communities mitigate and prepare for disasters offers a valuable opportunity to form a clearer picture of the vulnerabilities, capacities and priorities that exist at a local level – thereby pointing the way for other actors to play a role in building resilience.

The challenge for humanitarian organizations is to avoid imposing on communities a preconceived agenda of physical mitigation measures, to be completed within donor-driven timelines. Only a careful analysis of the nature of vulnerability and resilience at community level – which accounts both for hazards *and* for the social, political and economic reasons underlying vulnerability – can provide the basis for framing the right interventions.

Inevitably, however, such an analysis will identify far more problems – and raise far more expectations – than any single organization can solve. However, the value of CBDP lies in opening the door to these issues and encouraging other actors – whether community-based organizations, development agencies, government authorities or private sector companies – to integrate their efforts in a wider approach to reducing vulnerability, of which hazard reduction is just a small part. This does not mean humanitarian organizations need to abandon their areas of expertise to take on entirely new roles, but rather to increase cooperation with other agents who have expertise in different areas.

Attempts to strengthen resilience to disasters can only succeed and be sustained within the context of a developmental approach, which integrates not only different sectors (e.g. hazard management, health, water and sanitation, education, livelihoods) but also different levels (local, municipal, national, regional and international). The Philippine government is currently piloting such an approach, through a community-based forest management programme in Southern Leyte (see Box 5.3).

CHAPTER 5

Box 5.3 Integrating disaster resilience and development

The Philippine government's department of the environment and natural resources (DENR) has combined vulnerability-reduction goals with livelihood-centred sustainable development objectives in its community-based resource management programme. Under this programme, a forestry project has been established in Southern Leyte with national government funding. The upland project site was selected as a 'hot spot' for illegal logging activities.

Under the scheme, participants formed a local people's organization and were allocated individual parcels of (government-controlled) land of up to five hectares. For each plot, 80 per cent was planted with designated types of seedling trees, and the remaining 20 per cent set aside for growing cash crops or vegetables.

Once the trees have fully matured (in 20 to 25 years), participants will be allowed to fell them. For each plot, 70 per cent of the logging proceeds will go to the people's organization; the remaining 30 per cent belongs to the government. Of this 30 per cent, half is to be invested in expanding the programme into new areas, while the national treasury will claim the remainder. Participants in the project may also be periodically paid to plant seedlings provided by DENR in designated areas, for a normal daily labouring wage. Members of the people's organization are expected to patrol the project area to deter illegal logging activities.

Behind the programme lies a recognition that DENR can neither carry out reforestation alone, nor maintain sustainable upland management practices. Rather than enforcing the protection of upland areas by driving settlers out, the government has decided instead to endorse land use that meets its project criteria.

Working through local organizations provides a network of participants and a monitoring structure. An NGO called 'LABRADOR' (Leyte and Samar rural development workers' association) has organized the community and given local participants technical training. Other government agencies, such as the department of agriculture and the department of health, have also provided technical assistance. Agricultural training has included the prevention of soil erosion through 'alley farming' techniques and the establishment of hedgerows and terraces. Organic farming methods and health service provision have also been included.

Project elements designed to prevent soil erosion not only contribute to more effective agricultural practice, but also lessen the likelihood or severity of landslides in upland regions. Other forms of disaster preparedness have been incorporated in the project. These include regulating the flow of water in irrigation canals to alleviate flooding, and the introduction of drought-resistant upland rice varieties as an alternative source of food in times of water scarcity. Following recommendations from the Philippine Red Cross, forest firebreaks were established, lined with fire-resistant trees. Such risk reduction measures are more likely to be sustained by the community if they are integrated into a broader developmental approach than if they were simply stand-alone features of a hazard-focused programme. ∎

The government of the Philippines has realized that its intervention will be required to prevent the recurrence of tragedies such as the December 2003 landslides. Following those disasters, President Arroyo directed the government's department of the environment and natural resources to "get a comprehensive plan in place to restore ecological stability in the areas affected by this recent tragedy". Reforestation has become a government priority and responsibility. "We have to sustain the environment and, at the same time, provide alternative sources of income for the people so they will be encouraged to plant trees and build forests," said President Arroyo on 23 December 2003, according to the *Philippine Star* newspaper. This approach implicitly recognizes the reality that, in order to reduce the risks of disaster, local people need the long-term support of government and other powerful agencies across a range of development issues.

Within this context, CBDP clearly does not provide a complete solution – nor does it claim to. But it has the potential to play an important role in enabling local communities to protect themselves from disaster. This can be achieved partly by self-help but also, crucially, by helping local people to promote their needs among policy-makers and resource-holders in government and non-governmental circles.

Community-based disaster preparedness goes much further than traditional disaster management in focusing on locally specific vulnerabilities, coping strategies and resilience. However, in practice, CBDP approaches have tended to address the symptoms of vulnerability rather than its root causes. Ensuring that disaster mitigation and preparedness measures are both appropriate and sustainable will require rooting vulnerability reduction within a wider developmental approach. Some recommendations for humanitarian actors, based on field research in the Philippines, include:

- **Analyse the root causes of vulnerability to disaster.** Start by assessing vulnerability to disaster, not simply the recurrence of natural hazards. Ensure donor support for this approach.
- **Understand the strengths of local livelihoods and capacities.** Analyse local capacities to cope with and recover from crisis. Understand the cumulative impact on livelihoods of recurrent events such as floods. Ensure disaster preparedness measures do not undermine people's livelihoods or capacities.
- **Listen to community perspectives and priorities.** Resist the urge to impose definitions of vulnerability upon community actors. Build consensus around what needs to be done – ensuring all the different groups within the community are engaged. Consulting communities is not enough: projects must be people-centred and community-led to succeed.
- **Include other actors from the start,** so that the burden of risk reduction can be shared. Collaboration across sectors and between different government and non-governmental agents is very important.

■ **Advocate around issues that the community itself cannot tackle,** such as insecure land tenure, environmental degradation or representing the priorities of the marginalized. Collaboration between different actors could lead to joint advocacy for change in such areas.

■ **Advocate the integration of risk reduction into development planning** at all levels of government and with development policy-makers and planners. This will address the potentially disempowering effect of local disaster preparedness. Community capacity building should not be allowed to release the government, development agencies or donors from their responsibilities to address the root causes of disaster. Make clear the limitations of CBDP – it is not a panacea, but a place to start.

The principal contributor to this chapter and Boxes 5.2 and 5.3 was Katrina Allen, a research associate in the sociology department at the University of Leicester, UK. The Philippine National Red Cross contributed Box 5.1. The chapter draws primarily on research carried out during 1998-2002. The project was funded by the International Federation and supported by the PNRC and the Flood Hazard Research Centre, Middlesex University, UK.

Sources and further information

Bankoff, G., Frerks, G. and Hilhorst, D. (eds) *Mapping Vulnerability. Disasters, Development and People.* London: Earthscan, 2004.

Blaikie, P., Cannon, T., Davis, I. and Wisner, B. *At Risk: natural hazards, people's vulnerability, and disasters.* London: Routledge, 1994.

Christie, F. and Hanlon, J. *African Issues: Mozambique and the Great Flood of 2000.* Oxford and Bloomington, IN: James Currey and Indiana University Press, in association with the African International Institute, 2000.

Eade, D. *Capacity-Building: An Approach to People-Centred Development.* Oxford: Oxfam, 1997.

Government of the Philippines. (1999). *The Philippines' Initial National Communication on Climate Change: December 1999.* Manila: Inter-Agency Committee on Climate Change, Department of the Environment and Natural Resources, 1999.

Hewitt, K. (ed.) *Interpretations of Calamity from the Viewpoint of Human Ecology.* London: Allen and Unwin, 1983.

Hewitt, K. (ed.) *Regions of Risk: A Geographical Introduction to Disasters.* Harlow: Longman, 1997.

Hewitt, K. 'Excluded Perspectives in the Social Construction of Disaster' in Quarantelli (ed.), *What is a Disaster?* London: Routledge, 1998.

International Federation of Red Cross and Red Crescent Societies. *Strategy 2010: To improve the lives of vulnerable people by mobilizing the power of humanity.* Geneva: International Federation, 1999.

International Federation
of Red Cross and Red Crescent Societies

International Institute for Disaster Risk Management (IDRM). *Cambodian Red Cross Community-Based Disaster Preparedness Program (CRC-CBDP) Evaluation Report.* Makati City, Philippines: IDRM, 2002.

Lavell, A. 'Prevention and Mitigation of Disasters in Central America: Vulnerability to Disasters at the Local Level' in Varley, A. (ed.), *Disasters, Development and Environment.* Chichester: John Wiley and Sons, 1994.

Lewis, J. *Development in Disaster Prone Places: Studies of Vulnerability.* London: Intermediate Technology Publications, 1999.

Mahmud, N. 'Disasters and Population Displacement: the case of Ormoc City, the Philippines' in Parker, D.J. (ed.), *Floods* (Vol. I). London: Routledge, Hazards and Disasters Series, 2000.

Ozerdem, A. and Barakat, S. 'After the Marmara Earthquake: lessons for avoiding short cuts to disasters' in *Third World Quarterly,* 21(3), 2000.

Pelling, M. (ed.) *Natural Disasters and Development in a Globalizing World.* London: Routledge, 2003.

Rocha, J.L. and Christoplos, I. 'Disaster Mitigation and Preparedness on the Nicaraguan Post-Mitch Agenda' in *Disasters,* 25(3), 2001.

The Philippine National Red Cross (PNRC). *A Report and Proceedings of the ICDPP-DMS Integration Workshop, July 12-16, 1999.* Manila: PNRC, 1999.

Tobin, G. A. (1999). 'Sustainability and Community Resilience: the holy grail of hazards planning?' in *Environmental Hazards* 1, 1999.

Twigg, J. and Bhatt, M.R. (eds) *Understanding Vulnerability: South Asian Perspectives.* London: Intermediate Technology Publications (on behalf of Duryog Nivaran), 1998.

Twigg, J. *Physician Heal Thyself? The politics of disaster mitigation.* Disaster Management Working Paper 1/2001. Available online at: http://www.anglia.ac.uk/geography/radix.htm

Web sites

Asia Disaster Preparedness Center (ADPC)
   http://www.adpc.ait.ac.th/AUDMP/cambodia.html
Manila Bulletin **http://www.mb.co.ph**
Manila Times **http://www.manilatimes.net**
Philippine Star **http://www.philstar.com**

**Focus on
community
resilience**

International Federation
of Red Cross and Red Crescent Societies

AIDS: Communities pulling out of downward spiral

The people in the farming community of Evusweni, central Swaziland, were horrified. Some were outraged. Had the old man lost his mind? Chief Delezi Masilela, a respected farmer and community leader, had stood up and said he was HIV positive. Worse, he had publicly announced that many of his neighbours were too. A shudder ran through Evusweni's scattered homesteads and his family counselled him to be silent. He was, they said, bringing shame upon them. One of his wives soon left him.

The traditional chief, who already suffered from tuberculosis (the most common AIDS-related cause of death), could have expected it. Although he lives in a country with the world's highest prevalence of HIV/AIDS, the stigma around it is so great that the disease is kept in the shadows.

Officially, almost 40 per cent of Swazi adults are said to be infected. The true picture is probably worse. With prevalence climbing, there are well-founded fears that in parts of southern Africa the figure could soon be upwards of 50 per cent. But as things are, few of an estimated 20,000 Swazis infected each year will ever be open about it. They will be afraid to. People do care for HIV-infected relatives, but most ostracize others living with the virus. Even in death the stigma remains. Rather than AIDS, people die of tuberculosis (TB) and opportunistic disease. The symptoms are acknowledged, but not the cause.

But the chief had to break the silence. He saw more and more people dying around him and life as he knew it was unravelling. The impact of AIDS on agriculture, the poverty left in its wake, the plight of children orphaned and women widowed had left him fearful. Unless people spoke up and faced the spread of HIV, his community was doomed, he believed. "If things don't change, it will just die off," he told this writer.

The chief was witnessing a pernicious process that is now consuming southern Africa. HIV/AIDS is consorting with food insecurity, poverty, failed health care, common disease and mismanagement to bring a region to its knees. This combination has created an unprecedented disaster that conventional intervention can no longer contain: community erosion, the slow but inexorable destruction of southern Africa's social fabric. HIV/AIDS is not only a killer but, with other factors, is a malignant force weakening the ways in which people bounce back from adversity, their age-old coping mechanisms.

Photo opposite page: HIV/AIDS killed at least 2.2 million people across sub-Saharan Africa in 2003. The pandemic is eroding communities' capacities to cope with crisis.

© Marko Kokic/ International Federation.

Poor and worsening access to health care, the accelerated spread of TB, malaria and other disease, a widespread shortage of safe water and sanitation, uncontrolled urbanization and ineffective agriculture are among the aggravating factors. If something is bad, HIV finds it and joins forces. It is an alliance of ills, covertly conspiring, feeding and exploiting one another.

Chief Masilela saw the evidence every day. He spelt out what AIDS does to farming. "The people who are dying should be out there ploughing and planting the fields," he said. "Swazi culture is such that when a farmer dies, others in the community step in, help work the land. But even they have died. There is no one to assist anymore." Land lies idle as a consequence. From his own hillside homestead, the old man pointed to the households of troubled neighbours. Nothing bothered him more than women and children plunged into chronic poverty by the loss of husbands and parents. He was doing what he could to assist them. But the truth facing Evusweni is the truth facing much of southern Africa: life is becoming unsustainable.

Scenarios are familiar, rural and urban. When farmers fall ill with AIDS, wives leave the fields to nurse them. Fewer hands mean fewer crops and, coupled with drought, may bring famine. But rain or no rain, there is poverty because the farmers who die leave their widows with little but a virus. They struggle on until their own health fails, wondering how to feed their children and pay for their education. With the land producing little, they fall into debt or destitution.

When they are gone, the eldest child takes over. Many of southern Africa's 4 million children orphaned by AIDS are in 'child-headed households', where neither tomorrow's meal nor education is certain. These 'sibling families' account for 10 per cent of all households in Swaziland alone. "Of course, that's not a family," says Stephen Lewis, the United Nations (UN) Secretary-General's Special Envoy for HIV/AIDS in Africa, "it's a brutal rupture of the family constellation, where every child is vulnerable and at risk, and no child has a childhood." Schools exclude those who cannot pay the fees or buy exercise books and uniforms. While one generation dies of AIDS, another is denied a future (see Box 6.1).

Corroding the capacity to cope

Many youngsters drift to towns, where the greedy and perverse wait to exploit them as cheap, casual labour or as sex workers. But other urban ills are growing as well. In the humanitarian crisis gripping the region, aid efforts (although still inadequate) have been greatest in rural areas. The needs of urban and shanty populations have been overshadowed, although often they are more acute. The capacity to care has been saturated, structures have been overwhelmed and the consequences for community life are devastating. Social anarchy is taking over.

International Federation of Red Cross and Red Crescent Societies

According to Pierson Ntata, senior programme officer at the Learning Support Office in Malawi: "While in the past households may have coped using various strategies, they are no longer able to do so in the face of HIV/AIDS." Previously, during the 'hungry season' or in emergencies, by far the most important coping strategy for Malawian families was *ganyu* (paid casual work), followed by reducing the number of meals per day, sending children to stay with wealthier relatives in the cities, or selling some livestock. Significantly, however, none of these coping strategies undermined the household's ability to recover its normal livelihood status after the crisis.

HIV/AIDS has changed all this (see Box 6.2). By weakening and removing the families' strongest members in the prime of their lives, the pandemic not only jeopardizes the household's capacity to produce food but also prevents them from adopting the coping strategies that in the past would have sustained them in times of food shortage. As Ntata points out: "Chronic illness and the amount of time needed to look after the sick result in both patients and carers not being in a position to engage effectively in *ganyu*. Sending children to urban areas is increasingly being undermined by high rates of death of relatives resulting from the high HIV infections in these areas."

Irrespective of calamitous climatic hazards and their influence on food supply, the grip on southern Africa of chronic and enduring disaster is tightening. The scarcity of labour means more people depend on fewer and fewer breadwinners. Zimbabwe will have lost a fifth of its workforce by 2005. As agricultural production falls, HIV-affected households are hit hardest, because among them the burden of care is causing an average 60 per cent reduction in crops, compounded by the loss of productive family members. Moreover, as access to food falls, so too does the life expectancy of people living with HIV.

Women are disproportionately affected. They are infected at twice the rate of men, and account for more than half the people who live with the virus. Yet they are the sustaining force of the family and form 70 per cent of the agricultural labour force. It is they who nurse the sick and they who are plunged into poverty as their husbands become ill and die. Widows struggle not only to put food on the family table, but to pay for their children's education. Whether the youngsters should eat or continue their schooling is often a desperate dilemma for their mothers. What they must pay in school fees, and for obligatory books and uniforms, can buy a significant amount of maize.

All sections of society are affected. Household poverty and debt are increasing – driven partly by the costs of health care and medicine (*if* they are available). School dropouts (currently 25 per cent in Zimbabwe) are rising. Skills and knowledge in agriculture are being lost, and people with no other options to survive are being forced to migrate.

Box 6.1 Orphans suffer neglect and abuse

The orphans' crime had been that they were hungry. For much of the day, they had laboured at a well – a slight 12-year-old boy and his younger sister, drawing water for villagers in the Berea district of Lesotho. They were paid in food for their services.

At home the youngsters, who had lost their parents to AIDS, waited for their uncle, a guardian who cared little for them and vented his displeasure in ill-treatment. The man was often away, drinking with his cronies, but the children were forbidden from eating unless he was present at the table. As the hours passed their hunger increased and eventually they ate from the day's food takings. When the uncle returned, drunk as usual, and discovered the misdemeanour, he beat the children savagely.

Such tales are common in southern Africa where more than 4 million children orphaned by AIDS bring a new definition to the term 'most vulnerable'. Alongside the trauma and poverty that the loss of parents brings, abuse and exploitation are increasingly disturbing problems. Red Cross National Societies report that, without the protection of parents, cruelty, food for sex, cheap or forced child labour, child rape and even coerced commercial sex are blighting the lives of more and more young people.

Bongai Mundeta, the International Federation's Harare-based HIV/AIDS coordinator, has catalogued orphan abuse and misery across the region and condemns the slow pace of intervention. In the Lesotho case, the Red Cross reported the abuse to the local chief and saw to it that the uncle got a warning: stop or face prosecution. The beatings ended and so did their toil at the well. Now the children are assisted by an integrated home-based care programme that provides structured support to orphans.

But Mundeta says, "When you compare what is being done and the enormous number of children, you must conclude there is a great deal more talking going on than action. We need to mobilize communities."

Her case is backed by chilling evidence, such as the story of three little girls living alone since the death of their parents in Zambia's Copper Belt. An 11-year-old girl and her sisters, aged 9 and 4, were sexually abused daily by a neighbour. Red Cross appeals to intervene were rejected by the police. The man was too influential, they said. A legal process was initiated to get the children into sanctuary, but it was so agonizingly slow that the sisters were traumatized by the time the Red Cross could complete it. It didn't end there. The man was HIV positive and had infected them.

When asked, urban orphans place their safety above all else, and sexual abuse is one of their greatest fears. The scenario can only get worse. Zimbabwe alone had 980,000 children orphaned by AIDS in 2003 and the figure is expected to rise to more than 1.1 million by 2005.

Sometimes the suffering comes from simply being unwanted. Spiwa was 8, an orphan and HIV positive through mother-to-child transmission. She weighed just 14 kilos. What was happening to her in the industrial town of Chitungwiza, south of Harare, was a gross denial of children's rights – yet she was not even living on the streets.

She and her three elder sisters had been found by Ruth Mutukwa, a Red Cross home-care volunteer, who became a frequent caller and brought them food, clothing, blankets

International Federation
of Red Cross and Red Crescent Societies

and some auntie-like attention. Then she discovered that half the food was being taken from them – by their grandfather. "It's terrible," she said. "What can these children do against a full-grown man?" She would intervene, but carefully. She did not want him harming the children as a consequence.

Spiwa shared one small room with Florence, 18, Jane, 17, Ottile, 16, and the eldest girl's own toddler in what used to be the family home. Their father had died in 1996, their mother four years later. After that, their grandfather, who lived elsewhere in the neighbourhood, had rented out the rest of the place. He made a profit from the tenants but didn't share the money with his grandchildren. Florence was working on a food stall to earn a little cash. She was hoping to make the equivalent of US$ 3 or 4 a month.

The room was two metres by one and a half. Newspaper pages were taped to the wall as decoration. There was one small plant in a corner. The girls hadn't got much, but they were trying to make a home of it.

Jane looked after Spiwa. When their mother died, they had all moved up one in the family hierarchy. Florence had become the breadwinner and Jane had taken her place caring for the youngest children. She had taken Spiwa to hospital after the Red Cross suspected she had tuberculosis. If the sputum tests confirmed it, treatment would be free. The system would take care of that.

What it would not take care of was the severe skin infection over much of her body. She was in pain and had been for the past month. The sores on her face and head were awful. The hospital had prescribed treatment, but someone had to pay for the ointment and medication before it could be dispensed. A social welfare letter could exempt her from payment, but she needed a birth certificate for that and, through no fault of her own, she didn't have one.

Couldn't her grandfather pay? Jane had asked and reluctantly he had said he would, when he felt like it. The child sat on the floor of her concrete room and waited. Appalled, Red Cross workers gave Jane the money themselves but they knew they hadn't solved the problem. There were far too many similar cases.

Child negligence is a criminal act. Except, it seems, in southern Africa where – hastened by the burden of HIV/AIDS, uncaring bureaucracy, underfunding and mismanagement – health care is falling apart and access for the poor and orphaned gets ever worse. ■

Analyst Alex de Waal makes clear the consequences for communities across southern Africa: "Afflicted households do not 'cope' in the sense of succeeding to preserve an acceptable livelihood, but rather they 'struggle' and in fact commonly dissolve entirely. The very concept of 'coping' distracts policy-makers from the enormity of the crisis."

Policy outpaced – new paradigm needed

Humanitarian organizations are deep inside uncharted territory and doing business as usual will not halt the slide. The map from the past will not serve as a guide through the future. Aid policy – whether of agencies, donors or governments – is lagging behind the accelerating challenges. Despite knowing about the gravity of the HIV/AIDS pandemic since at least the mid-1990s, aid organizations have been very slow to respond.

Since 2002–2003, when a pre-emptive intervention of food aid helped to fend off widespread starvation in southern Africa, responsible voices have been crying out that the analysis must change. Prompt international action lifted the threat of famine for an estimated 14 million people, but it only postponed disaster. Hunger was not the root problem, only a symptom of a wider, complex crisis that remains untouched to this day. All the food aid in the world cannot stop it.

Alex de Waal characterized the implications of an HIV/AIDS epidemic interacting with acute food insecurity as "new variant famine". He argued that the disease left international models of food security in need of dramatic revision. "The basic assumptions built into economic and development analysis, farming systems research, livelihoods studies, and coping strategies research, that a household can command basic food entitlements in 'normal' times, need to be questioned," he and co-author Joseph Tumushabe warned in a report last year to the United Kingdom's Department for International Development (DFID).

De Waal and Tumushabe said the disproportionate effect of HIV/AIDS on agriculture was not due to higher rates of the disease among agricultural workers, but because the sector was less able than others to absorb the impacts of lost labour. With over 70 per cent of Africa's population dependent on agriculture for their livelihood, the impact would be far reaching. HIV/AIDS was intensifying labour bottlenecks, increasing malnutrition, proving a barrier to traditional support mechanisms, massively adding to the problems of rural women and deepening macroeconomic crises by reducing agricultural exports. Referring to the pre-existing fragility of most African farming systems, distortions built into international markets in agricultural produce and the role of agriculture as an unacknowledged social safety net, they went on: "Under the strain of the HIV/AIDS epidemic, the more vulnerable farming systems are simply breaking down, threatening a social calamity on a scale not witnessed before in the continent."

The emergency continues to revolve in ever more vicious circles. "AIDS has changed the face of disaster in southern Africa," says Dr Hakan Sandbladh, head of relief health for the International Federation of Red Cross and Red Crescent Societies. "Everyone must change with it. Unless they do, the apocalypse of AIDS will soon be unstoppable."

Sandbladh is the co-author (with Khanya Mabuza, secretary general of the Swaziland Red Cross, and Richard Blewitt of the British Red Cross) of an options assessment entitled *Not Business As Usual,* the basis of the International Federation's regional

Box 6.2 Selling cows, selling sex

The cattle trucks heading north for the meat markets of Zambia's Copper Belt bore testimony to the corrosion of 'coping' strategies. By selling off their last and most precious assets, farming families were denying themselves the chance of recovery. The cows sold for a pittance and, fattened up in the north, made a fortune for middlemen.

But what were the farmers' options? A third consecutive failed harvest neared and even the relatively well-off were in trouble. Farmer Leonard Njoolo glumly surveyed the nine hectares he had planted with maize and sorghum. The parched earth had failed to produce anything. Now, years of hard work and careful development were being wiped out because he had nothing to fall back on. He was selling his cows, he said, to feed his family. Less proud neighbours were asking for food aid.

Failing struggle was evident in the graves behind Belita's hut in Zambia's Sinazonge village. Her son, a daughter and a son-in-law were buried there. Close by lay a second, ailing daughter. Like the others before her, she had AIDS and when she died Belita would mourn a whole generation. A divorcee in her seventies, Belita was already caring for her seven grandchildren and her own blind mother. With the breadwinners gone she was penniless and, in the enduring food shortage, depended entirely on food rations the Red Cross planned as supplementary. She simply had nothing for the rations to supplement.

She had seen bad times before, she said, and a serious drought had occurred in the early 1990s. Only then the men were there, her children pulled together – somehow they coped. "Now when the food runs out we go to the woods and search for roots and wild vegetables," she said. For infirm, elderly people living alone because AIDS has robbed them of their caregivers, the predicament is worse still. Even neighbours who would once have helped them are now struggling and no longer able to assist.

Unless something changes, Belita's position will worsen. Food is only one of her problems. HIV/AIDS has done more than exacerbate the consequences of erratic climate. It has thrown her into chronic poverty that now threatens her grandchildren's future. School fees must be paid, books and uniforms bought, and there is no exemption on the grounds of poverty. Like many of her friends, Belita's granddaughter Prisca stopped going to school when she could no longer pay the fees. Like them she has been jobless since. "I am sad about it," she said. "I liked school and did well." Once she had hopes of becoming a nurse, but today has lost hope of anything. "I think of my parents and feel helpless."

Other girls in Sinazonge have lost more than hope. Authorities report a rise in prostitution. In the coal-mining township of Maamba, Dr Isaac Kasaro, executive director of the district hospital and social advisor to the Zambia Red Cross, said AIDS-related poverty was driving women to it. "Before, you could count the prostitutes on the fingers of your hand," he said. "Now they are all over and the tragedy is there are school-age girls among them." They spread the disease, completing a vicious circle. ■

strategy since summer 2003. "The combined effect of the interacting elements is horrifying," he says. "No one can accurately predict what the future holds and at every level, be it household, community or government, people are struggling and unable to cope. Southern Africa is caught in a dangerous downward spiral which is further fuelling the spread of HIV/AIDS and making people ever more vulnerable to common diseases and poverty."

Adds Sandbladh: "Above all, it has become painfully clear that HIV/AIDS efforts to prevent further new infections have failed to have any major impact. But then how is it possible to reduce the number of new HIV infections when families in deepest distress and desperation, their coping mechanisms exhausted, are forced to send their women into prostitution?" By the same token, how can anyone expect a hungry person living in appalling, unsanitary conditions – and with no access to care – to prioritize changes in sexual behaviour? Unfortunately the policy of the world's donors and their agents suggests that many of them expect exactly that. Desist or be damned is the attitude.

The facts suggest this approach is failing to work. Where HIV prevalence is highest, projections foresee life expectancy dropping below 20 years by 2020. Between a fifth and a third of all children below the age of 15 will have lost one or both of their parents by 2010. The UN's human development indicators reveal a rapid slide into

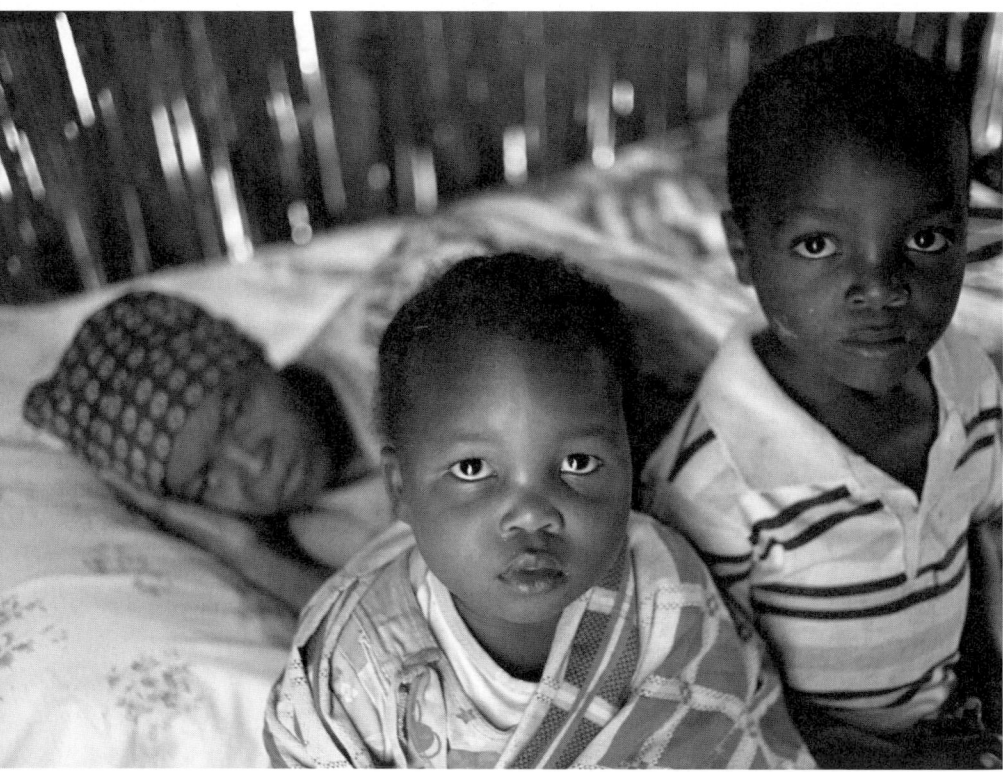

Across sub-Saharan Africa, 12-3 million children have been orphaned by AIDS (4 million of them in southern Africa). They are among the continent's most vulnerable people. Many fall prey to abuse or sexual exploitation.

© Marko Kokic/ International Federation.

deep poverty. More than 87 per cent of the Zambian population now lives in abject poverty and Zimbabwe has seen the fastest fall in gross domestic product in the world. Life expectancy is 38 in Malawi, 34 in Zimbabwe, less than 33 in Zambia and is expected to continue falling.

An even gloomier picture emerges as the indicators reveal increased vulnerability to common diseases such as respiratory tract infections, measles, malaria and TB, all of which are spreading like wildfire. Meanwhile, government investment in national health-care systems is very low – less than US$ 50 per person per year – making it almost impossible to vaccinate all children and meet the increasing demand for basic health care and prevention of disease. Poor and sometimes absent health-care structures present problems over the management of antiretroviral drugs if, as is hoped, they are made widely available to African people living with HIV/AIDS.

If people receive the right drug treatment at the right time, they may live for another 20 years. But people living with AIDS in developing countries can only expect to last a maximum of five years at present. Many governments and multinational drug companies have been far too slow in making affordable drugs available to extend the lives of those infected in sub-Saharan Africa – as well as to prevent the transmission of the virus from mother to child.

The bottom line is that without fresh approaches to tackle the HIV/AIDS pandemic, a dramatic fall in life expectancy, a decimation of the workforce and agricultural production, and the destitution of whole communities are inevitable. "It is critical that the full scenario is understood when we look at how to respond. We must challenge our own thinking. There is need of more sophisticated analysis of the situation," says Sandbladh. "A new paradigm is required." And not only for sub-Saharan Africa – the HIV/AIDS pandemic is threatening to get out of control on other continents too (see Box 6.3).

Food aid – false sense of relief

Supporting households at community level is vital to contain the crisis and develop long-term strategies to return places like Evusweni to normality. Chief Masilela would concur. His own quest is for fundamental change and part of the same equation.

The removal of stigma around HIV/AIDS is but a first step that leads to new cultural standards and practices in a traditionally polygamous society. Multiple sexual partners are the norm in Swaziland, casual sex is highly prevalent and pre-marital sex starts young – all habits from a time when life expectancy was low and infant mortality high. Things that assisted community survival then are now the seeds of its destruction.

Box 6.3 Alarm bells ring in China

An HIV/AIDS epidemic is spreading rapidly through China, the world's most populous nation. Unless it can be effectively controlled, not only will social stability and economic development be affected, but national security and prosperity will be threatened.

The assessment is official. According to a joint report from China's Ministry of Health and the UN theme group on HIV/AIDS in China, the virus has not been contained among high-risk groups and is now reaching the general population, threatening a widespread epidemic. Already, severe social and economic burdens are being felt.

Cesar Chelala, a public health consultant for the UN, wrote in the *South China Morning Post* recently: "The mainland is now facing an emergency of titanic proportions." The country's health minister, Wu Yi, has warned that without greater efforts, "the consequences will be very grievous".

China's leaders are making enormous efforts to mobilize the country. If the authorities were in the past seen as reticent to acknowledge publicly the extent of the disease, their language is now forthright. The official *China Daily* newspaper quoted one Beijing health official as saying, "This is what we have all been waiting for."

Ever since World AIDS Day 2003, when prime minister Wen Jiabao and health minister Wu made a much-publicized visit to AIDS patients, open discussion has increased remarkably. Wu's subsequent high-profile visit to AIDS-devastated villages in Henan province, where HIV prevalence among former blood plasma donors has reached 60 per cent in some communities, further energized debate. In May, China's state council called for more urgency in fighting the disease. A circular said prevention should be taught in schools and colleges, and information campaigns should target "entertainment venues". The language was combative, particularly for recalcitrant officials. Anyone "hiding epidemic reports will be severely punished", the circular warned.

The minister herself has maintained the tough talking. China must continue to crack down on illegal blood collection, do more to limit prostitution and drug use, and promote the use of condoms and clean syringes, she has said. Until last year, a ban on sex in advertising precluded even condom commercials.

China is responding to what one official report described as the need "to seize the fast-disappearing window of opportunity for prevention and control, to keep the economic and personal losses caused by HIV/AIDS as low as possible". Another, unofficial assessment from experts was less circumspect. "China is on the verge of a catastrophe that could result in unimaginable human suffering, economic loss and social devastation," it warned.

Some 840,000 Chinese are said to be living with HIV/AIDS, 80,000 of them AIDS patients. But, as often with this pandemic, official statistics tell little of what is really happening. The absence of good data is a major challenge for the central government, as it endeavours to convert policy into practice in provinces where some authorities still turn a blind eye, harass activists and suppress information for fear that it will reflect badly on them. The most useful figure is an indicative one from UNAIDS, which says the number of infected people could rise to 10 million by 2010 – unless much greater action is undertaken.

International Federation of Red Cross and Red Crescent Societies

All 31 provinces have reported HIV infection. Transmission has been mainly through intravenous drug use and the sale of blood and plasma that has infected both recipients and donors, due to unsafe practices. Now the proportion of sexually-transmitted infections is growing.

The Ministry of Health/UN assessment pointed to the impact on China's social fabric in provinces like Henan and Anhui, where AIDS cases have been particularly high. The epidemic would drain health and social welfare resources, it warned. The numbers of the poor would increase, as would the disparity between richest and poorest. "Most people living with HIV/AIDS in China live in underdeveloped areas where there are few natural resources, where health and education resources are in short supply and where poverty is relatively high," the assessment said.

Poverty is exacerbated by AIDS-affected families having lower incomes and higher medical bills. Evidence shows that people who had risen out of poverty and begun to enjoy a secure income have been plunged back into poverty by the epidemic. The discrimination that the disease brings, combined with the loss of jobs and schooling, threaten to bring about social instability.

The public's misunderstanding of what is popularly perceived to be a self-inflicted disease encourages stigma and silence, which in turn accelerates the epidemic's spread. "While many people in China are aware of AIDS, few understand the routes of transmission and means of prevention," says Audrey Swift, the International Federation's HIV/AIDS coordinator in east Asia. "Worse, even those who do understand the transmission have incorrect beliefs about non-transmission. They assume that casual contact or proximity to people living with HIV/AIDS can transmit the virus. Accompanying the HIV/AIDS pandemic are epidemics of isolation and rejection, and of self-isolation and fear of rejection."

Survey findings are appalling. One among sex workers discovered that while most knew sexual intercourse could spread HIV, few knew a condom could protect them. And 88 per cent of people questioned in a Sichuan survey said those with the virus should not be in contact with other people.

Breaking down ignorance requires massive investment. Present budgets are far short of requirements in both prevention and care. The Chinese Red Cross has been working on prevention, care and support for people living with the disease since 1994, and has a government mandate to recruit and retain voluntary, unpaid blood donors. "What China needs is more than information campaigns," Swift says. "It needs people with the skills to change perceptions and behaviour."

Much Red Cross focus is on peer education, particularly youth education. "Research has shown that education and behaviour change is most effective and sustainable when it is delivered by peers passing on life skills," Swift argues. "Peer educators require training and confidence to raise sensitive topics and to address the others' risks constructively."

In Yunnan and Xinjiang provinces, the Red Cross is developing peer education by and for people living with HIV/AIDS. Swift describes it as China's first project to support their development, as educators and as people who have something to give to their communities. "It trains them to educate their neighbours, friends and family about HIV/AIDS and caring for those who are infected." ■

Some people are listening, although general surveys in Swaziland show risk-taking behaviour has not altered despite information campaigns that have supposedly brought widespread awareness. The chief has found success in another area. He persuaded the elders to set aside land to feed the growing number of orphans and has advocated communal farming and crop sharing, making the most of idle or poorly used land to help the ailing and infected. "I know how difficult it is," he said. "I am no longer able to plough my own land myself and must rely on other people."

He is also concerned about water. Irrigation would end farmers' dependence on erratic rains, and there is tremendous need for safe domestic water. Cholera is now endemic, diarrhoeal disease rampant and with other common ills they compound catastrophe. Outside help with water schemes would be welcome. The chief is not a lover of food aid. Humanitarian assistance, he said, could far better focus on helping the community to help itself. The recovery of agriculture and the introduction of irrigation were high on his agenda. Chief Masilela knows the needs of his own community and if Evusweni is to recover, he and his neighbours – or those who survive them – will be central to the solution. It is a simple premise all too often forgotten.

An evaluation, on behalf of the UK-based Disasters Emergency Committee, of the humanitarian response to the 2002–2003 food crisis argued that, although the response successfully reduced suffering and deferred deaths, aid agencies "did not always have a deep enough understanding of the communities in which they worked". For example, international organizations' attempts to target food aid at the most vulnerable households in southern Africa backfired, as villagers subsequently redistributed the food to everyone in the community. A number of evaluations have found that aid agencies' targeting actually undermined the cohesion and cooperation of rural communities, which traditionally share resources during times of hardship. A report by Save the Children, a British non-governmental organization (NGO), provided evidence from village members that those villagers who had not been targeted for food aid were then unwilling to fulfil other community responsibilities.

No one talked to Rhoda Siamena before providing assistance to her village in the Sinazongwe region of Zambia's southern province. Rhoda, a mother of four still in her twenties, came to the attention of a Catholic priest as she sought to pacify her youngest, malnourished daughter when her crying disrupted Sunday service. She tried to suckle the child but her breasts were withered and the infant only howled the louder. With nothing else at hand, Rhoda broke clay from the wall of the church and desperately fed it to her.

Life has always been hard in Sinazongwe and villages like Rhoda's are not new to food shortages. Before, though, they had managed to cope. She and her husband would eat less in order to feed the children. She would supplement meals with wild plants she gathered and neighbours would help one another. Not any more. Everyone was struggling and there were days when all she had to eat were grass and leaves. Had AIDS tipped the balance? No one mentioned the disease, but people said TB was now common. They had long lived life on the edge and something was finally pushing them over.

Food aid did reach Sinazongwe. An international agency was delivering maize, a standard amount per family per month, regardless of family numbers. The food kept them alive but covered at most two-thirds of the month – insufficient to dull their hunger. The women struggled on, walking all day, searching for something to bridge the gap and ease the pain of their children's malnutrition.

After two consecutive failed harvests, they had planted maize and sorghum as usual when the rain began in November 2002. It ceased before the end of the month, enough to germinate the seed and set plants growing but not enough to sustain them. Another long, dry spell followed, stunting, scorching and shrivelling what in March and April would have been a harvest. Fresh hope had come with rain at the end of January. The women dug into the earth again, planting maize from the food aid, sacrificing a meal in a desperate attempt to claw themselves back from crisis. Their efforts were in vain. Even if the maize had germinated, what was left of the growing season was too short ever to produce a harvest.

Rhoda took to setting out at dawn, her youngest child on her back, walking several hours to the shore of Lake Kariba. She sometimes found work there, in a few small, irrigated fields. When in luck, she would weed through the heat of day and be paid at the end with some pumpkins. She would then have enough for an evening meal and perhaps to see her family through tomorrow.

If ever a picture were false, it is of Africa waiting with its hand out. No struggle was ever greater, no people more determined, more deserving of assistance that doesn't simply dump food then run when the crisis momentarily seems to subside.

Together we can go far

What Chief Masilela and Rhoda illustrate to would-be helpers prepared to change is that a people-centred approach involving the community is crucial for success. This means that vertical, sector-specific aid programming should end. Hakan Sandbladh argues: "We must recognize that the pandemic affects everyone in the community and *all* aspects of people's lives, not just their health. It follows that the responsibility for tackling epidemics like HIV/AIDS will no longer be borne solely by the health sector." Tackling hunger, strengthening livelihoods, spreading awareness, dispelling stigma and changing behaviour are equally vital tools in building resilience to the disease and its impacts.

It's not enough for aid organizations alone to wield these tools – every community member has a role to play. The courage, determination and resilience of ordinary people are the foundations upon which a solution to the pandemic must be built. People like Ruth Musiego from Kenya, who considered the day when she first accepted her HIV-positive status as the start of her new life. Ruth trained as a home-based carer and peer educator, and went on to tell schoolchildren her story (see Box 6.4).

The leap from greater awareness to changing behaviour is unlikely to happen unless the message is delivered in a culturally appropriate way. Mombasa, for example, is a predominantly Moslem city on the coast of Kenya, where religious leaders have become increasingly vocal in countering the stigma attached to HIV/AIDS. Sheikh Khitamy is imam of the Mandhry mosque, the oldest in Mombasa: "Nobody can advocate things to these communities effectively from their ivory towers in Nairobi or faraway foreign cities. Things will have to happen here, right here, to have an effect," he says, adding: "Change in our Muslim communities starts from the mosques. Our people deal with their issues through the mosques, through their religious leaders." Sheikh Khitamy uses the opportunity of evening prayers to address the faithful on the subject of the pandemic. "These are our sons and daughters, our neighbours, us who are infected, affected and dying. We need to speak up, especially we, the religious leaders."

For the Red Cross, Sandbladh advocates a programme of comprehensive community support, incorporating income generation and community self-help into existing home-based care and disease prevention programmes – as well as long-term safety nets for affected families. Three key issues must be addressed:

- Stop the accelerating trend towards poverty.
- Reduce the incidence of new HIV infections.
- Start reducing vulnerability to disease and disasters.

The major causes of the slide from well-being to poverty are clear: HIV/AIDS, tuberculosis, malaria, other common diseases, poor water and sanitation, the burden of care related to orphans and vulnerable children, insecurity and lack of protection, failing agriculture, unplanned urbanization, and poor access to schooling and health care.

Creating the right kind of aid programme means carrying out multi-sectoral vulnerability and capacity assessments. Translating such assessments into programmes requires a commitment by donors to holistic rather than sectoral programming. And dealing with such a range of risks requires a comprehensive package of measures, implemented by a consortium of partners with special interests and capacities.

The comparative advantage of National Red Cross or Red Crescent Societies is their closeness and access to the community. They can deliver, when it comes to mobilizing

Box 6.4 Ruth Musiego – a positive life

Ruth had a nasty rash on her arms and legs when I saw her for the first time. Three weeks later, it is worse. Her spirits, upbeat during the first visit, are low. One of the mantras of HIV-positive people is to live positively. They talk about it all the time, and it is drummed into them by counsellors and pamphlets. But it isn't always easy.

Ruth's husband was big and strong. With hindsight, he may already have been HIV positive when they met. But a year or so after they tied the knot, he grew frailer and started getting sick. "He was drinking a lot, so I thought that was what was eating into him," Ruth says. "He never told me about dying or having HIV. One day, four years ago, he just passed away. We were left with absolutely nothing to lean on to.

"I started having these questions, since I had heard about AIDS, but I never believed it was the reason for me being sick, too. I had rashes. I had blisters. People around me started telling me that I had AIDS," Ruth says. She confides that she was shy and never left the house. Her friends abandoned her. "Finally, in 2002, I went to a voluntary counselling and testing clinic and got tested. I was shocked: it was positive. I felt like dying then and there. I was thinking about killing myself.

"It was my children who dragged me out of this black hole. Who would care for them if I took my life? I decide to fight back. I went to counselling and asked the counsellor about half-a-million questions," she says. Ruth was directed to a man called Hassan Musa, who

is not only an HIV/AIDS counsellor, but also responsible for a ground-breaking Kenya Red Cross home-based care project in the Mombasa district of Majengo. "He got me to accept my status. He told me it is senseless to waste my life on thoughts that will change nothing. If it had not been for him, I might still be in some stage of denial. Or dead – who knows!

"I will die anyway one day. There is no reason for me to act dead before my time actually comes. That was the start of my new life," says Ruth.

Ruth believes she has been HIV positive for at least five years. "I had already passed through stigma, passed through discrimination. My family, my friends, employers... You name it. I reckoned I was qualified to come out in the open." When she met Hassan Musa for the first time, she had only told two other people of her status. Her mother was one – and she continued to love her daughter despite what others chose to do.

Hassan told Ruth about the Majengo project, and she enthusiastically volunteered to join it. She was the first participant to go public about being HIV positive, later becoming one of the first to be trained as a home-based caregiver by the Red Cross's Mombasa branch. The three-week training gave her new skills and a new meaning to life. Since then, she has been trained as peer educator by another organization. Now she visits schools, telling children her story and disseminating information about HIV/AIDS. ■

community resources and volunteers, or providing such things as basic public health education, home-based care or local first aid to target common diseases. They can also provide water and sanitation, targeted food aid, seeds and tools.

The Rwandan Red Cross (RRC), for example, has encouraged groups of people living with HIV/AIDS to form self-help associations. One 46-member group has given itself the name 'Let's preserve life'. Their aims are to provide each other with moral support, start breaking down the stigma associated with HIV/AIDS in their community, and strengthen their livelihoods. To this end, the RRC is supporting the association by buying them goats to breed and sell, providing seeds, tools and fertilizer for a market garden, and giving school materials to their children.

For more complicated programmes, however, partnership is crucial. The Swaziland Red Cross has developed partnerships with food security specialists, universities and the government in order to implement a programme that combines home-based care, improved farming methods through irrigation, and income-generation activities such as poultry breeding and vegetable gardening. Meanwhile in Zimbabwe, the International Federation is working with nutritionists at the University of Zimbabwe to develop an ideal food basket for infected people, since better nutrition significantly boosts the immune systems of people living with HIV/AIDS and greatly reduces loss of life.

Partners will also be needed for technical support in areas such as large-scale agriculture, veterinary services, sustained behavioural change, strategies for TB control, voluntary testing and counselling for HIV, and preventing mother-to-child transmission of the virus. Any or all of these factors could be essential elements of the approach needed to help communities pull themselves out of a downward spiral and get back on their feet. Where it has no expertise, the Red Cross Red Crescent can help identify needs and introduce partners to meet those needs. A Zen tenet is required in southern Africa: "Together we can go far."

Ray of hope?

Interest in Chief Masilela and millions of others like him has waned. The news last year that mass starvation in southern Africa had apparently been averted left an impression that the emergency was over. The very success of a humanitarian intervention that for once was ahead of the game seemed to be backfiring. Indeed, there were those who questioned whether 14 million people had ever been in grave danger, as aid agencies had estimated. Had the humanitarians hyped it? No bodies, no disaster.

The television images had been missing, the ones that have always defined disaster in Africa. There were no skeletal figures traipsing across the landscape, no agonizing evidence of malnutrition, no hunger camps, no endless lines of fly-eyed, wasting children.

God forbid, they may come again, but those are yesterday's images. Today's disaster is a silent one and most of those dying are dying at home. A ubiquitous disaster has befallen them. There is no escape so no mass migration is happening, except to the place where people were born. Care can be found more easily there and the funerals won't be expensive.

Out of sight and out of mind of a world largely indifferent, if response is any indicator, millions of people are dying. People like Abraham, a 45-year-old sugar-cane cutter. When AIDS began to debilitate him, he went back to the family homestead of earth and stone dwellings in southern Swaziland. His ailing younger sister, Ntombikayise, did too, taking her children with her. Muzi, three, a gaunt little boy, was already ill and five-month-old Valesa soon would be.

Abraham died on a clear March morning. As he succumbed in one hut, his sister and the youngsters lay chronically ill in another. Valesa, her little body wasted, died the very same day. Muzi went a week later. Grace, their doting old grandmother was inconsolable, the grief in the homestead dreadful. But in no way was this exceptional. Such is the face of contemporary disaster in southern Africa. Within the next ten years, Swaziland can expect that half its working-age population will die of AIDS. Besides the grief, they will leave ever more orphans and unturned land, and a poorly skilled generation facing social meltdown.

Yet even in such a scenario, a ray of hope can emerge. The day Abraham died, Mummsy Sithebe, a 38-year-old Red Cross volunteer, was in the compound. In her unpaid job providing home care to her scattered rural community, particularly to people infected and affected by HIV/AIDS, she sees more than her fair share of funerals. By week's end three more clients would be gone.

But all was not lost. Each morning she continued to walk down the rocky hillside track to the homestead. Through the long dark weeks that followed the deaths, she cared for Ntombikayise. She nursed, cooked, cleaned, listened and counselled. She helped the stricken Grace through her anguish. She brought food, hygiene parcels and medicine which she ensured Ntombikayise took on time.

The woman survived. Three months later she could stand again. There were good days and bad. Her steps were measured. But she could take a bus to the nearest hospital, visit a doctor and be dispensed a supply of drugs. It wasn't a miracle. What laid her low was TB. Up to 50 per cent of people living with HIV/AIDS develop it, but treatment is effective if timely and consistent. It needs to be. HIV is largely responsible for the accelerated spread of TB in sub-Saharan Africa and, in the course of a year, one case of open pulmonary TB can, if untreated, affect another 10 to 15 people. It calls for vigilance and the home-based care programme that the Swaziland Red Cross has introduced to the region has made care facilitators like Mummsy the eyes and ears of the community.

Most of their clients are chronically ill with AIDS-related problems, but the wider well-being of the community – its health and welfare – is what they are there to protect. The provision of health education is part of it, whether on HIV or hygiene. The care programme is centred on a clinic in the small community of Silele, which serves ten districts in a radius of 40 kilometres. Importantly, the home care is linked to targeted food distribution and much-needed water and sanitation programmes.

"Most people have no latrines," said water and sanitation officer Mduduzi Nkonyane. "People defecate in the bush. They do not cover their faeces and do not wash their hands because water isn't close. When it rains the faeces are washed into the rivers. People drink from the rivers, the water is dirty, it is kept in dirty containers and nothing is done to purify it. Often homesteads do not have refuse pits. You find cow dung all over the yard. Food like vegetables isn't washed before cooking or eating and flies are everywhere."

Nkonyane was busy changing things. In the hills close by, streams were fed into filtration and purification tanks and a pipeline carried water down to the clinic. A mountain of coiled pipe revealed other plans: to take the clean water into hundreds of homesteads. The digging of trenches had started. It was the first such project in the area and other communities were interested – evidence that health information campaigns were paying dividends.

But other needs loomed – agricultural, infrastructural – and given community momentum, it was time for new partners to step in and support the Red Cross. If it is the coping capacity of the *whole* community that needs to be strengthened, not simply that of the most vulnerable, who would be the partners?

According to Milly Katana, a member of the Commission on HIV/AIDS and Governance in Africa (established last year by UN Secretary-General Kofi Annan): "In Africa it's only governments that have the capacity to do things [nationally]. The NGOs have good intentions, but their capacity just cannot match the needs." For its part, Swaziland's government has taken some proactive steps to combat the pandemic (see Box 6.5).

Build response on local resilience

The HIV/AIDS pandemic has exposed a weak link in the chain of international aid – the link between relief and development. The colossal US$ 600 million intervention during 2002–2003 to provide 14 million people across sub-Saharan Africa with food aid was hailed as a successful new form of pre-emptive humanitarian action. Yet it achieved little more than deferring death. At worst, it sent the wrong signal to the international community that 'disaster' was averted – when in fact, an ongoing, chronic disaster continues day in, day out across the continent. Last year, AIDS claimed over 3 million victims worldwide, according to UNAIDS, of whom between 2.2 million and 2.4 million died in sub-Saharan Africa alone.

Box 6.5 How can Swaziland cope with HIV/AIDS?

To ask the question is to recognize that Swaziland is a vivid microcosm of all the similarly afflicted countries of southern Africa. At the grass roots, where it counts, there's a superhuman determination to bring the pandemic to heel, and to overcome the tremendous assault on the human condition. I'm not romanticizing: in the midst of the worst the world has to offer, the people of Swaziland simply refuse to succumb, and they're fighting back with every means available. In three areas in particular, the response is inspired.

First, Swaziland intends to put between 4,000 and 4,500 people into antiretroviral treatment by the end of this year (there are about 1,500 in treatment now); 10,000 to 13,000 by the end of next year. That will represent almost 50 per cent of those who are eligible for treatment, a much higher ratio than most other countries. Can they pull it off? The answer would appear to be yes, because the National Emergency Response Council on HIV/AIDS (NERCHA) is extraordinarily impressive, well led and single-minded. More, it has devised a computer tracking system for drugs and adherence and side effects, available to physicians in the public and private sectors to follow patients, while sealed in absolute confidentiality.

Second, in order to deal with the vast numbers of orphans, NERCHA is proposing to establish a cadre of 10,000 women to act as a kind of surrogate parent for the children. These are women who have families of their own, still do all of the tasks related to those families, still care for the others who are vulnerable in their villages, but on top of all of that, will somehow find several hours of the day to feed and support the orphans. It's a classic example of how women sustain African society, usually unheralded and uncompensated. NERCHA is asking donors that the 10,000 women be paid for the specific work they will undertake with the orphans. Predictably, it's a very modest stipend, roughly US$ 40 a month. But it's explicitly in recognition of the additional work over and above all the other work that is normally done. It will be monitored carefully, and the money will be paid.

Third, given the surfeit of orphans, schooling and feeding are vital. In Swaziland, you have the predicament characteristic of many other countries: school fees prevent school attendance. In response, NERCHA, UNICEF and WFP, working with powerful local chiefs, have fashioned a truly imaginative initiative, serving as a model in a number of communities. The communities are offered a grant (through UNICEF) to be used as they see fit (including school fees, but sometimes teachers or materials or refurbishing of classrooms), and the entire purpose is to get kids back into school. Tens of thousands of children are currently out of school.

It's working. The children are returning in large numbers; WFP feeds them a couple of meals a day; school gardens are planted to give the children some agricultural experience and to enhance the diet; it's organized around 'neighbourhood care points' – points in a chiefdom where villagers gather for the purpose of attending to children, and NERCHA is overseeing the construction of a number of social centres to serve as a focal point for all community and orphan activity. It's quite the model, and it's giving joy and hope to a lot of orphan kids. ■

Of all contemporary catastrophes, HIV/AIDS most powerfully exposes the futility of applying a temporary 'band-aid' solution to a complex but deadly problem. Food aid is certainly a vital reinforcement for communities on the cusp of crisis – but stopping at food aid is simply not enough. As James Morris, the executive director of the World Food Programme and special envoy of the UN Secretary-General for humanitarian needs in Southern Africa, wrote in 2002, in relation to the HIV/AIDS pandemic: "The traditional pattern of humanitarian assistance, which at times may attempt to replace a weakened government sector in order to achieve its lifesaving objectives, is simply not a viable option for Southern Africa at this time, as it would merely postpone an eventual collapse."

Much closer cooperation between humanitarian and development actors – and governments – is needed to create a long-term strategy of response and recovery. HIV/AIDS raises humanitarian challenges for development, such as welfare support for those left destitute. But only a developmental, participatory approach to this long-term crisis, with a detailed understanding of local needs and capacities at its heart, can ensure that interventions are appropriate, effective and sustainable. To achieve the depth of analysis and engagement needed, international aid organizations will have to seek the partnership of community groups, local NGOs, churches, mosques, local authorities and governments in tackling this crisis. The crucial challenge is to establish working connections between the actors and develop strong regional partnerships.

Meanwhile, a focus that isolates HIV/AIDS prevention and treatment alone is unlikely to succeed. Recent revision of the Sphere handbook recognizes that HIV/AIDS is a cross-cutting issue. A multi-dimensional response is needed, which incorporates support for local economies and livelihoods, agricultural irrigation and production, urban food security, education, clean water and sanitation – as well as prevention of the disease and care for those who succumb to its effects.

Above all, among the many voices that are raised around the world demanding that something be done, we must seek out the voices of those at greatest risk. The voice of Chief Masilela, who spoke out about his own illness to help save his village, who called not for food aid but for irrigation – so that his village could feed itself. Success in the war on AIDS will be based on the courage and skills of those who wake up to the disease's impacts every day of their lives. People like Rhoda Siamena, who walked for hours each dawn and dusk to till fields in return for a pumpkin to feed her family, or Red Cross volunteer Mummsy Sithebe, who has devoted her life to caring for the sick and dying. These are the human qualities of resilience on which every intervention must build.

International Federation
of Red Cross and Red Crescent Societies

John Sparrow, the International Federation's regional information delegate in east Asia and formerly based in southern Africa, was principal contributor to this chapter and Boxes 6.1, 6.2 and 6.3. Pekka Reinikainen of the International Federation contributed Box 6.4. Box 6.5 is an excerpt from a press briefing delivered on 31 March 2004 by Stephen Lewis, UN Secretary-General's Special Envoy for HIV/AIDS in Africa.

Sources and further information

Active Learning Network for Accountability and Performance in Humanitarian Action (ALNAP). *Review of Humanitarian Action in 2003.* London: ALNAP, 2004.

de Waal, Alex and Tumushabe, Joseph. *HIV/AIDS and food security in Africa.* A report for DFID, 2003. Available at: http://www.sarpn.org.za/documents/d0000235/P227_AIDS_Food_Security.pdf

Harvey, Paul. *HIV/AIDS and humanitarian action.* HPG Research Report 16. London: Overseas Development Institute, 2004.

Inter-Agency Standing Committee (IASC). *Guidelines for HIV/AIDS interventions in emergency settings.* IASC, 2003. Available at: http://www.humanitarianinfo.org/iasc/publications.asp

Joint United Nations Programme on HIV/AIDS (UNAIDS). *AIDS Epidemic Update 2003.* Geneva: UNAIDS, 2003.

Lewis, Stephen. *Report Back on Swaziland.* Notes for press briefing, United Nations, New York, 31 March 2004. Available at: http://www.stephenlewisfoundation.org/docs/2004-03-31-PressBriefingSwaziland.doc

Morris, James. *Report on the First Mission to Lesotho, Malawi, Mozambique, Swaziland, Zimbabwe, and Zambia 3–15 September 2002.* Rome: World Food Programme, 2002.

Ntata, Pierson. *Improving the Emergency Programme's Focus on the Needs of Individuals, Households and Communities Affected by the HIV/AIDS Pandemic in Malawi.* Learning Support Office, Malawi, 2003.

Sandbladh, Hakan, Mabuza, Khanya and Blewitt, Richard. *Not Business As Usual,* Geneva: International Federation, 2003.

Valid International. *A Stitch in Time? Independent Evaluation of the Disasters Emergency Committee's Southern Africa Crisis Appeal, July 2002 to June 2003.* London: Valid International, 2003.

Web sites

Averting HIV/AIDS **http://www.avert.org**
International Federation **http://www.ifrc.org**
South Africa: The Official Gateway **http://www.southafrica.info**
South African Regional Poverty Network **http://www.sarpn.org.za**
UN-OCHA Integrated Regional Information Network **http://www.plusnews.org**

Focus on community resilience

International Federation
of Red Cross and Red Crescent Societies

Surviving in the slums

"When we first came here, the settlements were at a distance from the riverbed, and seasonal change in the water levels wasn't a concern," says Azlam, who brought his family to Delhi from the state of West Bengal in the early 1960s. "But over the years," he continues, "overcrowding has led to soil erosion, with slums virtually kissing the river. Even normal monsoon rains now result in floods."

Nor are the floods as they used to be. The overflowing river now carries the sewage, garbage and industrial waste that the city produces but cannot dispose of properly. This pollutes people's daily water supply, as well as making annual floods more hazardous, threatening the well-being of local residents all year round.

Although it may seem the obvious solution, moving away is not as easy or attractive as it sounds. There is no safer land – or land of any kind – available to Azlam within many miles of his work. Low-income families lack the money to compete in the property market, leaving them no option but to reside as informal squatters on land owned by the government or private individuals.

The 'illegal' status of Azlam and his neighbours increases the risks they face. They cannot ask the government to help them mitigate the impacts of floods. If they try to protect themselves from polluted flood waters by raising their homes or creating a community drainage system, they will arouse the attention of the authorities, increasing the risk of eviction. Whereas the floods occur once a year, the possibility of eviction is ever present. Between the two kinds of risk, avoiding eviction is what informal settlers usually prioritize. They keep a low profile and deal with the floods through adapting as best they can when the rains come. Meanwhile, the polluted water supply just becomes part of daily life, inevitably leading to illness and missed days from work or school.

Azlam's story is not unique. Millions more like him around the world have similar tales to tell. Their stories may feature different risks, but two common elements will remain:

- The process of rapid, unplanned urbanization is altering the nature and magnitude of 'traditional' environmental risks, sometimes creating new risks altogether.
- The same process of urbanization, while rendering people's traditional coping mechanisms less effective, can also provide new, alternative ways of coping with risk.

Photo opposite page: Worldwide, 2.2 million people a year die from diseases due to dirty water and sanitation – many of them children in urban slums.

© Charles Page/ International Federation.

While the growth of 'mega-cities' and 'mega-risks' like earthquakes capture the headlines, far more lives are lost to smaller, everyday disasters caused by dirty drinking water and inadequate sanitation. If governments and aid organizations are successfully to enhance the resilience of slum dwellers to disaster, they will have to understand how risk and coping in the city have themselves become urbanized, and plan their actions accordingly. Some fundamental questions must be asked. What is distinctive about risks and opportunities in urban settings? Which risks do slum dwellers themselves prioritize and how do they cope with them? What are the implications for governments, municipalities and aid organizations?

This chapter aims to start exploring these important questions, drawing on field research undertaken in Mumbai, India, which examined the relationship between community coping and livelihood strategies for slum dwellers. Although the research is specific to Mumbai, its conclusions may be applicable to city slums in other developing countries. As we shall discover below, despite the overwhelming risks that slum dwellers face, there are opportunities for (and examples of) poor urban communities creating joint partnerships with local municipalities to begin crafting a safer and healthier future.

Southern cities soaring in size

Nearly half the world lives in urban areas, and the numbers are accelerating. Why? Globalization, the perception of new opportunities in the 'big bright city', the quest to diversify stressed rural livelihoods: these are just a few reasons. The United Nations (UN) estimates that, by 2007, every third urban dweller will live in poverty, with little or no access to shelter, basic services and social amenities. In another decade, there may be more people living in urban slums than there were people on this planet a century ago. And increasingly, urban and rural areas are starting to overlap.

Over the next two decades, 90 per cent of population growth in developing countries will be urban – a trend that is already well under way. From 1970 to 1985, India contributed the largest absolute increase in urban population of any country: 87 million. Some estimates suggest that Indian cities are growing by 600,000 people each month. In Mumbai alone, an estimated 500 families are believed to enter the city each day.

Many municipalities, such as Mumbai, have found it impossible to keep up. City authorities often lack the financial, human or technical capacity necessary to ensure that adequate and appropriate space is prepared for the right number of families; that homes, schools and infrastructure are built to sufficient standards; that enough jobs are available; that industrial areas remain apart from living areas; and so on. Systems of governance needed to help communities manage their own growth, in partnership with the city, are frequently not in place.

So urban expansion is usually uncontrolled and informal, with too many people occupying too small a space, depending on inadequate water, sanitation and drainage services. Urban planning becomes, instead, urban 'catch-up' in pursuit of the spontaneous and often chaotic growth that has already occurred. In Mumbai, 60 per cent of the city's 23 million inhabitants occupy just 6 per cent of its total area – implying an average density of around 2,000 people per hectare (200,000 per square kilometre). In some of these slums, as many as 50 families have to share a single toilet.

Urban slums' distinctive risks

Rapid and uncontrolled urban growth not only exacerbates the scope and scale of hazard events, it also increases the vulnerability of many city inhabitants (especially slum dwellers) to those hazards. The enormous pressures placed on living space by the convergence of so many people means that the rich tend to buy homes in safer and more desirable areas, while the poor have no choice but to live in densely packed districts, often located on inappropriate and unsafe land. Slum settlements in Mumbai have sprung up wherever land could be found: on steep slopes, by open gutters and streams, on low-lying flood plains, under high-voltage wires, beneath stone quarries, along railway lines and highways, and inside industrial zones.

'Catch-up' urban planning normally reaches slum communities too late to be effective. In some of Mumbai's hill communities, remarks Dr Subramanyam, a geologist from the Indian Institute of Technology, you can no longer *see* the slopes to be able to determine what kind of techniques would have been required to stabilize them.

Natural hazards become more destructive as a result. For example, the crowded and unplanned spread of buildings and roads alters natural watershed patterns. Rainwater can no longer soak into the earth and, if drainage infrastructure is inadequate, it simply flows through the city's streets, alleys and homes, often creating floods where none existed before. As nearby wooded slopes become denuded by people seeking fuel or building materials, the consequent erosion and landslides add to the hazards facing those below.

In Mumbai, the monsoon's flood waters may only remain for a few days in well-planned and well-serviced areas of the city. But the same flood waters can stay for a month at a time in the informal, un-serviced districts, where the earth is vanishing beneath the slums and storm drains are nowhere to be seen. In

Kumbharwadi slum, monsoon floods have been getting worse. Every year the community raises the height of the concrete blocks that dam the waters threatening their homes.

Meanwhile, the dirty drinking water and poor sanitation characteristic of slums are not just inconveniences – they are killers. Worldwide, more than 2.2 million people, in urban and rural areas, die from water and sanitation-related diseases every year – many of them children in slums. Garbage and sewage are often left out in the open, since the municipality either lacks the resources to remove it or refuses to provide those services in an 'illegal' area. As a result, the land and water table become polluted, and the prevalence of bacteria and communicable diseases, especially in children, increases dramatically.

The infant mortality rate in Bangladesh's squatter settlements during 1991 was more than twice the rural rate. The crude death rate in central Mumbai during the 1990s was twice that of the suburbs, and three times higher than in well-to-do districts. Similarly, unregulated air pollution, created by congested traffic and industrial emissions, causes chronic bronchial infections which shorten lives and reduce people's strength and well-being.

In Mumbai's slums, natural and technological hazards can quickly combine. In the same square kilometre where 150,000 or 200,000 people live, you could easily find a school right next to a tanning factory, spilling acids and industrial waste into the open gutter; meanwhile, the lack of adequate toilets, drainage and rubbish collection means waste of all descriptions builds up. As flood waters rise in that same square kilometre, they now carry with them a hazardous mixture of chemicals, sewage, garbage and housing debris – flowing through an area already congested by innumerable living and working spaces. This uniquely urban combination of risks can be devastating for slum dwellers' health, safety and livelihoods – as well as having knock-on effects such as reducing the time children spend at school.

The sheer density of poorly built structures exacerbates the vulnerability of those living and working in such slums. A relatively minor earth tremor can wreak widespread destruction. Small fires can rapidly spread out of control. In the densely populated Delhi slum of Yamuna Pushta, a savage fire destroyed 2,000 squatter homes in November 2002 – just 20 days after a smaller fire destroyed 200–300 homes in the same area. In both cases, the cause was a small fire, built by inhabitants to counter the chill of the winter night, which was left momentarily unattended. Since most dwellers use highly inflammable polythene sheets on their roofs to keep the rain out, it only takes a moment of negligence to spark a full-scale disaster. What's more, the lack of urban planning means slums can trap their inhabitants in a labyrinth of alleys and dead ends, beyond the reach of rescue vehicles.

Livelihoods tied to market and money

The lives and livelihoods of Mumbai's informal settlers are inextricably bound to the marketplace. With so many people concentrated in a small area, the immediate environment cannot produce the resources (such as food, water and fuel) that every household needs. So resources have to be brought in, rather than being found or produced within the household. This usually costs money.

Moreover, poor urban families often lack the space or security to keep stocks of goods for consumption at a later date. Instead, they tend to buy things when they need them, which exposes them to the risk of unpredictable price rises. As a result, slum dwellers may be unable to access vital supplies during times of crisis. Their high dependence on the ability to buy and sell clearly puts greater emphasis on money and income generation than on any other livelihood asset.

Typically, urban dwellers will have fewer kinds of livelihood assets (or a weaker balance of assets) than many inhabitants of rural areas, who may have access to some cash, subsistence farming, livestock, forms of communal exchange, savings and family land. The poorest rural households across the world rely on the natural resource base of their surrounding area for up to 25 per cent of their yearly household income. But in urban areas, these resources are far less available (although the potential for urban farming has grown considerably in the past 20 years, especially in Africa). Meanwhile, the change from rural, communal livelihoods to more of a market-based strategy reduces the scope for social cohesion among urban neighbours and even extended family members, as people's household livelihoods are no longer inextricably linked.

Dependence on the market means that financial poverty can be a crippling factor in urban vulnerability, simply because so few other assets are available in emergencies. Many urban dwellers are dependent on a single source of income – for example, rickshaw driving, hawking, petty trading or working on a building site. If the market sustains a shock and the local currency devalues, if companies or industries go out of business, if the family breadwinner falls ill, or if the make-up of income-generation activities within a household changes, people can lose the foundation of their entire livelihood strategy.

One slum-dwelling woman interviewed in Mumbai earned her income selling tea on the streets. A year before, she had caught malaria from mosquitoes breeding in stagnant monsoon flood waters near her home. She was so ill that her husband stayed in the city to care for her, instead of travelling back to his village to sell his labour during the harvest, as he normally does. Although many of their belongings were seriously damaged in the monsoon, neither of them considered the flood to be the disaster. The disaster was their devastating loss of income due to her illness, at just the time when they needed it most.

Meanwhile, many rural migrants seeking new opportunities in the city often find themselves ill-prepared to find employment, even if the city offers a wider range of possible livelihoods. They may not have the appropriate urban experience or income-generating skills needed to compete for jobs; they may lack the financial capital or access to affordable credit needed to start a business; or the day-labour market may simply be saturated – leaving them more vulnerable to risks and shocks.

Money-based livelihoods can also lead to environmental degradation. In rural areas, there is an incentive to look after the land on which your livestock grazes or in which your crops grow. In urban slums, your livelihood depends less on the land, so that incentive disappears. And the resources (e.g., time, money and energy) it takes to look after your surrounding area are probably needed elsewhere, so the environment may deteriorate as a result.

Different ways to protect livelihoods

Given the dependence of slum dwellers on the market, it will come as no surprise that they attach a very high priority to protecting their ability to earn money. However, the measures necessary to safeguard an income can vary widely from household to household.

The house, as a physical location in which to earn a living and maintain as healthy a lifestyle as possible, is very important to many slum dwellers. One Mumbai woman, interviewed in a particularly flood-prone slum, had decided two years earlier to invest her livelihood assets into raising the floor of her house above the flood level, despite the enormous expense. She did so because her sole method of earning an income was beading fabric in her one-room home, and she needed the assurance of being able to continue working throughout the monsoon season. Direct mitigation against the floods was, for her, a strategic method of maintaining or increasing her livelihood capability.

Her neighbour, on the other hand, worked outside the home as a housekeeper for a wealthy family. Raising the floor of her home would not have been such a strategic move, as her livelihood did not depend on it. She decided to invest her assets in other directions that would be of greater use in protecting her own livelihood outcomes. To the naked eye, the apparent risk experienced by the households was identical, but in fact the difference was great – and led to different ways of coping and adapting.

Clearly, the way in which slum dwellers choose to boost their resilience depends fundamentally on how they perceive the risks that threaten them. This is an important point to highlight. If the risk is seen as lost earnings rather than a physical event, then people will not necessarily try to prevent the flood itself, but rather try to reduce future losses of income – and there are many more ways of going about that than by building a flood defence. So, just as many disasters are unrecognizable or 'hidden' to the uninformed eye, so many strategies to strengthen resilience are equally hidden.

In the case of the woman who raised her floor, the only reason researchers recognized her strategy was because it happened to coincide with a widely held perception of what a flood defence should look like. But a common problem with external actors is that, when they observe that the flood isn't being tackled directly, they assume that no mitigation is being carried out, and therefore that increasing resilience to disasters is not a priority. But things often *are* happening – they are simply beyond the observers' perception (see Box 7.1).

Box 7.1 Rational long-term resilience in Mumbai

During research in the slums of Mumbai, one of the people interviewed was a woman who lived by herself in a derelict plastic-sheet tent under a bridge. Nevertheless, among her personal possessions was a television, powered by a clandestine electrical connection wired into the city's main power line. Her living situation seemed highly precarious – at risk from flooding, fire or eviction. A hasty appraisal of her condition would probably conclude that the woman was either ignorant of the risks she faced or simply didn't prioritize risk reduction.

On the contrary, the woman had a very conscious and coherent risk mitigation strategy. She was the owner of a simple, yet well-built flat in an established neighbourhood somewhere else in Mumbai. Having a school-aged daughter, and relying on relatively few skills herself with which to compete for employment, she placed the greatest importance on protecting the one specific livelihood asset that could assure a

better future for herself and her family – her daughter.

In order to afford sending her daughter away to school, she rented out her safe home and lived in a dwelling which, although precarious, would be easy to replace if damaged by a natural hazard. By opting to live in a place of increased short-term risk, she was actually decreasing her long-term risk.

Researchers had approached the woman in search of a case study which exposed a poor mitigation strategy. Instead, they discovered one of the most successful examples of long-term resilience. It was an important lesson. It illustrated that external actors are bound to overlook the inherently rational coping strategies that slum dwellers employ, unless they understand:

■ which risks slum dwellers prioritize;
■ what they are doing or would like to do to mitigate those risks; and
■ how they are using their livelihood assets to achieve those goals. ■

Urban governance – agent of disaster?

Urban governance is all about how a city is run. Rather than simply being a synonym for 'government', governance is the arena in which *everyone* in the city (including the government, civil society and the private sector) negotiates for their share of space, resources and entitlements to fulfil their needs and develop their interests. Governance is about who gets to make decisions, how those decisions are made and for whose benefit. Equally, it is the arena in which citizens share responsibilities for ensuring equitable health and well-being. Urban lives and livelihoods are closely intertwined with urban governance. In slums, most people rely on *access* to resources, such as fuel and food, rather than on their ability to *produce* those resources themselves – and governance is all about who controls access to resources and how they manage that control.

However, the poor often find themselves excluded from a place at the negotiating table, so their needs and livelihood constraints are not taken into consideration when city policies are made. If, for example, enough land is not made available at prices the poor can afford, they find themselves with no option but to squat in informal settlements outside legal boundaries. Similarly, to register a new business requires time and financial resources that the poor all too often lack. As economist Hernando de Soto puts it: "Migrants do not so much break the law as the law breaks them – and they opt out of the system." In Mumbai, members of this informal sector comprise an estimated 92 per cent of the city's population.

So starts a downwards spiral. 'Illegal' status renders slum dwellers unable to negotiate their interests and participate in the development process. It seriously affects their ability to raise loans, voice concerns with the police, call emergency services, vote for the person who would best represent their interests, or even send their child to the local school or clinic. And, being outside the law, households often have no way of claiming basic amenities, services or infrastructure from the formal system. In Mumbai, entire neighbourhoods of thousands of inhabitants function without electricity, locally available water, drainage or appropriate sanitation, because they have no recognized right to ask for it or install it themselves.

Poor governance keeps slum dwellers vulnerable, because it denies them access to the kinds of support, such as credit or basic services, that they need to help enhance their resilience to risks. For example, they lack the option of raising a loan to pay for better housing materials or designs, often making slum dwellings risky places to live. Studies estimate that only 9 per cent of Mumbai's 3 million slum dwellings are made of reinforced concrete (and many of these may not be up to acceptable standards). According to the officer in charge of the disaster management plan for Mumbai, an earthquake measuring just 6 on the Richter scale would be enough to bring down most of the city's informal housing. Yet these slum pockets do not even fall within his jurisdiction because of their extra-legal status. For the same reason, municipalities often refuse to provide informal settlements with the refuse collection, clean water and sanitation services vital to people's health and well-being.

City authorities often perpetuate or increase risk by failing to take responsibility for imposing high construction standards. For example, Mumbai's public works department does not conduct risk analyses or environmental impact assessments before initiating major infrastructure projects. Building codes only specify earthquake-resistant standards for government buildings, and pollution control remains minimal, for fear of driving away big industry.

A similar lack of oversight is evident in public-private partnerships in Mumbai. One disturbing example is a shelter scheme, initiated by the state government in the 1990s, through which private developers are contracted to provide tower-block housing for authorized slum dwellers. The developers make their profit from the private sale of any additional flats they build. Mr Malvankar, secretary of the state of Maharashtra's slum rehabilitation authority (SRA), admitted to the research team that the government absolves itself of all responsibility for the quality and safety standards of the work they have contracted out in this programme. Everything from the choice of construction materials to the strength and earthquake resistance of the building design is left to the discretion of the profit-driven developer.

Slum dwellers account for 92 per cent of Mumbai's 23 million inhabitants. Population densities reach 200,000 per square km and 50 families may share a single toilet.

© Mark Henley/ Panos.

CHAPTER 7

Even when households may be capable and willing to reduce their own risks, poor governance can undermine this capacity for resilience. For example, a number of skilled Mumbai masons living in informal settlements were interviewed to discover why their homes were not better protected against monsoon floods, when homes just a couple of alleys back (well hidden from the main road) had been successfully raised above the flood level. They said they had built their homes without legal permission. If the authorities saw that improvements were being made to the homes, they would evict the masons and rent out the dwellings to other people willing to pay good money for the extra protection. The masons' argument was, "If you fear eviction, why invest in something that you can't take with you when you're forced out?"

Herein lies the sad irony of the relationship between poor urban governance and coping: not only is the municipality often unable or unwilling to invest in mitigation measures on behalf of, or in partnership with, informal settlers, but it actually *incapacitates* these communities (sometimes unwittingly, sometimes in full knowledge) from coping with and adapting to risk on their own initiative. Such exclusionary urban governance makes more work for the municipality itself – since the very partners whose resources the authorities could harness to reduce urban risks are denied the chance to cooperate, leaving all the city's colossal problems on the doorstep of the municipality.

Barriers to coping and adapting

Apart from – or perhaps because of – the failure of urban municipalities to increase resilience to risk, there are social and psychological barriers to better coping and adapting. The attitude towards risk reduction of those slum dwellers interviewed by researchers has turned progressively more pessimistic, due to the very magnitude of urban risk and the lack of municipal commitment to tackle it.

In the case of Azlam and his neighbours at the riverside, they had long-since accepted that some of the most pervasive and chronic disasters they faced – ill health and even premature death from polluted water – were simply facts of life. A sad yet understandable outlook: it is very hard to keep your open gutters clean and your drinking water unpolluted, when those gutters are clogged with the rubbish of hundreds of thousands of other urban residents living outside your neighbourhood, and when there is no authority willing to coordinate clean-up and maintenance.

Individuals and households feel as if they have few options, when the capacity for effectively improving their neighbourhood shifts out of their hands in this way. So people tend to make minor adjustments to cope with immediate risk (e.g., buying water at extortionate prices from the black market) or adapt to the consequences of that risk within their livelihood strategy (e.g., taking a child out of school to make up for the reduced income entering the home). While such strategies may be examples of

International Federation
of Red Cross and Red Crescent Societies

individual resilience in the face of inescapable risks, they do not address the *causes* of those risks.

Urban slum communities are often marked by less social cohesion than rural villages, as people become more focused on developing their individual ability to exchange goods or services in the marketplace. In some informal urban settlements, where space is particularly scarce, families will not risk returning to their rural villages to participate in the harvest for fear that, while they are away, their neighbours will occupy the dwellings they have tenuously claimed for themselves.

This means slum households don't naturally group together to share disaster preparedness measures or to develop communal support mechanisms. So, although communities may have a latent capacity to enhance their resilience to the risks threatening them, their own lack of social cohesion is the barrier preventing that from taking place. There are, of course, some notable exceptions; for example, the potters of Kumbharwadi slum in Mumbai, whose shared source of livelihood motivated them to cooperate in protecting themselves from the hazards around them (see Box 7.2).

Box 7.2 Building resilience around a shared livelihood

Kumbharwadi is a district of Mumbai's Dharavi slum, where families of Gujarati potters have lived for over a century. These artisans have nurtured a sense of social cohesion, rooted in their shared livelihoods, as a way of increasing their resilience to risk.

The potters of Kumbharwadi have five *bhalties* (kilns) between them, which they have jointly protected with tin roofs. This means they can continue working during the rainy monsoon season, albeit at a reduced rate of production. Similarly, the families have agreed on a bond of trust to store a number of their wares for trading during the heaviest rains, when production suffers the most – thereby reducing the risk to their livelihoods during that time.

To further protect themselves from the precariousness of their situation, a 'chit fund' and rotating loan have been set up between families (without any external support), to be accessed by their households in times of trouble. The families also collect an extra 5 rupees per month from each household to pay for cleaning the gutters in the area, safeguarding their health and livelihood assets.

The success factor behind the resilience of the potters of Kumbharwadi is not that they are wealthier than other families in the area. In fact, other neighbourhoods with stronger financial resources are far less proactive in mitigating the risks they face. For the Kumbharwadi potters, risk mitigation has become an integral part of their livelihoods, because:

■ hazard mitigation measures were identified as the optimal use of resources to protect and enhance their livelihoods; and
■ they have the social cohesion required to make it happen – based on their shared source of livelihood. ■

However, across Mumbai's slums, public areas and communal buildings remain dangerous or vulnerable, even when the only asset missing to improve them is team labour or the collection of a few rupees per household. The inevitable floods will continue to take lives unnecessarily, as long as slum communities lack the consensus and resources needed to establish early warning systems or evacuation plans. Meanwhile, the continued absence of a waste management system will be blamed on the municipality, yet the slum dwellers' own social organization won't be strong enough to begin one of its own accord.

Change for the better

Yet experience from other urban slums suggests that community cohesion can be generated and harnessed for the better. Numerous aid organizations have found they can play a key role as catalysts for change. From Lusaka to Manila, from Cairo to Santo Domingo, there are success stories of slum communities and non-governmental organizations (NGOs) cooperating in waste management, recycling or income-generating initiatives. For example, the Orangi Pilot Project in Karachi, Pakistan is a long-term community-based sanitation initiative, which harnessed the skills and resources of the urban poor to build a low-cost underground sewer system. In the space of ten years, infant mortality rates in Orangi district fell from 130 to 37 per 1,000 live births.

Nevertheless, the sheer magnitude and complexity of urban risk – which combines inadequate infrastructure, poor water and sanitation, pollution, deforestation, high population density, recurrent natural hazards, fragile livelihoods and weak governance – means that the responsibility for building resilience to risk cannot be left to either at-risk communities or municipalities alone. While slum households may be able to protect themselves in very localized ways (such as raising their homes above flood waters), the degree to which they can build wider resilience to risk fundamentally depends on the way in which they relate to the municipality.

The rules of engagement between urban stakeholders have to change, to unlock the doors currently barring people from addressing their own risks and assuming their roles as responsible caretakers of the city. This is a key role that 'external' organizations can take on: helping improve the relationship between authorities and slum dwellers to transform the nature of urban governance. Often, this may entail overcoming mutual mistrust between the city's bureaucrats and its citizens (see Box 7.3).

It also means that donors and aid organizations must not only work with citizens' associations, but also support, rather than circumvent, municipal authorities. For, despite its failings, the municipality remains the authority best placed to coordinate and facilitate large-scale urban development and risk reduction. And, as Mark Pelling,

International Federation
of Red Cross and Red Crescent Societies

Santo Domingo is the capital of the Dominican Republic in the Caribbean and home to about 5 million people. The city is exposed to episodic shocks from hurricanes and earthquakes. With two-thirds of the city's population unable to access adequate housing and basic services, vulnerability to chronic environmental health hazards is also high.

The city and country have long histories of authoritarian government. Civil society is vibrant but political violence has left little trust between community groups and the state. The municipality is under-financed and unable to meet the basic service needs of a growing population. Despite these structural constraints, the commitment for change in the city has led to constructive, collaborative governance and disaster resilience. Two examples, responding to episodic and chronic risk, follow.

Following Hurricane Georges in September 1998, about 4,000 of the 10,000 households in Sabana Perdida, one of the capital's rapidly growing informal settlements or *barrios*, were made homeless. Before the hurricane, a number of local groups existed in the *barrio*. In devising a response strategy, the United Nations Development Programme encouraged these community groups and political activists to collaborate on a local action plan, which led to the reconstruction of 530 homes, a seamstress's school for women and a sports court. The municipality contributed building materials from part of its reconstruction budget. Early intervention and the involvement of local actors, including the municipality, gave the programme legitimacy and allowed people to continue living and working in the *barrio*, thereby avoiding displacement and homelessness.

In Los Manguitos, an informal settlement of 33,000 people, environmental health risks were high, mainly because of uncollected household waste. In 1992, six community-based organizations came together – with the help of IDDI (a Dominican NGO), initial financial support from the United States Agency for International Development and collaboration from the city municipality – to form UCOREBAM, a community-managed household waste collection business. That these nine organizations, from across the social and political spectrum, were able to come together to address a risk issue shows what can be done when the will for collaboration is mobilized. Not only has the environmental health hazard been reduced, but the project has also generated livelihood opportunities for waste collectors and increased the management expertise of the community groups in Los Manguitos.

Across Santo Domingo, there are many more examples of collaboration between local and non-local actors, as well as between civil society and the public sector, leading to greater disaster resilience – building trust and increasing the skills and experience of those involved. But there is more to be done. Not all the most vulnerable are represented in community groups. Political partisanship continues to distort local and municipal agendas. And regulation of construction standards and land-use remains problematic. Meanwhile, the twin goals of international donors – to support civil society groups and strengthen democracy through an effective and transparent municipal government – have created tensions. Finally, the private sector has so far played only a limited role in supporting disaster resilience, despite the sector's involvement in water, waste management and communications. ∎

author of *The vulnerability of cities,* points out: "The municipality is a democratically governed body, which many [organizations] in civil society are not."

"Now we're unstoppable"

Where this support to municipalities has been tried, there have been some promising results. For example, the Slum Sanitation Programme in Greater Mumbai was created in 1997 to provide a number of slum pockets with proper sanitation facilities. The critical state of health among some of the city's more crowded slums made the intervention an urgent priority. The programme sought to introduce a community-based approach to toilet provision, which was different from anything previously attempted.

The World Bank sponsored the building of the physical infrastructure, while local community-based organizations (CBOs) took responsibility for the ownership, administration and management of the facilities. During the process of planning and construction, the municipality helped enhance the CBOs' administration and management skills, based on the needs and capacities of each individual group. The municipality also supported the development of the project design, the user payment scheme and the management strategy, according to the particular needs of each community.

The toilets are now administered by CBOs on a pay-per-use or monthly fee basis. Unlike municipality-owned facilities, the money never leaves the community. Any funds left over from repairs and upkeep are reinvested into the neighbourhood, through new or ongoing local projects of the community's choosing.

A similar grass-roots approach was adopted with the Slum Adoption Scheme, which aims to tackle the chronic problems of garbage and waste matter contaminating Mumbai's slums, exacerbating flood and fire risks, and contributing to chronic ill-health. In this scheme, each household pays a local CBO a certain amount per month for the removal of garbage and the maintenance of clean gutters and drains. Usually, unemployed youths or marginalized community members are hired to do the work, thereby creating a source of income for the poorest in the community.

The money raised is matched on a one-to-one basis by the municipality, which supplies basic equipment and helps to enhance local administration and management capacities. As with the Slum Sanitation Programme, the profit made each month by the scheme is reinvested into the community, through the creation of local projects chosen by the participants.

Both schemes have increased resilience in slum areas by stimulating the growth of social cohesion and creating a mechanism for that unity to begin producing tangible

International Federation
of Red Cross and Red Crescent Societies

results. The schemes draw on community money and then reinvest it back into projects of communal benefit. The resources unlocked have been used for both direct and indirect risk reduction measures. Communal buildings have been reinforced; businesses and other income-generating ventures have been started up; counselling services have appeared; and political participation is increasing.

When asked about the future of one particularly proactive CBO participating in the Slum Sanitation Programme, a community leader responded: "We started with toilets, now we're unstoppable."

The principal lesson to be learned from these two cases is that, while poor governance practices shift power to manage risk out of the household, good governance has the ability to put it back. The burden on the municipality to design, implement and maintain tens of thousands of new toilets effectively would have been overwhelming – and the results would probably have been poor. Changing the rules of engagement to create joint ownership of that process with the end-users resulted in a successful sanitation programme that created community coping benefits beyond the sum of its parts. The catalytic role of the external agency in facilitating this relationship was crucial.

It is worth emphasizing the need for joint ownership, as too much decentralization of responsibility for the provision of services from municipal to community level could simply be seen as another form of privatization and rolling back of the state.

Supporting resilience in urban slums

Based on research in Mumbai into urban risks and coping strategies, a number of implications arise for 'external' humanitarian and development actors, as well as for governments and municipalities, seeking to support community resilience in urban areas:

- **Understand what urban dwellers perceive as disasters.** How are they already coping with and adapting to these threats? The answers are not as obvious as one might assume. Slum dwellers make rational decisions in the face of different risks, based on what's best for their long-term livelihoods. A mitigation measure that is useful for one household may be irrelevant for a neighbouring household. So donor strategies must enable local actors to shape their own agendas.
- **Explore barriers that constrain people from coping.** This too may not be as obvious as it initially appears. Is the barrier internal to the household (e.g., lack of knowledge, funds, social unity) or is it external (e.g., threat of eviction, inability to access public support, lack of a recognized right to improve safety in an area)? Given the risks of eviction, aid organizations must be aware that some types of support may put slum communities at greater risk.

- **Link measures supporting resilience to income generation.** Research has shown that slum dwellers are more willing to dedicate time, energy and commitment to increasing their resilience to risks, if it directly contributes to the security of their incomes. The creation of savings groups, for example, simultaneously boosts financial stability and creates community cohesion.
- **Improve relations between municipalities and slum dwellers,** so that responsibility for creating resilience to urban risks does not fall completely on the shoulders of one party or the other, but rests rather on a dynamic partnership between authorities and end-users. While not every aid organization can address structural governance problems, all agencies should aim to get beyond bilateral relationships with either communities or governments and strive to create a culture of engagement between all those with a stake in creating a healthier, safer city.

Jennifer Rowell, urban technical adviser at CARE International (UK), was principal contributor to this chapter and Boxes 7.1 and 7.2. Mark Pelling, author of The vulnerability of cities: natural disasters and social resilience, *contributed Box 7.3.*

Sources and further information

Blaikie, Piers; Cannon, Terry; Davis, Ian; and Wisner, Ben. *At Risk: Natural Hazards, People's Vulnerability and Disasters.* London: Routledge, 2004 (second edition).

Devas, Nick and Rakodi, Carole. 'The Urban Challenge' in Devas and Radoki (eds), *Managing Fast Growing Cities.* Essex, UK and New York: Longman Group and John Wiley & Sons, Inc., 1993.

Kreimer, A. and Munasingle, M. *Environmental Management and Urban Vulnerability.* Discussion Paper. Washington DC: World Bank, 1992.

Pelling, Mark. *The vulnerability of cities: natural disasters and social resilience.* London: Earthscan, 2003.

Rahman, S.U. 'The Plight of Slum Dwellers in Delhi' in *The Milli Gazette.* New Delhi, 26 November 2002.

Rowell, Jennifer. *Mainstreaming Risk Management in the Slums of Mumbai: A Livelihoods Perspective.* Unpublished Masters thesis; Cranfield University, UK, 2002.

Sanderson, David. *The Urbanisation of Poverty.* London: CARE International UK, 2002. Available at: http://www.careinternational.org.uk/resource_centre/urban.htm

Twigg, John. 'Disaster risk reduction: Mitigation and preparedness in development and emergency planning' in *Good Practice Review,* Number 9, March 2004. Humanitarian Practice Network, Overseas Development Institute, London.

United Nations Human Settlements Programme (UN-HABITAT). *Slums of the World: The face of urban poverty in the new millennium.* Nairobi: UN-HABITAT, 2003.

Web sites

CARE International UK **http://www.careinternational.org.uk**
Overseas Development Institute **http://www.odi.org.uk**
UN-HABITAT **http://www.unhabitat.org**
World Bank **http://www.worldbank.org**

Tracking
the system

From 1994 to 2003, deaths per reported disaster were on average seven times higher in countries of low human development than in highly developed countries.

© Marko Kokic, International Federation.

International Federation
of Red Cross and Red Crescent Societies

Disaster data:
key trends and statistics

As in previous years, the *World Disasters Report* features the latest reported data on disasters with a natural or technological trigger from the past decade (1994–2003). However, our statistics do *not* cover the effects of war, conflict-related famine, disease or epidemics such as HIV/AIDS.

Our 'natural' disaster data are divided into hydro-meteorological and geophysical disasters, in order to track the changing impact of weather-related hazards. We analyse the data not only by country and continent, but according to levels of human development, to highlight the relationship between development and disasters.

All disasters on the rise

Over the past decade, the number of natural and technological disasters has inexorably climbed (see Figure 8.1). From 1994 to 1998, reported disasters averaged 428 per year – from 1999 to 2003, this figure shot up by two-thirds to an average 707 disaster events each year. The biggest rise was in countries of low human development, which suffered an increase of 142 per cent.

A closer analysis of the figures reveals that transport accidents registered the biggest rise, climbing 75 per cent during the second half of the decade to average 229 events per year. Transport accidents now account for half of all natural and technological disasters reported in Africa. However, our tables only account for reported transport accidents where at least ten people have been killed or 100 affected by a single incident (see disaster definitions below). Hence, the full number and impact of global road traffic accidents, for example, is not captured by the data.

Both hydro-meteorological and geophysical disasters have become more common, becoming respectively 68 per cent and 62 per cent more frequent over the decade. This reflects longer-term trends: between 1960 and 2003, the number of reported hydro-meteorological disasters has

Figure 8.1

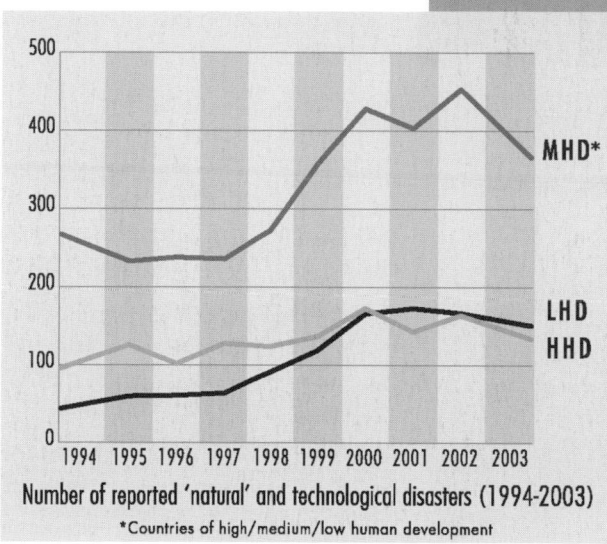

Number of reported 'natural' and technological disasters (1994-2003)
*Countries of high/medium/low human development

multiplied more than seven times, while geophysical disasters have multiplied five times.

However, reported weather-related disasters still outnumber geophysical disasters by nine to one over the past ten years. Among natural disasters, floods are the most common event in Africa, Asia and Europe, while windstorms are the most reported disaster in the Americas and Oceania.

Famine, earthquake, heat: the deadliest

Last year's death toll of nearly 77,000 was triple the total for 2002 – with countries of medium and high development hit hardest. Disasters cost around 31,000 lives in Europe last year – mainly due to the August heatwave. This figure was eight times higher than the average annual death toll from disasters in Europe for the previous nine years. The earthquake that devastated the Iranian city of Bam claimed at least 26,000 lives. Meanwhile, deaths in countries of low human development (LHD) last year fell to their lowest level for nine years. However, over the decade, more than half of those killed by natural disasters lived in LHD countries.

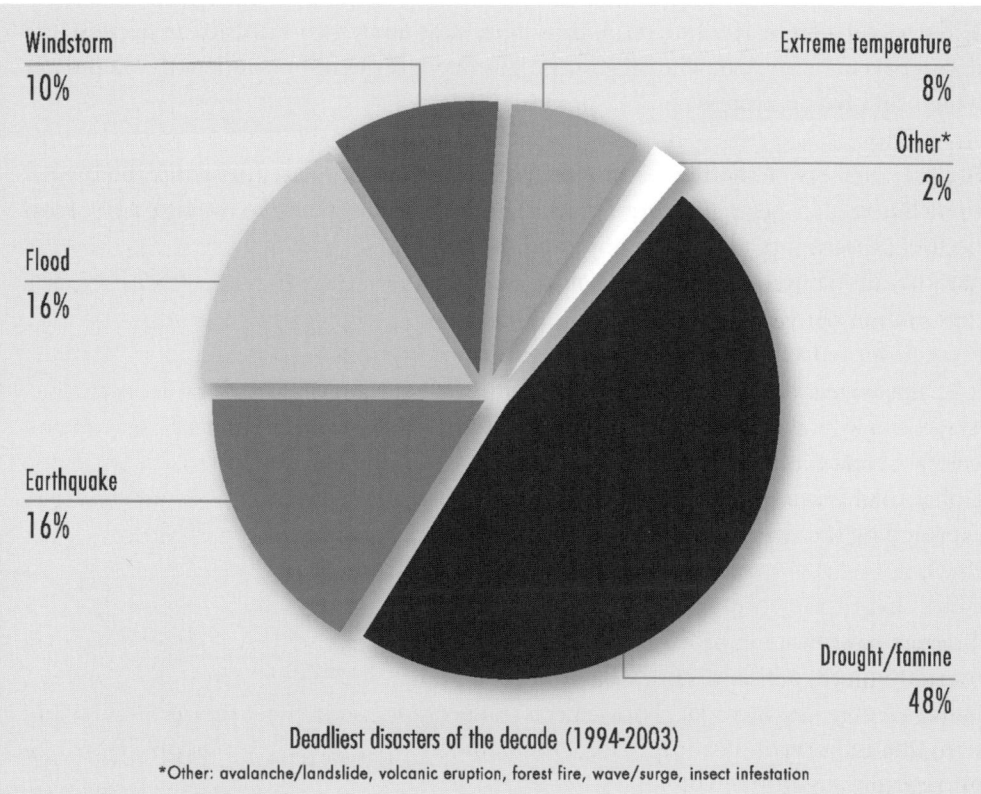

Windstorm
10%

Extreme temperature
8%

Other*
2%

Flood
16%

Earthquake
16%

Drought/famine
48%

Deadliest disasters of the decade (1994-2003)
*Other: avalanche/landslide, volcanic eruption, forest fire, wave/surge, insect infestation

Figure 8.2

International Federation
of Red Cross and Red Crescent Societies

Drought and famine have proved the deadliest disaster of the decade worldwide, accounting for at least 275,000 deaths since 1994 – nearly half the total for all natural disasters (see Figure 8.2). The food crisis in the Democratic People's Republic of Korea from 1995 to 1999 accounted for much of this figure. Comparing data on the frequency and mortality of disasters over the past decade, drought/famine was again the deadliest, claiming over 1,000 lives per reported disaster. Earthquakes killed an average of 370 people per disaster, while extreme temperatures claimed over 300 lives per disaster. By contrast, each windstorm and flood which was reported killed an average of 70 to 80 people. Nearly three-quarters of all reported deaths over the last ten years occurred during hydro-meteorological disasters.

Deaths drop, numbers affected climb

Despite the increased number of disasters reported over the decade, average annual death tolls dropped from over 75,000 per year (1994–1998) to 59,000 per year (1999–2003). However, over the same period, the numbers affected continued to climb. For the first five years of the decade, an average of 213 million people were affected – almost all by natural disasters. The second half of the decade saw this figure rise by over 40 per cent to an average of 303 million per year, driven by the colossal numbers reported affected in 2002 (when drought in India affected 300 million people). Last year, 150 million Chinese were affected by one flood in July alone. Asia is the most disaster-prone continent, accounting for 91 per cent of those reported affected.

Analysing the past two decades of data reveals similar trends. Deaths reported from natural and technological disasters between 1984 and 1993 averaged 102,000 per year. This toll dropped by a third to average around 67,000 deaths per year from 1994 to 2003. Over the same 20 years, the numbers of people reported affected by disasters climbed by 59 per cent from an average of 163 million per year (1984–1993) to 258 million per year (1994–2003).

The reason less people are dying from hydro-meteorological disasters, in particular, may be partly explained by better satellite forecasting and early warning systems, which enable those in the path of disaster to seek shelter or evacuate before it is too late. Equally, systematic disaster preparedness at community level, in countries such as Bangladesh and India where seasonal disasters are frequent, has helped reduce death tolls.

The fact that more people are being affected by disasters reflects a range of factors. Overall numbers of reported disasters are increasing, driven partly by a more variable global climate. Meanwhile, a rapid increase of population in poorer parts of the world – combined with rapid, unplanned development (particularly in urban areas) – is putting more people at risk.

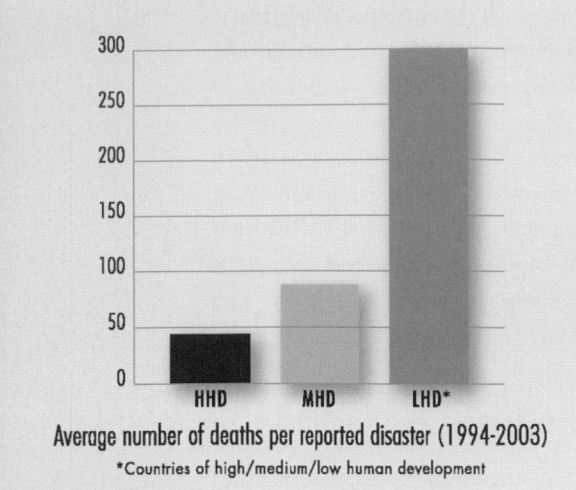

Average number of deaths per reported disaster (1994-2003)
*Countries of high/medium/low human development

Figure 8.3

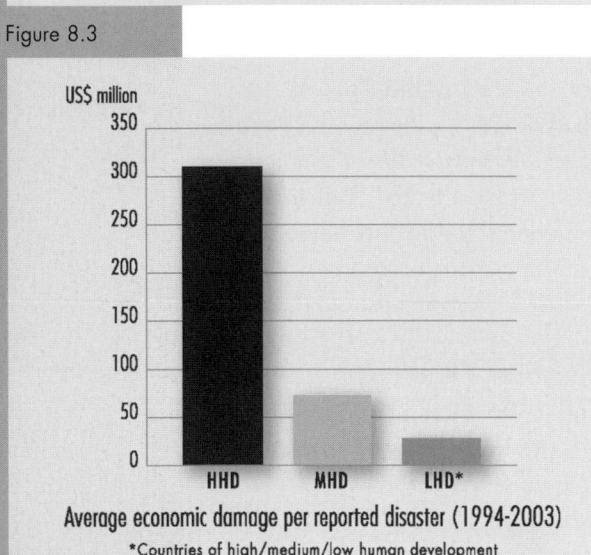

US$ million

Average economic damage per reported disaster (1994-2003)
*Countries of high/medium/low human development

Figure 8.4

Development level determines disaster costs

Impacts vary enormously according to the level of human development achieved in the country where disaster strikes. Levels of development for each country are taken from the United Nations Development Programme's (UNDP) Human Development Index (HDI). One simple way of analysing disaster impacts is to compare reported deaths and costs against the number of disasters reported. Over the past decade, this calculation reveals that natural and technological disasters in countries of high human development (HHD) killed an average of 44 people per event, while disasters in LHD countries killed an average of 300 people each (see Figure 8.3).

Estimated costs of damage, however, play the other way. Disasters in HHD countries inflicted an average of US$ 318 million worth of damage per event – over 11 times higher than the US$ 28 million recorded per disaster in LHD countries (see Figure 8.4). These figures reflect the fact that rich countries have more high-value infrastructure exposed to disasters than poorer countries. However, the statistics fail to capture the fact that disasters have a far more devastating impact on gross domestic product (GDP) in poor countries than in rich countries.

Over the past decade, HHD countries were most commonly afflicted by windstorms (mainly in the United States), which accounted for nearly half of all those affected by disasters. However, extreme temperatures (particularly 2003's heatwave in Europe) caused more than half of all deaths reported in highly developed countries since 1994. Meanwhile earthquakes (particularly Japan's Kobe quake) inflicted at least US$206 billion of damage over the ten-year period, double the cost of windstorms, the next most expensive disaster.

In countries of medium human development (MHD), transport accidents proved most common from 1994 to 2003, driven by a more mobile population and accelerating economic development in countries such as India and China. However, a combination of earthquakes, floods and windstorms accounted for nearly three-

International Federation
of Red Cross and Red Crescent Societies

quarters of all disaster deaths in MHD countries over the decade. Of all those reported affected by disasters in MHD countries, 58 per cent suffered from floods, which caused at least US$ 107 billion of damage over the period.

Transport accidents also accounted for the highest number of disasters reported in LHD countries. However, drought and famine proved by far the most devastating disaster in these countries, accounting for 84 per cent of the decade's death toll and three-quarters of all those affected. Floods, meanwhile, cost LHD countries the most, accounting for three-quarters of all reported economic damage.

Aid flows climb

Official development assistance (ODA) from members of the Development Assistance Committee (DAC) of the Organisation for Economic Co-operation and Development (OECD) grew significantly to US$ 58.3 billion in 2002 (the latest year for which statistics are available), a gross increase of 11.3 per cent compared to 2001 (see Figure 8.5). When taking into account both inflation and exchange rate movements, the rise is still a significant 7.2 per cent in real terms. Canada, France, Greece, Ireland and Italy increased their contributions by more than 30 per cent (see Figure 8.6). The biggest individual increases came from France (up US$ 1.28 billion) and the United States (up US$ 1.86 billion).

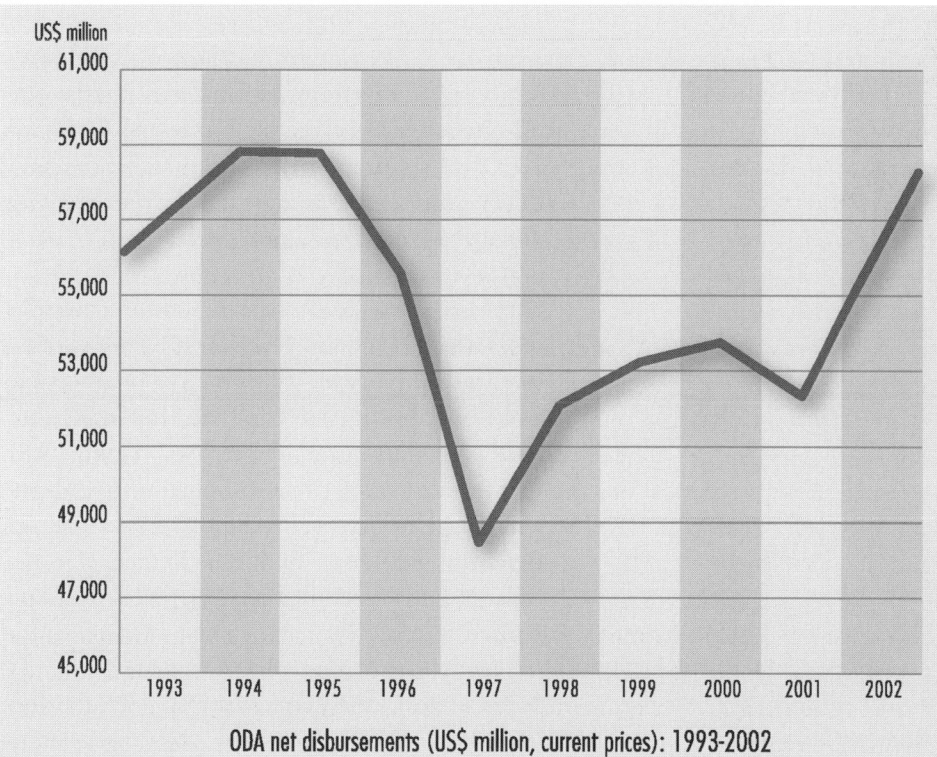

ODA net disbursements (US$ million, current prices): 1993-2002

Figure 8.5

Figure 8.6

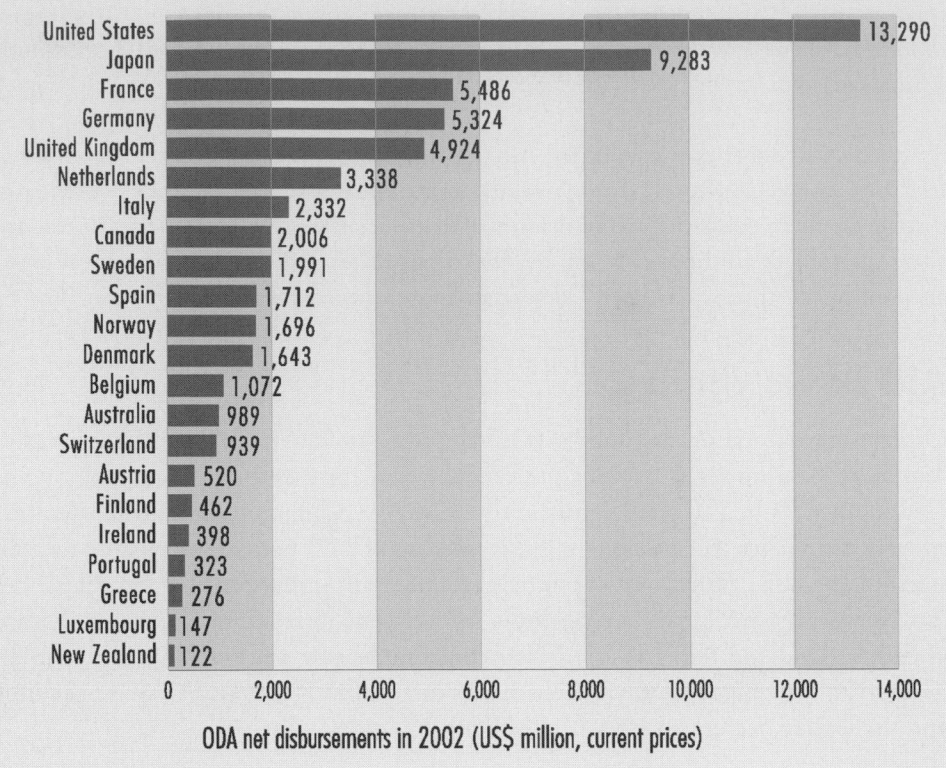

ODA net disbursements in 2002 (US$ million, current prices)

Among the five biggest donors, aid from the United States has grown significantly since 1997 (see Figure 8.7). Meanwhile, contributions from the United Kingdom over the past decade have steadily increased to match levels given by France and Germany, whose aid has declined since the mid-1990s. Japan was the world's largest donor of ODA until 2000, after which levels fell below donations from the United States.

Expressed as a percentage of donor countries' gross national income (GNI), only five countries (Denmark, Norway, Sweden, the Netherlands and Luxembourg) exceeded the United Nations' (UN) 0.7 per cent target (see Figure 8.8). Compared to 2001, the proportion of aid as a percentage of their GNI increased for Australia, Belgium, Canada, Finland, France, Greece, Ireland, Italy, Norway, Portugal, Sweden and the United States.

Meanwhile emergency/distress relief (not including relief provided by multilateral

Figure 8.7

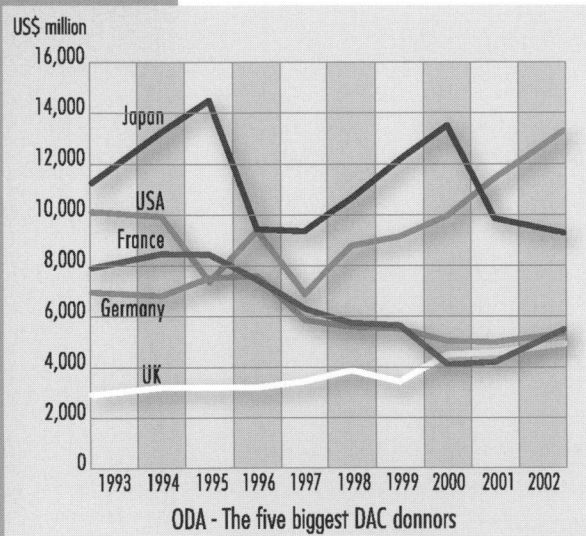

ODA - The five biggest DAC donnors

International Federation
of Red Cross and Red Crescent Societies

Figure 8.8

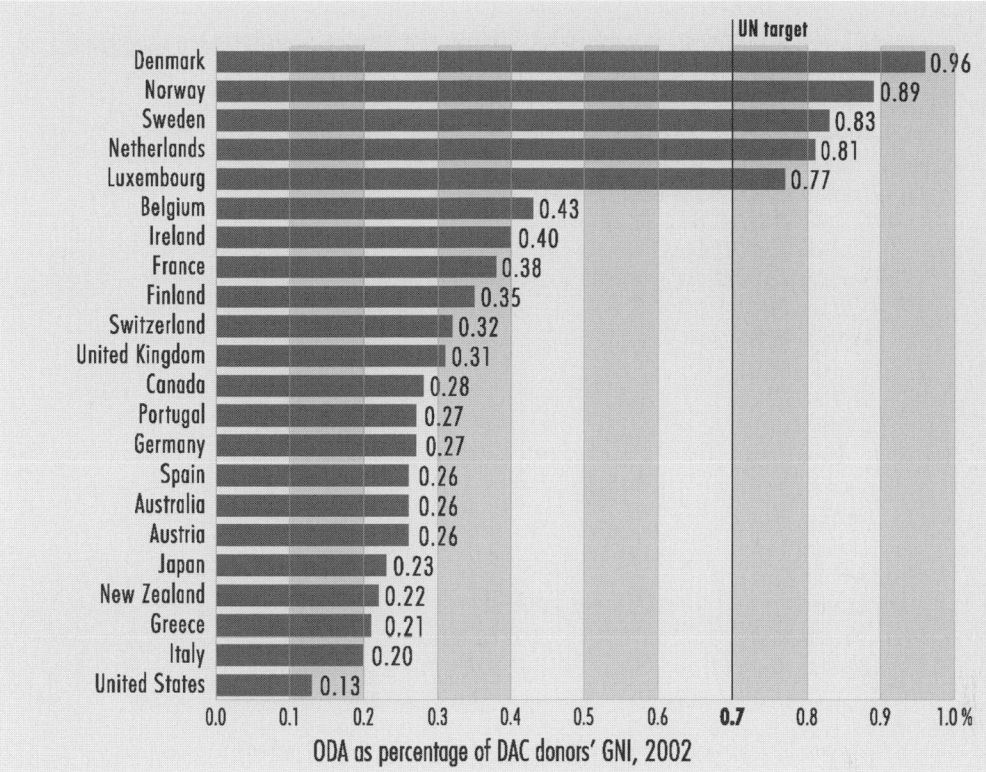

ODA as percentage of DAC donors' GNI, 2002

institutions and non-governmental organizations (NGOs)) grew from US$ 3.3 billion in 2001 to US$ 3.9 billion in 2002 – an increase of 18 per cent (see Figure 8.9). As in previous years, the United States was the biggest donor of emergency/distress relief, accounting for 36 per cent of all donations. However, DAC rules allow donors to define spending on refugees hosted in donor countries as part of their emergency/distress relief (this amounted to 25 per cent of the total in 2001).

Calculating the full amount spent on humanitarian relief is notoriously difficult, as different donors account for their relief contributions in different ways. The total of US$ 3.9 billion for emergency relief quoted above does not present the full picture. A recent independent report, *Global Humanitarian Assistance 2003,* sponsored by the United Kingdom's Department for International Development, has tried to arrive at a more accurate figure. According to the report, "global humanitarian assistance totals at least $10 billion a year". Breaking down the total for 2001, the report calculated the following contributions:

- OECD DAC donors' humanitarian aid (not including expenditure on domestic refugees): US$ 4.2 billion.
- OECD DAC donors' spending on post-conflict peace activities: US$ 4 billion.
- Humanitarian assistance from non-DAC donors (especially Saudi Arabia and the Republic of Korea): US$ 500 million.

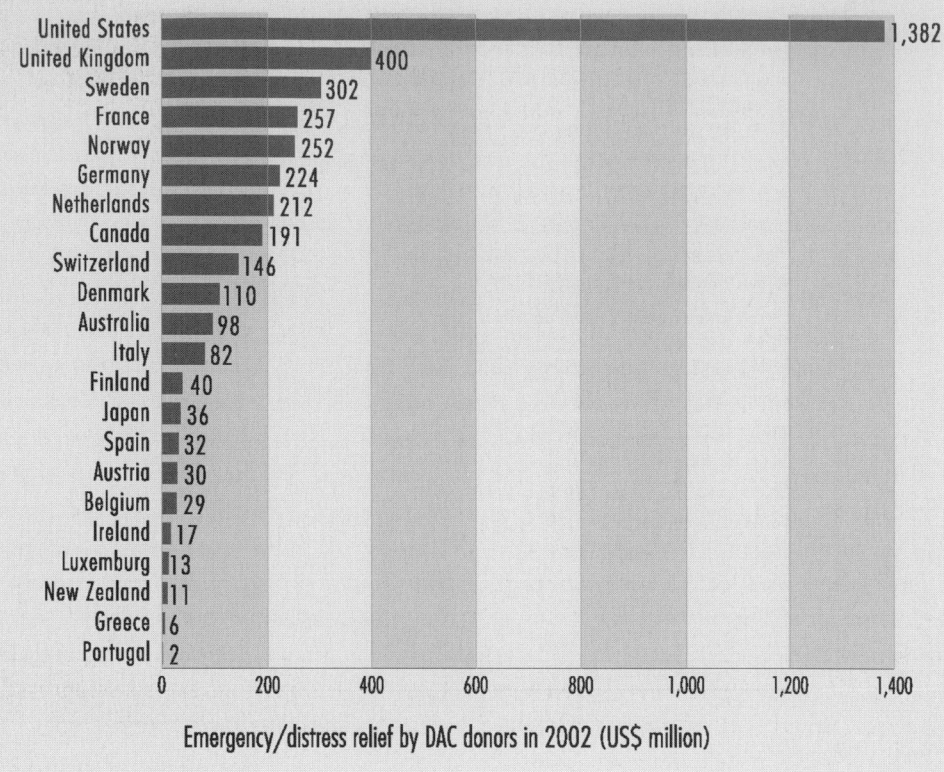

Figure 8.9

Country	Emergency/distress relief by DAC donors in 2002 (US$ million)
United States	1,382
United Kingdom	400
Sweden	302
France	257
Norway	252
Germany	224
Netherlands	212
Canada	191
Switzerland	146
Denmark	110
Australia	98
Italy	82
Finland	40
Japan	36
Spain	32
Austria	30
Belgium	29
Ireland	17
Luxemburg	13
New Zealand	11
Greece	6
Portugal	2

Emergency/distress relief by DAC donors in 2002 (US$ million)

- Voluntary contributions from the public via NGOs: US$ 700 million–US$ 1.5 billion.
- Multilateral humanitarian aid (via NGOs, UN, international organizations) not captured by DAC statistics: US$ 400 million.

For more detail on these data, visit: www.globalhumanitarianassistance.org

Disaster definitions

Data in Tables 1 to 13 are provided by CRED, the Belgium-based Centre for Research on the Epidemiology of Disasters (see Box 8.1). CRED defines a disaster as a "situation or event, which overwhelms local capacity, necessitating a request to national or international level for external assistance; an unforeseen and often sudden event that causes great damage, destruction and human suffering". For a disaster to be entered into its EM-DAT database, at least one of the following criteria must be fulfilled:

- ten or more people reported killed;
- 100 people reported affected;
- declaration of a state of emergency;
- call for international assistance.

International Federation
of Red Cross and Red Crescent Societies

Box 8.1 EM-DAT: a specialized disaster database

Tables 1 to 13 on disasters and their human impacts over the last decade were drawn from EM-DAT and documented by CRED. Established in 1973 as a non-profit institution, CRED is based at the School of Public Health of the Catholic University of Louvain in Belgium and became a World Health Organization (WHO) collaborating centre in 1980. Although CRED's main focus is on public health, the centre also studies the socio-economic and long-term effects of large-scale disasters.

Since 1988, with the sponsorship of USAID's Office of Foreign Disaster Assistance (OFDA), CRED has maintained EM-DAT, a worldwide database on disasters. It contains essential core data on the occurrence and effects of over 14,000 disasters in the world from 1900 to the present.

The database is compiled from various sources, including UN agencies, NGOs, insurance companies, research institutes and press agencies. The entries are constantly reviewed for redundancies, inconsistencies and the completion of missing data.

CRED consolidates and updates data on a daily basis. A further check is made at three-month intervals. Revisions are entered annually at the end of the calendar year. Priority is given to data from UN agencies, followed by OFDA, governments and the International Federation. This priority is not a reflection of the quality or value of the data but the recognition that most reporting sources do not cover all disasters or have political limitations that may affect the figures.

The database's main objective is to assist humanitarian action at both national and international levels. It aims to rationalize decision-making for disaster preparedness, as well as providing an objective basis for vulnerability assessment and priority setting.
Dr. D. Guha-Sapir, Director, CRED, WHO Collaborating Centre, School of Public Health, Catholic University of Louvain, 30.94, Clos Chapelle-aux-Champs, 1200 Brussels, Belgium.
Tel.: +32 2 764 3327
Fax: +32 2 764 3441
E-mail: sapir@epid.ucl.ac.be
Web: http://www.cred.be ■

The number of people killed includes "persons confirmed as dead and persons missing and presumed dead"; people affected are those "requiring immediate assistance during a period of emergency, i.e. requiring basic survival needs such as food, water, shelter, sanitation and immediate medical assistance". People reported injured or homeless in the tables are aggregated with those reported affected to produce a "total number of people affected".

The economic impact of a disaster usually consists of direct losses (e.g., damage to infrastructure, crops, housing) and indirect losses (e.g., loss of revenues, unemployment, market destabilization) to the local economy. EM-DAT's figures represent only the value of direct losses at the moment of the event, expressed in US dollars (2003 prices).

Box 8.2 US Committee for Refugees

The United States Committee for Refugees (USCR) is the public information and advocacy arm of Immigration and Refugee Services of America, a non-governmental organization. USCR's activities are twofold: it reports on issues affecting refugees, asylum seekers and internally displaced people; and encourages the public, policy-makers and the international community to respond appropriately and effectively to the needs of uprooted populations.

USCR travels to the scene of refugee emergencies to gather testimony from uprooted people, to assess their needs and to gauge governmental and international response. The committee conducts public briefings to present its findings and recommendations, testifies before the United States Congress, communicates concerns directly to governments and provides first-hand assessments to the media. USCR publishes the annual *World Refugee Survey*, the monthly *Refugee Reports* and issue papers.

The data in Tables 14–16 were provided by USCR. The quality of the data in these tables is affected by the less-than-ideal conditions often associated with flight. Unsettled conditions, the biases of governments and opposition groups, and the need to use population estimates to plan for providing humanitarian assistance can each contribute to inaccurate estimates. The estimates reproduced in these tables are USCR's preliminary year-end figures for 2003.

Table 14 lists refugees and asylum seekers by country of origin, while Table 15 lists the two groups by host country. Refugees are people who are outside their home country and are unable or unwilling to return to that country because they fear persecution or armed conflict. Asylum seekers are people who claim to be refugees; many are awaiting a determination of their refugee status. While not all asylum seekers are refugees, they are nonetheless entitled to certain protections under international refugee law, at least until they are determined not to be refugees. USCR also includes persons granted various forms of humanitarian relief if that relief is based on factors related to the UN refugee definition, as distinct from, for example, relief granted because of natural disaster.

Table 16 concerns internally displaced people (IDPs). Like refugees and asylum seekers, IDPs have fled their homes, but have remained in their home country. No universally accepted definition of IDPs exists. USCR generally considers people who are uprooted within their country because of armed conflict or persecution – and thus would be refugees if they were to cross an international border – to be internally displaced. Broader definitions are employed by some agencies, however, who sometimes include people who are uprooted by natural or human-made disasters or other causes not directly related to human rights. IDPs often live in war-torn areas and are neither registered nor counted in any systematic way. Estimates of the size of IDP populations are frequently subject to great margins of error.

US Committee for Refugees,
1717 Massachusetts Avenue NW, Suite 200,
Washington DC 20036, USA.
Tel.: +1 202 347 3507
Fax: +1 202 347 3418
E-mail: uscr@irsa-uscr.org
Web: http://www.refugees.org ∎

International Federation
of Red Cross and Red Crescent Societies

EM-DAT distinguishes two generic categories for disasters (natural and technological), divided into 15 main categories, each themselves covering more than 50 sub-categories. For these tables, natural disasters are split into hydro-meteorological disasters (avalanches/landslides; droughts/famines; extreme temperatures; floods; forest/scrub fires; windstorms; and other disasters: insect infestations and waves/surges) and geophysical disasters (earthquakes and volcanic eruptions). Meanwhile, technological disasters include industrial accidents (chemical spills; collapses of industrial infrastructure; explosions; fires; gas leaks; poisoning; radiation), transport accidents (by air, rail, road or water) and miscellaneous accidents (collapses of domestic/non-industrial structures; explosions; fires). In Tables 1 to 13, "disasters" refer to disasters with a natural and technological trigger only, and do not include wars, conflict-related famines, diseases or epidemics.

The classification of countries as high, medium or low human development is based on UNDP's 2003 HDI. To classify countries not listed in the HDI, the World Bank's 2004 Development Indicators are used, classing low-income countries as low human development, lower middle income and upper middle income as medium human development, and high income as high human development. Islands and territories that are dependencies of a state are classed in the same category as the state. Niue and Tuvalu are classed according to the World Bank's 1998 Development Indicators.

Caveats

Key problems with disaster data include the lack of standardized collection methodologies and definitions. The original information, collected from a variety of public sources, is not specifically gathered for statistical purposes. So, even when the compilation applies strict definitions for disaster events and parameters, the original suppliers of information may not. Moreover, data are not always complete for each disaster. The completeness may vary according the type of disaster (e.g., the number of people injured or affected by transport accidents is rarely reported) or its country of occurrence.

For natural disasters over the last decade, data on deaths are missing for one-tenth of disasters; data on numbers affected are missing for one-fifth of disasters; and data on economic damage are missing for 70 per cent of disasters. Meanwhile, data on economic damage inflicted by technological disasters are missing for 97 per cent of reported disasters. The figures should therefore be regarded as indicative. Relative changes and trends are more useful to look at than absolute, isolated figures.

Information systems have improved vastly in the past 25 years and statistical data are now more easily available. However, despite efforts to verify and review data, the quality of disaster databases can only be as good as the reporting system. The lack of systematization and standardization of data collection is proving a major problem for long-term planning. Fortunately, due to increased pressures for accountability from various sources, many donors and development agencies have started to prioritize data collection and methodologies.

Data can be skewed because of the rationale behind data gathering. Reinsurance companies, for instance, systematically gather data on disaster occurrence to assess insurance risk, but only in countries where disaster insurance is widespread. Their data may miss out poor disaster-affected regions where insurance is unaffordable or unavailable.

Data on the numbers of people affected by a disaster can provide some of the most potentially useful figures, for planning disaster preparedness and response, yet these are sometimes poorly reported. Moreover, the definition of "affected" is open to interpretation, political or otherwise. Even if manipulation is absent, data are often extrapolated from old census information, with assumptions being made about the percentage of an area's population affected.

Dates can be a source of ambiguity. For example, a declared date for a famine is both necessary and meaningless – famines do not occur on a single day. In such cases, the date the appropriate body declares an official emergency has been used. Changes in national boundaries also cause ambiguities in the data and may make the analysis of long-term trends more complicated.

Part of the solution to this data problem lies in retrospective analysis. Data are most often publicly quoted and reported during a disaster, but it is only long after the event, once the relief operation is over, that estimates of damage and death can be verified. Some data gatherers, like CRED, do this, which means retrospective annual disaster figures can change one, two or even three years after the event.

A more detailed analysis of the challenges facing the gathering, standardizing and assessing of disaster data can be found in Chapter 7 of the *World Disasters Report 2003*.

In the following tables, some totals may not correspond due to rounding.

This analysis was contributed by Jonathan Walter, editor of the World Disasters Report, *and by CRED team members Philippe Hoyois, senior research fellow; Regina Below, EM-DAT disaster database manager; and Debarati Guha-Sapir, director.*

Table 1 Total number of reported disasters,[1] by continent and by year (1994 to 2003)

	1994	1995	1996	1997	1998	1999	2000	2001	2002	2003	Total
Africa	59	63	58	56	83	144	196	186	201	163	1,209
Americas	80	99	95	102	112	137	147	128	153	119	1,172
Asia	182	177	176	195	209	240	289	295	301	264	2,328
Europe	69	72	55	60	66	78	122	92	111	85	810
Oceania	17	8	17	15	17	15	13	18	18	20	158
High human development[2]	96	126	102	128	124	137	173	143	164	134	1,327
Medium human development	267	233	238	236	272	358	428	403	453	366	3,254
Low human development	44	60	61	64	91	119	166	173	167	151	1,096
Total	**407**	**419**	**401**	**428**	**487**	**614**	**767**	**719**	**784**	**651**	**5,677**

Source: EM-DAT, CRED, University of Louvain, Belgium

[1] In Tables 1–13, 'disasters' refer to those with a natural and technological trigger only, and do not include wars, conflict-related famines, diseases or epidemics.

[2] See note on UNDP's Human Development Index country status in the section on disaster definitions in the introduction to this chapter.

In 2003, Asia remained the continent most frequently struck by disasters, with 41 per cent of the total number of disasters recorded in EM-DAT.

Disasters reported worldwide over the first half of the decade (1994–1998) averaged 428 per year, increasing by 65 per cent during the second half of the decade (1999–2003) to average 707 per year.

Countries of low human development recorded the biggest rise in reported disasters (up 142 per cent during the second half of the decade), with Africa worst affected. By comparison, disasters in countries of high human development increased by just 30 per cent over the same period.

However, disasters reported in 2003 fell by 17 per cent compared with 2002.

Table 2 Total number of people reported killed, by continent and by year (1994 to 2003)

	1994	1995	1996	1997	1998	1999	2000	2001	2002	2003	Total
Africa	3,144	2,962	3,484	4,064	7,006	2,688	5,756	4,462	8,272	5,810	47,648
Americas	2,874	2,628	2,541	3,069	21,865	33,989	1,820	3,460	2,285	2,026	76,557
Asia	13,328	75,590	69,706	71,033	82,373	75,890	11,608	29,255	13,358	37,860	480,001
Europe	2,340	3,366	1,204	1,166	1,434	19,448	1,627	2,196	1,699	31,046	65,526
Oceania	103	24	111	388	2,227	116	205	9	91	64	3,338
High human development¹	2,462	8,145	2,062	2,450	2,893	3,250	2,039	1,849	1,895	31,619	58,664
Medium human development	15,874	18,815	16,465	18,122	42,244	72,023	13,198	33,498	14,754	41,275	286,268
Low human development	3,453	57,610	58,519	59,148	69,768	56,858	5,779	4,035	9,056	3,912	328,138
Total	**21,789**	**84,570**	**77,046**	**79,720**	**114,905**	**132,131**	**21,016**	**39,382**	**25,705**	**76,806**	**673,070**

Source: EM-DAT, CRED, University of Louvain, Belgium

¹ See note on UNDP's Human Development Index country status in the section on disaster definitions in the introduction to this chapter.

As discussed in the introduction, numbers of people reported killed are underestimated. On the basis of the available data, of the total number of people reported killed by disasters over the decade, 71 per cent are in Asia. Countries of high human development account for 9 per cent of deaths from 1994–2003; those of medium human development for 42 per cent; and those of low human development for 49 per cent.

However, 2003 was highly unusual: deaths in Europe were five times higher than the decade's average, due to a heatwave which killed nearly 30,000 people. Meanwhile, the earthquake that hit the Iranian city of Bam in December 2003 killed at least 26,000 people. By contrast, countries of low human development reported eight times fewer deaths during 2003 than the decade's average.

Table 3 Total number of people reported affected, by continent and by year (1994 to 2003) in thousands

	1994	1995	1996	1997	1998	1999	2000	2001	2002	2003	Total
Africa	16,234	9,535	4,282	7,736	10,150	14,362	23,044	18,386	31,736	20,951	156,417
Americas	2,722	1,152	2,380	2,711	16,966	5,008	1,348	11,246	2,046	3,739	49,318
Asia	166,210	225,621	207,163	56,269	315,714	188,605	230,044	141,177	583,216	228,895	2,342,913
Europe	909	8,220	30	679	622	6,549	2,907	786	1,205	1,121	23,028
Oceania	5,914	2,682	652	730	328	151	7	32	41	38	10,575
High human development[1]	6,472	11,584	2,614	1,972	2,663	5,586	1,055	6,710	2,078	813	41,546
Medium human development	167,064	220,337	203,040	57,480	334,179	196,636	228,922	143,339	585,110	232,922	2,369,029
Low human development	18,453	15,289	8,853	8,673	6,938	12,453	27,373	21,579	31,055	21,011	171,676
Total	**191,988**	**247,210**	**214,507**	**68,125**	**343,780**	**214,675**	**257,350**	**171,627**	**618,243**	**254,745**	**2,582,251**

Source: EM-DAT, CRED, University of Louvain, Belgium

[1] See note on UNDP's Human Development Index country status in the section on disaster definitions in the introduction to this chapter.

As discussed in the introduction, numbers of people reported affected are underestimated. Numbers affected in 2003 were just under the decade's average of 258 million people affected by disasters every year.

A flood in China during July 2003 affected 150 million people, accounting for over half of the year's total. In India, two floods in August and September affected 7.6 million people. Over the last ten years, 91 per cent of those reported affected lived in Asia.

CHAPTER 8

Table 4 Total amount of disaster estimated damage, by continent and by year (1994 to 2003) in millions of US dollars (2003 prices)

	1994	1995	1996	1997	1998	1999	2000	2001	2002	2003	Total
Africa	532	200	130	22	358	803	160	331	140	5,537	8,213
Americas	36,916	27,051	14,489	11,408	19,614	14,288	3,503	10,831	3,453	13,901	155,455
Asia	15,298	188,387	35,058	30,109	32,377	29,513	17,648	16,760	7,644	17,304	390,099
Europe	12,667	15,326	387	11,141	5,300	39,679	8,857	874	16,627	18,611	129,468
Oceania	2,102	1,547	1,100	284	319	944	540	355	399	601	8,191
High human development[i]	50,664	202,625	15,805	20,817	18,502	33,551	11,394	10,507	19,048	39,480	422,391
Medium human development	16,251	11,615	31,727	32,127	39,275	51,658	12,615	18,115	9,165	16,122	238,671
Low human development	600	18,272	3,633	18	191	19	6,699	530	51	353	30,365
Total	**67,515**	**232,511**	**51,165**	**52,963**	**57,968**	**85,227**	**30,708**	**29,152**	**28,264**	**55,954**	**691,426**

Source: EM-DAT, CRED, University of Louvain, Belgium

[i] See note on UNDP's Human Development Index country status in the section on disaster definitions in the introduction to this chapter.

As discussed in the introduction, damage estimations are notoriously unreliable. Data are missing for more than 80 per cent of reported disasters. Even for the existing data, methodologies are not standardized and the coverage of damages may vary widely.

Countries of high human development account for 61 per cent of disaster damage over the past decade, due to higher value infrastructure and greater insurance penetration, which leads to somewhat better reporting. Nations of low human development account for just 4 per cent of estimated damage.

The most damaging disaster in 2003 was the heatwave in Europe, which inflicted around US$ 13 billion in property damage alone (in agriculture and due to forest fires). Typhoon Maemi, which devastated Japan and the Republic of Korea in September, caused an estimated US$ 5.5 billion of economic damage. Four other disasters each inflicted US$ 5 billion of damage: an earthquake in Mexico in January; a tornado in the United States in March; an earthquake in Algeria in May; and Hurricane Isabel in Canada and the United States in September.

However, 2003's total bill of US$ 56 billion was well below the decade's average of US$ 69 billion per year.

Table 5 Total number of reported disasters, by type of phenomenon and by year (1994 to 2003)

	1994	1995	1996	1997	1998	1999	2000	2001	2002	2003	Total
Avalanches/landslides	8	15	24	13	21	15	29	21	19	21	186
Droughts/famines	10	16	8	18	34	30	48	47	41	21	273
Earthquakes	23	25	11	17	17	33	31	25	35	40	257
Extreme temperatures	10	13	5	13	13	8	31	23	15	18	149
Floods	78	95	70	76	88	112	152	159	172	158	1,160
Forest/scrub fires	13	7	5	15	16	22	30	14	22	14	158
Volcanic eruptions	6	5	5	4	4	5	5	6	7	2	49
Windstorms	67	59	63	68	72	86	101	98	112	76	802
Other natural disasters[1]	1	4	2	3	2	2	4	2	1	0	21
Subtotal hydro-meteorological disasters	*187*	*209*	*177*	*206*	*246*	*275*	*395*	*364*	*382*	*308*	*2,749*
Subtotal geophysical disasters	*29*	*30*	*16*	*21*	*21*	*38*	*36*	*31*	*42*	*42*	*306*
Total natural disasters	**216**	**239**	**193**	**227**	**267**	**313**	**431**	**395**	**424**	**350**	**3,055**
Industrial accidents	34	45	35	35	43	36	50	54	48	46	426
Miscellaneous accidents	30	29	37	30	29	51	47	49	52	44	398
Transport accidents	127	106	136	136	148	214	239	221	260	211	1,798
Total technological disasters	**191**	**180**	**208**	**201**	**220**	**301**	**336**	**324**	**360**	**301**	**2,622**
Total	**407**	**419**	**401**	**428**	**487**	**614**	**767**	**719**	**784**	**651**	**5,677**

Source: EM-DAT, CRED, University of Louvain, Belgium

[1] Insect infestations and waves/surges.

In 2003, the highest number of reported disasters were transport accidents (32 per cent of all disasters), followed by floods (24 per cent). Hydro-meteorological disasters reported worldwide over the first half of the decade (1994–1998) averaged 205 per year, increasing by 68 per cent during the second half of the decade (1999–2003) to average 345 per year. Over the same period, transport accidents increased by 75 per cent, from an average of 131 per year (1994–1998) to an average of 229 per year (1999–2003). Geophysical disasters increased 62 per cent over the same period.

Floods and windstorms account for 64 per cent of all natural disasters, while transport accidents account for 68 per cent of all technological accidents.

Table 6 Total number of people reported killed, by type of phenomenon and by year (1994 to 2003)

	1994	1995	1996	1997	1998	1999	2000	2001	2002	2003	Total
Avalanches/landslides	280	1,497	1,129	801	981	351	1,099	692	1,149	700	8,679
Droughts/famines	n.a.	54,000	54,000	54,520	57,875	54,029	370	199	538	9	275,540
Earthquakes	1,242	7,966	584	3,039	7,417	21,870	204	21,355	1,606	29,617	94,900
Extreme temperatures	416	1,730	300	619	3,225	771	922	1,653	3,369	32,403	45,408
Floods	6,403	8,145	7,309	6,958	9,695	34,366	6,330	4,678	4,354	4,050	92,288
Forest/scrub fires	84	29	45	32	109	70	47	33	6	53	508
Volcanic eruptions	101	n.a.	4	53	n.a.	n.a.	n.a.	n.a.	254	n.a.	412
Windstorms	4,081	3,724	4,380	5,330	24,657	11,899	1,129	1,864	1,093	995	59,152
Other natural disasters[1]	31	n.a.	32	400	2,182	3	1	n.a.	n.a.	ndr	2,649
Subtotal hydro-meteorological disasters	11,295	69,125	67,195	68,660	98,724	101,489	9,898	9,119	10,509	38,210	484,224
Subtotal geophysical disasters	1,343	7,966	588	3,092	7,417	21,870	204	21,355	1,860	29,617	95,312
Total natural disasters	**12,638**	**77,091**	**67,783**	**71,752**	**106,141**	**123,359**	**10,102**	**30,474**	**12,369**	**67,827**	**579,536**
Industrial accidents	779	513	674	1,033	1,942	742	1,743	1,271	1,147	1,101	10,945
Miscellaneous accidents	1,719	1,711	1,159	1,277	748	1,330	1,112	1,783	2,023	1,361	14,223
Transport accidents	6,653	5,255	7,430	5,658	6,074	6,700	8,059	5,854	10,166	6,517	68,366
Total technological disasters	**9,151**	**7,479**	**9,263**	**7,968**	**8,764**	**8,772**	**10,914**	**8,908**	**13,336**	**8,979**	**93,534**
Total	**21,789**	**84,570**	**77,046**	**79,720**	**114,905**	**132,131**	**21,016**	**39,382**	**25,705**	**76,806**	**673,070**

Source: EM-DAT, CRED, University of Louvain, Belgium

[1] Insect infestations and waves/surges

Note: n.a. signifies no data available; ndr signifies no disaster reported. For more information, see section on caveats in introductory text.

Extreme temperatures – mainly the European heatwave – caused the most fatalities during 2003, accounting for 42 per cent of all the year's disaster deaths. Natural disasters accounted for 86 per cent of all reported disaster fatalities over the decade, although 2000 and 2002 saw technological disasters claim more lives than natural disasters. Hydro-meteorological disasters claimed 484,224 lives (72 per cent of all disaster deaths).

Drought/famine is the deadliest disaster by far, accounting for 48 per cent of all deaths from natural disasters, while floods and earthquakes account for 16 per cent each. The high drought/famine figures are due to the disaster in the Democratic People's Republic of Korea from 1995 to 1999.

Table 7 Total number of people reported affected, by type of phenomenon and by year (1994 to 2003) in thousands

	1994	1995	1996	1997	1998	1999	2000	2001	2002	2003	Total
Avalanches/landslides	298	1,122	9	34	209	15	208	67	771	459	3,194
Droughts/famines	20,515	30,431	5,836	8,016	24,495	38,647	176,477	86,757	338,536	70,274	799,985
Earthquakes	730	3,029	2,018	634	1,878	3,893	2,458	19,307	548	3,956	38,452
Extreme temperatures	1,108	535	n.a.	615	36	725	28	213	104	1,840	5,204
Floods	127,688	198,233	178,451	44,956	290,073	150,167	62,506	34,500	167,186	166,828	1,420,587
Forest/scrub fires	3,067	12	6	53	167	19	39	6	26	9	3,404
Volcanic eruptions	236	26	7	7	8	34	119	78	298	25	837
Windstorms	38,311	13,771	28,144	13,594	26,784	21,153	15,459	30,645	110,709	10,781	309,354
Other natural disasters[1]	n.a.	n.a.	n.a.	29	10	1	17	n.a.	2	ndr	59
Subtotal hydro-meteorological disasters	190,988	244,105	212,446	67,297	341,775	210,727	254,734	152,189	617,334	250,191	2,541,786
Subtotal geophysical disasters	966	3,055	2,025	641	1,886	3,928	2,577	19,386	845	3,981	39,290
Total natural disasters	191,954	247,160	214,470	67,939	343,661	214,655	257,312	171,574	618,180	254,171	2,581,076
Industrial accidents	19	27	16	163	63	3	17	19	2	555	885
Miscellaneous accidents	11	19	18	20	52	12	15	30	56	14	249
Transport accidents	3	3	3	3	4	5	6	3	5	4	41
Total technological disasters	34	50	36	186	119	21	38	53	63	574	1,174
Total	191,988	247,210	214,507	68,125	343,780	214,675	257,350	171,627	618,243	254,745	2,582,251

Source: EM-DAT, CRED, University of Louvain, Belgium

[1] Insect infestations and waves/surges

Note: n.a. signifies no data available; ndr signifies no disaster reported. For more information, see section on caveats in introductory text.

Over the decade, hydro-meteorological disasters accounted for 98 per cent of all those reported affected by disasters. Floods affect an average of 142 million people every year, accounting for 55 per cent of the decade's total. However, in 2003, floods affected 167 million people – 65 per cent of the year's total. The numbers affected by technological accidents are far lower, although the spill of 1.2 billion litres of toxic materials into two Brazilian rivers in April 2003 left 550,000 people without regular water supply.

CHAPTER 8

Table 8 Total amount of disaster estimated damage, by continent and by year (1994 to 2003) in millions of US dollars (2003 prices)

	1994	1995	1996	1997	1998	1999	2000	2001	2002	2003	Total
Avalanches/landslides	77	12	n.a.	19	n.a.	n.a.	180	74	13	51	427
Droughts/famines	1,522	6,990	1,410	470	510	7,581	6,764	3,939	1,494	710	31,392
Earthquakes	32,882	161,268	621	5,662	428	34,847	152	10,375	1,245	9,512	256,992
Extreme temperatures	809	1,010	0	3,451	4,185	1,107	133	208	n.a.	11,250	22,152
Floods	23,947	31,551	29,305	14,727	32,971	14,733	11,425	3,250	24,046	14,703	200,657
Forest/scrub fires	189	163	2,023	19,541	686	543	1,127	73	94	2,595	27,033
Volcanic eruptions	498	1	19	9	0	0	0	15	9	n.a.	552
Windstorms	6,182	29,540	14,690	8,629	18,987	26,191	10,332	11,207	1,311	17,134	144,202
Other natural disasters[1]	n.a.	126	n.a.	4	2	n.a.	128	n.a.	n.a.	ndr	260
Subtotal hydro-meteorological disasters	32,726	69,391	47,428	46,841	57,340	50,154	30,090	18,750	26,958	46,443	426,123
Subtotal geophysical disasters	33,380	161,628	640	5,671	428	34,847	152	10,391	1,254	9,512	257,544
Total natural disasters	**66,106**	**230,660**	**48,069**	**52,512**	**57,768**	**85,001**	**30,242**	**29,141**	**28,212**	**55,954**	**683,666**
Industrial accidents	56	754	1,417	438	146	3	n.a.	10	n.a.	n.a.	2,824
Miscellaneous accidents	733	267	1,436	n.a.	21	2	466	0	51	n.a.	2,977
Transport accidents	620	830	243	12	33	220	n.a.	n.a.	n.a.	n.a.	1,958
Total technological disasters	**1,409**	**1,851**	**3,096**	**450**	**200**	**226**	**466**	**10**	**51**	**n.a.**	**7,760**
Total	**67,515**	**232,511**	**51,165**	**52,963**	**57,968**	**85,227**	**30,708**	**29,152**	**28,264**	**55,954**	**691,426**

Source: EM-DAT, CRED, University of Louvain, Belgium

[1] Insect infestations and waves/surges

Note: n.a. signifies no data available; ndr signifies no disaster reported. For more information, see section on caveats in introductory text.

Estimates of damage from natural disasters should be treated with caution, as the financial value attached to infrastructure in more developed countries is much higher than that in developing countries. In 2003, windstorms caused the costliest damage (US$ 17 billion). However, the single most devastating event was the European heatwave (and associated forest fires), which caused damage amounting to US$ 13 billion.

Over the decade, earthquakes accounted for 37 per cent of estimated damage from natural and technological disasters, while floods accounted for 29 per cent and windstorms 21 per cent. The earthquake in Kobe, Japan, in 1995 caused over US$ 160 billion in damage, making it the decade's most expensive disaster.

International Federation
of Red Cross and Red Crescent Societies

Table 9 Total number of reported disasters, by continent and by type of phenomenon (1994 to 2003)

	Africa	Americas	Asia	Europe	Oceania	HHD[2]	MHD[2]	LHD[2]	Total
Avalanches/landslides	12	42	105	19	8	24	138	24	186
Droughts/famines	118	46	86	13	10	29	128	116	273
Earthquakes	11	47	145	45	9	51	185	21	257
Extreme temperatures	7	32	45	61	4	61	75	13	149
Floods	269	256	411	195	29	286	610	264	1,160
Forest/scrub fires	13	66	22	46	11	88	63	7	158
Volcanic eruptions	4	25	12	2	6	18	28	3	49
Windstorms	70	277	307	87	61	360	381	61	802
Other natural disasters[1]	3	5	10	1	2	1	16	4	21
Subtotal hydro-meteorological disasters	*492*	*724*	*986*	*422*	*125*	*849*	*1,411*	*489*	*2,749*
Subtotal geophysical disasters	*15*	*72*	*157*	*47*	*15*	*69*	*213*	*24*	*306*
Total natural disasters	**507**	**769**	**1,143**	**469**	**140**	**918**	**1,624**	**513**	**3,055**
Industrial accidents	39	50	262	73	2	75	308	43	426
Miscellaneous accidents	75	55	203	61	4	87	250	61	398
Transport accidents	588	271	720	207	12	247	1,072	479	1,798
Total technological disasters	**702**	**376**	**1,185**	**341**	**18**	**409**	**1,630**	**583**	**2,622**
Total	**1,209**	**1,172**	**2,328**	**810**	**158**	**1,327**	**3,254**	**1,096**	**5,677**

Source: EM-DAT, CRED, University of Louvain, Belgium

[1] Insect infestations and waves/surges
[2] HHD stands for high human development, MHD for medium human development, and LHD for low human development. See note on UNDP's Human Development Index country status in the section on disaster definitions in the introduction to this chapter.

Floods are the most commonly reported natural disasters in Africa, Asia and Europe, while windstorms are most common in the Americas and Oceania. However, transport accidents are even more common – accounting for 49 per cent of all reported disasters in Africa, 31 per cent in Asia and 26 per cent in Europe.

In high human development countries, windstorms are most common (largely occurring in the United States), while in medium and low human development countries, transport accidents are most common.

CHAPTER 8

Table 10 Total number of people reported killed, by continent and by type of phenomenon (1994 to 2003)

	Africa	Americas	Asia	Europe	Oceania	HHD[2]	MHD[2]	LHD[2]	Total
Avalanches/landslides	273	1,700	6,162	416	128	397	6,614	1,668	8,679
Droughts/famines	4,471	58	270,923	n.a.	88	n.a.	846	274,694	275,540
Earthquakes	2,497	3,299	68,376	20,710	18	5,993	80,317	8,590	94,900
Extreme temperatures	187	2,291	10,062	32,862	6	33,024	11,409	975	45,408
Floods	9,989	34,775	45,961	1,537	26	3,679	75,823	12,786	92,288
Forest/scrub fires	136	120	125	114	13	203	269	36	508
Volcanic eruptions	254	52	97	n.a.	9	52	106	254	412
Windstorms	1,463	23,444	33,270	726	249	3,678	52,288	3,186	59,152
Other natural disasters[1]	n.a.	15	452	n.a.	2,182	n.a.	2,649	n.a.	2,649
Subtotal hydro-meteorological disasters	16,519	62,403	366,955	35,655	2,692	40,981	149,898	293,345	484,224
Subtotal geophysical disasters	2,751	3,351	68,473	20,710	27	6,045	80,423	8,844	95,312
Total natural disasters	**19,270**	**65,754**	**435,428**	**56,365**	**2,719**	**47,026**	**230,321**	**302,189**	**579,536**
Industrial accidents	2,682	322	7,082	837	22	362	7,827	2,756	10,945
Miscellaneous accidents	2,821	1,997	8,053	1,306	46	2,635	9,328	2,260	14,223
Transport accidents	22,875	8,484	29,438	7,018	551	8,641	38,792	20,933	68,366
Total technological disasters	**28,378**	**10,803**	**44,573**	**9,161**	**619**	**11,638**	**55,947**	**25,949**	**93,534**
Total	**47,648**	**76,557**	**480,001**	**65,526**	**3,338**	**58,664**	**286,268**	**328,138**	**673,070**

Source: EM-DAT, CRED, University of Louvain, Belgium

[1] Insect infestations and waves/surges

[2] HHD stands for high human development, MHD for medium human development, and LHD for low human development. See note on UNDP's Human Development Index country status in the section on disaster definitions in the introduction to this chapter.

Note: n.a. signifies no data available. For more information, see section on caveats in introductory text.

Over the decade, more than half the people killed worldwide by natural disasters lived in low human development countries. Droughts/famines caused 84 per cent of all deaths in LHD countries; earthquakes, floods and windstorms caused 73 per cent of all deaths in medium human development countries; and extreme temperatures caused 56 per cent of all deaths in high human development countries.

Table 11 Total number of people reported affected, by continent and by type of phenomenon (1994 to 2003) in thousands

	Africa	Americas	Asia	Europe	Oceania	HHD²	MHD²	LHD²	Total
Avalanches/landslides	3	362	2,813	14	1	13	2,886	294	3,194
Droughts/famines	127,982	15,101	645,257	7,063	4,583	10,165	661,651	128,169	799,985
Earthquakes	327	3,645	32,310	2,140	30	2,654	34,233	1,566	38,452
Extreme temperatures	0	1,932	893	779	1,600	1,677	3,328	200	5,205
Floods	21,994	9,267	1,383,083	6,170	73	6,514	1,381,518	32,554	1,420,587
Forest/scrub fires	8	148	3,056	128	64	195	3,202	6	3,404
Volcanic eruptions	139	374	152	0	172	148	556	133	837
Windstorms	5,887	17,884	274,908	6,647	4,029	20,022	280,682	8,650	309,354
Other natural disasters¹	n.a.	3	47	n.a.	10	n.a.	30	29	59
Subtotal hydro-meteorological disasters	*155,873*	*44,696*	*2,310,056*	*20,800*	*10,360*	*38,587*	*2,333,297*	*169,902*	*2,541,787*
Subtotal geophysical disasters	*467*	*4,018*	*32,463*	*2,140*	*202*	*2,802*	*34,789*	*1,699*	*39,290*
Total natural disasters	**156,340**	**48,715**	**2,342,519**	**22,940**	**10,563**	**41,389**	**2,368,086**	**171,601**	**2,581,076**
Industrial accidents	5	586	216	77	0	131	750	4	885
Miscellaneous accidents	60	9	161	6	12	17	170	61	249
Transport accidents	11	8	17	4	0	9	22	9	41
Total technological disasters	**77**	**603**	**394**	**88**	**12**	**158**	**942**	**74**	**1,174**
Total	**156,417**	**49,318**	**2,342,913**	**23,028**	**10,575**	**41,546**	**2,369,029**	**171,676**	**2,582,251**

Source: EM-DAT, CRED, University of Louvain, Belgium

¹ Insect infestations and waves/surges

² HHD stands for high human development, MHD for medium human development, and LHD for low human development. See note on UNDP's Human Development Index country status in the section on disaster definitions in the introduction to this chapter.

Note: n.a. signifies no data available. For more information, see section on caveats in introductory text.

Floods in Asia accounted for 97 per cent of all those affected by floods worldwide over the decade. Windstorms accounted for 48 per cent of all those affected by disasters in high human development countries; while floods accounted for 58 per cent of those affected in medium human development countries. Droughts/famines accounted for three-quarters of those affected in low human development countries.

CHAPTER 8

CHAPTER 8

Table 12 Total amount of disaster estimated damage, by continent and by type of phenomenon (1994 to 2003) in millions of US dollars (2003 prices)

	Africa	Americas	Asia	Europe	Oceania	HHD[2]	MHD[2]	LHD[2]	Total
Avalanches/landslides	n.a.	189	212	26	n.a.	26	401	n.a.	427
Droughts/famines	434	3,561	14,109	10,401	2,887	15,557	15,441	394	31,392
Earthquakes	5,154	42,041	179,997	29,800	0	205,562	51,343	87	256,992
Extreme temperatures	1	6,128	3,447	12,369	208	18,025	4,127	n.a.	22,152
Floods	1,668	21,673	121,438	54,738	1,140	70,742	106,948	22,967	200,657
Forest/scrub fires	4	2,583	21,853	2,006	588	5,001	22,032	n.a.	27,033
Volcanic eruptions	9	21	1	23	498	32	511	9	552
Windstorms	856	75,548	46,761	18,309	2,727	101,355	36,165	6,682	144,202
Other natural disasters[1]	6	126	0	n.a.	128	128	126	6	261
Subtotal hydro-meteorological disasters	2,969	109,807	207,819	97,849	7,679	210,835	185,240	30,049	426,124
Subtotal geophysical disasters	5,164	42,063	179,997	29,822	498	205,594	51,854	96	257,544
Total natural disasters	**8,133**	**151,870**	**387,817**	**127,671**	**8,176**	**416,428**	**237,093**	**30,145**	**683,666**
Industrial accidents	10	1,289	808	702	15	2,017	602	206	2,824
Miscellaneous accidents	5	1,660	743	569	n.a.	2,899	73	5	2,977
Transport accidents	66	636	731	526	n.a	1,047	902	9	1,958
Total technological disasters	**81**	**3,585**	**2,282**	**1,797**	**15**	**5,963**	**1,577**	**220**	**7,760**
Total	**8,213**	**155,455**	**390,099**	**129,468**	**8,191**	**422,391**	**238,671**	**30,365**	**691,426**

Source: EM-DAT, CRED, University of Louvain, Belgium

[1] Insect infestations and waves/surges
[2] HHD stands for high human development, MHD for medium human development, and LHD for low human development. See note on UNDP's Human Development Index country status in the section on disaster definitions in the introduction to this chapter.

Note: n.a. signifies no data available. For more information, see section on caveats in introductory text.

Total damage reported from high human development countries was 14 times higher than that reported from low human development countries

International Federation
of Red Cross and Red Crescent Societies

Table 13 Total number of people reported killed and affected by disasters by country (1984 to 1993; 1994 to 2003; and 2003)

	Total number of people reported killed (1984-1993)	Total number of people reported affected (1984-1993)	Total number of people reported killed (1994-2003)	Total number of people reported affected (1994-2003)	Total number of people reported killed (2003)	Total number of people reported affected (2003)
Africa	**579,454**	**152,866,203**	**47,648**	**156,416,500**	**5,810**	**20,951,399**
Algeria	294	45,145	4,047	352,942	2,523	210,551
Angola	181	3,681,042	1,203	182,070	40	831
Benin	64	1,899,000	265	835,305	139	22
Botswana	8	3,348,307	23	144,276	ndr	ndr
Burkina Faso	16	2,835,396	45	176,700	17	12,350
Burundi	112	3,600	216	1,151,715	160	56
Cameroon	1,847	798,537	795	6,271	76	126
Canary Is. (SP)	ndr	ndr	38	730	15	n.a.
Cape Verde	29	5,500	18	46,306	ndr	ndr
Central African Republic	31	n.a.	158	80,666	32	270
Chad	3,093	3,382,212	131	932,436	ndr	ndr
Comoros	26	85,200	256	300	n.a.	300
Congo, DR of the[1]	722	327,959	2,250	284,207	411	24,296
Congo, Rep. of	521	50	200	83,631	ndr	ndr
Côte d'Ivoire	122	7,187	383	163	ndr	ndr
Djibouti	10	280,300	146	566,125	ndr	ndr
Egypt	1,670	37,359	2,333	170,037	116	168
Equatorial Guinea	15	313	2	1,000	n.a.	150
Eritrea[2]	28	1,615,700	105	2,873,025	n.a.	900,000
Ethiopia[2]	301,171	41,100,780	1,017	55,721,157	144	13,310,026
Gabon	102	10,000	31	n.a.	17	n.a.
Gambia	100	n.a.	78	46,769	3	8,019
Ghana	257	8,809	573	1,170,960	ndr	ndr
Guinea	373	6,066	386	220,136	ndr	ndr
Guinea-Bissau	1	10,050	217	101,500	n.a.	n.a.
Kenya	1,144	3,300,211	1,446	13,634,451	86	1,000,300
Lesotho	40	850,000	1	1,103,751	n.a.	270,000
Liberia	n.a.	1,000,000	80	7,000	ndr	ndr
Libyan AJ	310	121	103	10	ndr	ndr
Madagascar	538	1,834,593	736	4,311,789	105	786,120
Malawi	506	18,437,701	676	7,192,630	12	19,500
Mali	148	326,667	3,734	52,257	n.a.	10,000
Mauritania	2,270	2,091,707	182	823,599	3	441,000
Mauritius	160	12,007	8	4,350	ndr	ndr
Morocco	120	151	1,625	390,719	43	783

	Total number of people reported killed (1984-1993)	Total number of people reported affected (1984-1993)	Total number of people reported killed (1994-2003)	Total number of people reported affected (1994-2003)	Total number of people reported killed (2003)	Total number of people reported affected (2003)
Mozambique	105,912	7,178,571	1,657	7,142,928	69	713,013
Namibia	20	250,000	21	1,192,748	2	654,539
Niger	190	6,210,000	181	3,780,583	7	30,000
Nigeria	1,920	3,313,563	8,423	1,187,280	723	210,435
Reunion (F)	79	10,261	2	3,700	ndr	ndr
Rwanda	285	501,678	301	1,339,410	13	42,039
Saint Helena (UK)	ndr	ndr	n.a.	300	ndr	ndr
São Tomé and Principe	n.a.	n.a.	ndr	ndr	ndr	ndr
Senegal	131	18,425	2,203	623,290	31	7,804
Seychelles	ndr	ndr	5	8,037	ndr	ndr
Sierra Leone	222	n.a.	865	200,025	ndr	ndr
Somalia	844	633,500	2,726	4,245,889	1	300
South Africa	1,648	5,302,318	2,276	515,594	135	2,527
Sudan	150,617	24,112,044	1,230	9,201,128	240	325,219
Swaziland	53	1,067,500	30	512,059	ndr	ndr
Tanzania	443	3,328,368	2,261	9,854,555	84	1,902,141
Togo	n.a.	450,000	3	231,905	ndr	ndr
Tunisia	88	98,627	313	27,180	252	27,043
Uganda	346	949,580	923	1,266,381	146	12,275
Zambia	429	2,500,000	331	5,345,025	73	11,006
Zimbabwe	198	9,600,098	390	17,069,500	92	18,190
Americas	**59,390**	**32,250,982**	**76,557**	**49,317,904**	**2,026**	**3,739,486**
Anguilla (UK)	n.a.	n.a.	n.a.	150	ndr	ndr
Antigua and Barbuda	2	8,030	5	76,684	ndr	ndr
Argentina	447	6,395,965	428	883,237	52	163,901
Aruba (NL)	ndr	ndr	ndr	ndr	ndr	ndr
Bahamas	104	1,700	1	1,500	ndr	ndr
Barbados	n.a.	330	n.a.	2,000	ndr	ndr
Belize	n.a.	n.a.	66	145,170	ndr	ndr
Bermuda (UK)	28	40	22	n.a.	4	0
Bolivia	229	657,331	796	916,530	180	58,550
Brazil	3,642	6,092,427	2,348	12,736,613	406	810,797
Canada	483	79,066	433	578,238	9	2,670
Cayman Is. (UK)	ndr	ndr	n.a.	300	ndr	ndr
Chile	1,007	2,295,607	416	577,103	n.a.	285
Colombia	25,184	883,927	2,852	2,546,834	94	40,562
Costa Rica	119	393,870	126	873,073	3	2,635
Cuba	856	1,411,679	280	7,827,747	30	671
Dominica	2	10,710	15	3,891	ndr	ndr

International Federation
of Red Cross and Red Crescent Societies

	Total number of people reported killed (1984-1993)	Total number of people reported affected (1984-1993)	Total number of people reported killed (1994-2003)	Total number of people reported affected (1994-2003)	Total number of people reported killed (2003)	Total number of people reported affected (2003)
Dominican Republic	311	1,214,085	798	1,066,053	62	59,858
Ecuador	1,271	478,057	826	415,063	38	32,941
El Salvador	1,259	817,060	1,859	2,098,831	ndr	ndr
Falkland Is. (UK)	ndr	ndr	ndr	ndr	ndr	ndr
French Guiana (FR)	ndr	ndr	n.a.	70,000	ndr	ndr
Grenada	n.a.	1,000	n.a.	210	ndr	ndr
Guadeloupe (FR)	5	12,084	24	899	ndr	ndr
Guatemala	391	136,940	1,076	348,713	22	220
Guyana	n.a.	281	10	645,400	ndr	ndr
Haiti	2,379	2,066,686	2,447	1,781,896	142	162,590
Honduras	692	176,584	14,866	3,697,157	10	3,105
Jamaica	128	1,432,012	14	3,500	ndr	ndr
Martinique (FR)	10	4,510	n.a.	600	ndr	ndr
Mexico	11,566	836,675	3,641	2,468,505	88	241,673
Montserrat (UK)	11	12,040	32	13,000	ndr	ndr
Netherlands Antilles (NL)	n.a.	n.a.	17	40,004	ndr	ndr
Nicaragua	352	940,803	3,492	1,647,181	ndr	ndr
Panama	154	53,903	51	42,085	2	2,415
Paraguay	n.a.	125,575	118	505,194	ndr	ndr
Peru	2,622	3,955,185	3,392	3,608,024	445	1,904,877
Puerto Rico (USA)	760	2,534	128	117,939	2	2,505
Saint Kitts and Nevis	1	1,330	5	12,980	ndr	ndr
Saint Lucia	45	n.a.	4	1,125	ndr	ndr
Saint Pierre et Miquelon (FR)	ndr	ndr	ndr	ndr	ndr	ndr
Saint Vincent and the Grenadines	3	1,560	n.a.	100	ndr	ndr
Suriname	169	13	10	n.a.	ndr	ndr
Trinidad and Tobago	11	1,030	n.a.	617	ndr	ndr
Turks and Caicos Is. (UK)	n.a.	770	43	n.a.	ndr	ndr
United States	4,413	1,666,353	5,388	2,812,910	400	248,365
Uruguay	20	26,740	98	25,547	n.a.	200
Venezuela	714	46,490	30,419	715,298	37	666
Virgin Is. (UK)	n.a.	10,000	n.a.	3	ndr	ndr
Virgin Is. (USA)	ndr	ndr	11	10,000	ndr	ndr
Asia	**341,143**	**1,425,145,631**	**480,001**	**2,342,913,147**	**37,860**	**228,895,146**
Afghanistan	2,432	408,128	10,115	7,095,043	159	4,772
Armenia[3]	86	1,300,048	20	319,906	ndr	ndr

	Total number of people reported killed (1984-1993)	Total number of people reported affected (1984-1993)	Total number of people reported killed (1994-2003)	Total number of people reported affected (1994-2003)	Total number of people reported killed (2003)	Total number of people reported affected (2003)
Azerbaijan[3]	59	20	595	2,484,196	n.a.	31,500
Bahrain	10	n.a.	143	n.a.	ndr	ndr
Bangladesh	166,924	235,509,392	10,062	57,303,575	1,312	553,145
Bhutan	ndr	ndr	239	66,600	ndr	ndr
Brunei Darussalam	ndr	ndr	ndr	ndr	ndr	ndr
Cambodia	100	900,000	1,123	15,456,614	ndr	ndr
China, PR of[4]	23,088	531,462,124	33,137	1,382,461,945	2,403	216,352,042
East Timor[5]	ndr	ndr	4	3,508	3	1,000
Georgia[3]	541	266,746	91	1,238,486	ndr	ndr
Hong Kong (China)[4]	299	14,284	106	8,655	25	3,554
India	42,171	551,374,870	68,671	680,657,773	3,082	8,098,666
Indonesia	7,004	1,841,396	7,689	6,721,099	600	338,269
Iran, Islamic Rep. of	43,007	1,672,941	32,621	64,323,290	27,317	336,605
Iraq	796	500	135	808,007	22	n.a.
Israel	90	360	102	1,897	ndr	ndr
Japan	1,611	617,200	6,221	2,802,756	41	24,481
Jordan	34	18,279	134	330,352	22	25
Kazakhstan[3]	10	30,000	240	650,842	3	36,626
Korea, DPR of	774	22,967	270,449	10,561,915	ndr	ndr
Korea, Rep. of	2,241	1,119,833	2,646	916,330	562	80,246
Kuwait	ndr	ndr	2	200	ndr	ndr
Kyrgyzstan[3]	58	196,900	306	69,881	78	221
Lao PDR	54	1,371,462	185	3,198,905	ndr	ndr
Lebanon	70	105,575	48	555	38	28
Macau (China)	n.a.	3,986	ndr	ndr	ndr	ndr
Malaysia	674	113,943	598	68,615	8	18,800
Maldives	n.a.	24,149	10	n.a.	ndr	ndr
Mongolia	140	60,000	190	2,371,712	15	1,650
Myanmar	1,145	535,444	434	452,489	ndr	ndr
Nepal	3,224	1,321,651	3,199	653,590	379	59,273
Oman	ndr	ndr	83	91	30	n.a.
Pakistan	5,807	20,146,333	6,360	10,050,863	654	1,322,848
Palestine (West Bank/Gaza)[6]	ndr	ndr	14	20	ndr	ndr
Philippines	24,929	41,915,826	6,517	21,076,342	405	377,010
Qatar	ndr	ndr	ndr	ndr	ndr	ndr
Saudi Arabia	1,884	5,000	1,083	17,137	119	13,097
Singapore	27	237	n.a.	1,200	ndr	ndr
Sri Lanka	809	5,925,716	691	5,290,033	235	695,000

International Federation
of Red Cross and Red Crescent Societies

	Total number of people reported killed (1984-1993)	Total number of people reported affected (1984-1993)	Total number of people reported killed (1994-2003)	Total number of people reported affected (1994-2003)	Total number of people reported killed (2003)	Total number of people reported affected (2003)
Syrian Arab Republic	ndr	ndr	322	668,357	ndr	ndr
Taiwan (China)	912	23,603	3,545	766,051	33	172
Tajikistan[3]	1,718	140,461	199	3,343,769	7	7,936
Thailand	3,168	8,056,974	2,046	28,910,798	9	112,700
Turkmenistan[3]	n.a.	420	51	n.a.	ndr	ndr
United Arab Emirates	n.a.	100	140	39	ndr	ndr
Uzbekistan[3]	10	50,400	131	1,123,988	ndr	ndr
Viet Nam	4,922	16,649,823	8,269	30,373,867	191	425,437
Yemen[7]	252	908,540	1,035	261,856	108	43
Yemen, Arab Rep.[7]	38	150,000				
Yemen, DPR[7]	25	340,000				
Europe	**40,537**	**7,524,471**	**65,526**	**23,028,114**	**31,046**	**1,121,047**
Albania	196	3,242,801	10	218,384	ndr	ndr
Andorra	ndr	ndr	ndr	ndr	ndr	ndr
Austria	83	30	263	70,494	ndr	ndr
Azores (P)	172	n.a.	74	1,215	ndr	ndr
Belarus[3]	n.a.	40,000	92	23,468	31	n.a
Belgium	266	1,278	212	4,677	161	37
Bosnia and Herzegovina[8]	ndr	ndr	60	73,080	n.a	62,575
Bulgaria	121	8,179	17	1,740	ndr	ndr
Channel Is. (UK)	ndr	ndr	ndr	ndr	ndr	ndr
Croatia[8]	61	25	87	3,400	n.a	n.a.
Cyprus	n.a.	n.a.	59	4,337	n.a.	n.a.
Czech Republic[9]	ndr	ndr	84	302,146	19	35
Czechoslovakia[9]	94	95				
Denmark	55	100	8	n.a.	ndr	ndr
Estonia[3]	ndr	ndr	934	170	ndr	ndr
Faroe Is. (DK)	ndr	ndr	ndr	ndr	ndr	ndr
Finland	n.a.	n.a.	11	33	ndr	ndr
France	653	9,562	15,634	3,905,252	15,020	30,159
Germany[10]	346	106,150	5,616	477,311	5,267	1,020
German Dem. Rep.[10]	92	n.a.				
Germany, Fed. Rep. of[10]	164	4,327				
Gibraltar (UK)	ndr	ndr	ndr	ndr	ndr	ndr
Greece	1,254	47,488	521	215,890	37	534
Greenland (DK)	ndr	ndr	ndr	ndr	ndr	ndr
Hungary	20	0	229	147,248	38	12

	Total number of people reported killed (1984-1993)	Total number of people reported affected (1984-1993)	Total number of people reported killed (1994-2003)	Total number of people reported affected (1994-2003)	Total number of people reported killed (2003)	Total number of people reported affected (2003)
Iceland	n.a.	280	34	282	ndr	ndr
Ireland	357	3,500	29	1,000	ndr	ndr
Isle of Man (UK)	ndr	ndr	ndr	ndr	ndr	ndr
Italy	863	25,691	5,168	258,407	4,259	1,667
Latvia[3]	ndr	ndr	36	n.a.	15	n.a.
Liechtenstein	ndr	ndr	ndr	ndr	ndr	ndr
Lithuania[3]	6	n.a.	62	n.a.	ndr	ndr
Luxembourg	n.a.	n.a.	20	n.a.	ndr	ndr
Macedonia, FYR[8]	196	10,015	27	7,906	2	4,750
Malta	12	n.a.	283	n.a.	ndr	ndr
Moldova[3]	ndr	ndr	60	2,655,037	ndr	ndr
Monaco	ndr	ndr	ndr	ndr	ndr	ndr
Netherlands	80	12,656	1,306	253,251	1,200	n.a.
Norway	236	n.a.	270	6,130	ndr	ndr
Poland	263	39	976	240,768	ndr	ndr
Portugal	234	2,542	2,153	3,138	2,037	1,536
Romania	329	21,905	432	245,088	3	600
Russian Federation[3]	2,672	68,404	6,671	3,586,111	161	1,002,782
San Marino	ndr	ndr	ndr	ndr	ndr	ndr
Serbia and Montenegro[8]	1	6,000	128	79,716	ndr	ndr
Slovakia[9]	ndr	ndr	84	48,039	11	24
Slovenia[8]	ndr	ndr	n.a.	700	ndr	ndr
Soviet Union[3]	27,272	2,098,322				
Spain	561	62,514	766	6,071,287	214	265
Sweden	47	122	64	162	ndr	ndr
Switzerland	68	2,260	111	6,810	n.a.	7
Turkey	2,109	1,134,184	20,027	1,751,337	509	14,425
Ukraine[3]	61	409,000	578	2,073,812	17	619
United Kingdom	1,122	204,280	2,330	290,288	2,045	n.a.
Yugoslavia[8]	471	2,722				
Vatican	ndr	ndr	ndr	ndr	ndr	ndr
Oceania	**1,081**	**8,036,051**	**3,338**	**10,574,889**	**64**	**38,355**
American Samoa (USA)	25	n.a.	6	3	6	3
Australia	348	6,545,255	357	9,122,009	6	5,206
Cook Is.	6	2,000	19	1,644	ndr	ndr
Fiji	85	511,372	76	298,727	17	30,000
French Polynesia (F)	10	n.a.	13	511	ndr	ndr

International Federation
of Red Cross and Red Crescent Societies

	Total number of people reported killed (1984-1993)	Total number of people reported affected (1984-1993)	Total number of people reported killed (1994-2003)	Total number of people reported affected (1994-2003)	Total number of people reported killed (2003)	Total number of people reported affected (2003)
Guam (USA)	1	6,115	229	21,564	ndr	ndr
Kiribati	ndr	ndr	n.a.	84,000	ndr	ndr
Marshall Is.	n.a.	6,000	ndr	ndr	ndr	ndr
Micronesia Fed. States of	5	203	47	31,448	n.a.	1,000
Nauru	ndr	ndr	ndr	ndr	ndr	ndr
New Caledonia (F)	2	n.a.	2	1,100	2	1,100
New Zealand	23	20,320	24	3,417	20	n.a.
Niue	n.a.	200	ndr	ndr	ndr	ndr
Northern Mariana Is. (USA)	ndr	ndr	ndr	ndr	ndr	ndr
Palau	ndr	ndr	1	12,004	ndr	ndr
Papua New Guinea	345	223,240	2,500	947,732	13	621
Samoa	21	283,000	n.a.	n.a.	ndr	ndr
Solomon Is.	139	239,674	n.a.	1,905	n.a.	425
Tokelau (NZ)	n.a.	1,832	ndr	ndr	ndr	ndr
Tonga	1	3,103	n.a.	23,021	ndr	ndr
Tuvalu	n.a.	850	18	n.a.	ndr	ndr
Vanuatu	64	188,367	46	25,804	ndr	ndr
Wallis & Futuna (FR)	6	4,520	ndr	ndr	ndr	ndr
Total	**1,021,605**	**1,625,823,338**	**673,070**	**2,582,250,554**	**76,806**	**254,745,433**

Source: EM-DAT, CRED, University of Louvain, Belgium

[1] Democratic Republic of the Congo since 1997, previously: Zaire.

[2] Prior to 1993, Ethiopia was considered one country, after this date separate countries: Eritrea and Ethiopia.

[3] Prior to 1991, Soviet Union was considered one country, after this date separate countries. The western former republics of the USSR (Belarus, Estonia, Latvia, Lithuania, Moldova, Russian Federation, Ukraine) are included in Europe; the southern former republics (Armenia, Azerbaijan, Georgia, Kazakhstan, Kyrgyzstan, Tajikistan, Turkmenistan, Uzbekistan) are included in Asia.

[4] Hong Kong has been a Special Administrative Region of the People's Republic of China since July 1997; Macau since December 1999.

[5] Since May 2002, East Timor has been an independent country.

[6] Since September 1993 and the Israel-PLO Declaration of Principles, the Gaza Strip and West Bank have had a Palestinian self-government. Direct negotiations to determine the permanent status of these territories began in September 1999 but are far from reaching a permanent agreement.

[7] Prior to May 1990, Yemen was divided into Arab and People's Democratic Republics, after this date considered one country.

[8] Prior to 1992 Yugoslavia was considered one country, after this date separate countries: Bosnia and Herzegovina, Croatia, Serbia and Montenegro, Slovenia, FYR Macedonia.

[9] Prior to 1993, Czechoslovakia was considered one country, after this date separate countries: Czech Republic and Slovakia.

[10] Prior to October 1990, Germany was divided into Federal and Democratic Republics, after this date considered one country.

Note: n.a. signifies no data available; ndr signifies no disaster reported. For more information, see section on caveats in introductory text.

From 1984–1993, deaths reported from natural and technological disasters averaged 102,000 per year; this dropped by a third to an average of 67,000 deaths a year from 1994–2003. Over the same period, those reported affected by disasters rose 59 per cent from an average of 163 million per year (1984–1993) to 258 million per year (1994–2003).

In 2003, two disasters inflicted three-quarters of all global deaths: the heatwave in Western Europe (39 per cent) and the earthquake in the Bam region of Iran (36 per cent).

Disasters in China accounted for 85 per cent of all those reported affected during 2003.

International Federation
of Red Cross and Red Crescent Societies

Table 14 Refugees and asylum seekers by country/territory of origin (1997 to 2003)

	1997	1998	1999	2000	2001	2002	2003
Africa	**2,897,000**	**2,880,950**	**3,072,800**	**3,254,300**	**2,923,000**	**2,907,700**	**2,900,000**
Algeria	–	3,000	5,000	–	10,000	–	8,000
Angola[1]	223,000	303,300	339,300	400,000	445,000	402,000	300,000
Burundi[1]	248,000	281,000	311,000	421,000	375,000	395,000	330,000
Cameroon	–	–	–	–	2,000	–	5,000
Central African Republic	–	–	–	–	22,000	14,000	40,000
Chad	12,000	15,000	13,000	53,000	35,000	–	7,000
Congo, DR of[1]	132,000	136,000	229,000	342,000	355,000	393,000	350,000
Congo, Rep. of	40,000	20,000	25,000	22,000	30,000	15,000	23,000
Côte d'Ivoire[1]	–	–	–	–	–	22,000	20,000
Djibouti	5,000	3,000	1,000	1,000	–	–	–
Eritrea[1]	323,000	323,100	323,100	356,400	305,000	285,000	280,000
Ethiopia[1]	48,000	39,600	53,300	36,200	13,000	15,500	20,000
Ghana	12,000	11,000	10,000	10,000	10,000	10,000	10,000
Guinea	–	–	–	–	5,000	–	–
Guinea-Bissau	–	11,150	5,300	1,500	–	–	–
Kenya	–	8,000	5,000	–	–	–	–
Liberia[1]	475,000	310,000	249,000	196,000	215,000	255,300	260,000
Mali	16,000	3,000	2,000	–	–	–	3,000
Mauritania[1]	55,000	30,000	45,000	45,000	50,000	40,000	23,000
Namibia	–	–	1,000	–	–	–	1,000
Niger	10,000	–	–	–	–	–	–
Nigeria	–	–	–	–	10,000	15,000	30,000
Rwanda[1]	43,000	12,000	27,000	52,000	60,000	36,000	40,000
Senegal	17,000	10,000	10,000	10,000	10,000	11,000	10,000
Sierra Leone[1]	297,000	480,000	454,000	419,000	185,000	115,000	90,000
Somalia	486,000	414,600	415,600	370,000	300,000	282,900	290,000
Sudan[1]	353,000	352,200	423,200	392,200	440,000	471,000	575,000
Togo	6,000	3,000	3,000	2,000	–	–	5,000
Uganda	10,000	12,000	15,000	20,000	20,000	25,000	10,000
Western Sahara	86,000	100,000	105,000	105,000	110,000	105,000	165,000
Zimbabwe[1]	–	–	–	–	–	–	5,000
East Asia and Pacific	**723,000**	**763,200**	**864,100**	**1,056,000**	**1,078,500**	**1,172,100**	**1,224,400**
Cambodia	77,000	51,000	15,100	16,400	16,000	16,000	15,400
China (Tibet)	128,000	128,000	130,000	130,000	151,000	160,900	167,600
East Timor	–	–	120,000	120,000	80,000	28,000	2,300
Indonesia	8,000	8,000	8,000	6,150	5,500	5,100	21,000
Korea, DPR of	–	–	–	50,000	50,000	100,000	104,000
Lao PDR	14,000	12,100	13,900	400	–	–	15,000
Myanmar	215,000	238,100	240,100	380,250	450,000	509,100	525,000
Philippines	–	45,000	45,000	57,000	57,000	57,000	57,700
Viet Nam	281,000	281,000	292,000	295,800	295,000	296,000	316,400

	1997	1998	1999	2000	2001	2002	2003
South and central Asia	**2,966,000**	**2,928,700**	**2,906,750**	**3,832,700**	**4,961,500**	**3,878,600**	**2,752,000**
Afghanistan	2,622,000	2,628,600	2,561,050	3,520,350	4,500,000	3,532,900	2,400,000
Bangladesh	40,000	–	–	–	–	–	7,000
Bhutan	113,000	115,000	125,000	124,000	126,000	127,000	129,000
India	13,000	15,000	15,000	17,000	17,000	18,000	36,000
Kazakhstan	–	–	–	100	–	–	–
Pakistan	–	–	–	–	10,000	–	14,000
Sri Lanka	100,000	110,000	110,000	110,000	144,000	148,100	106,000
Tajikistan	32,000	15,100	62,500	59,750	55,000	52,600	60,000
Uzbekistan	46,000	45,000	33,200	1,500	–	–	–
Middle East	**4,304,000**	**4,397,700**	**3,987,050**	**5,426,500**	**4,428,000**	**3,244,500**	**3,335,000**
Iran	35,000	30,800	31,200	30,600	34,000	24,800	35,000
Iraq	526,000	555,800	534,450	409,300	300,000	237,400	300,000
Lebanon	–	–	–	4,400	–	1,200	–
Palestinian Territory, Occupied[2]	3,743,000	3,811,100	3,931,400	4,982,100	4,123,000	2,981,100	300,000
Syrian Arab Rep.	–	–	–	100	–	–	–
Europe	**1,343,100**	**1,241,300**	**1,238,100**	**755,900**	**674,000**	**517,500**	**583,400**
Albania	–	–	–	–	–	–	8,200
Armenia	188,000	180,000	188,400	–	9,000	–	7,800
Azerbaijan	218,000	218,000	230,000	–	–	–	4,300
Belarus	–	–	–	–	–	–	3,600
Bosnia and Herzegovina	342,600	80,350	250,000	234,600	210,000	156,100	142,200
Croatia	335,000	329,000	336,000	314,700	272,000	250,000	209,100
Georgia	11,000	23,000	2,800	22,400	21,000	11,400	25,000
Macedonia, FYR of	–	–	–	–	23,000	3,000	4,100
Romania	–	–	–	–	–	–	3,500
Russian Federation	–	500	12,350	22,700	18,000	27,900	51,000
Serbia and Montenegro	3,100	136,900	376,400	148,900	60,000	52,200	70,000
Slovakia	–	–	–	–	–	–	3,000
Slovenia	–	–	–	4,400	–	–	–
Turkey	11,000	11,300	11,800	12,600	43,000	16,900	40,000
Ukraine	–	–	–	–	10,000	–	11,600
Americas and Caribbean	**521,300**	**442,550**	**393,800**	**366,750**	**428,000**	**454,200**	**346,900**
Argentina	–	–	–	–	–	–	1,400
Brazil	–	–	–	–	–	–	1,400
Colombia	300	600	–	2,300	23,000	42,900	223,600
Costa Rica	–	–	–	–	–	–	1,500
Cuba	600	300	850	1,200	3,000	31,500	29,500
Dominican Republic	–	–	–	–	–	–	100
Ecuador	–	–	–	–	–	–	500
El Salvador[3]	12,000	250,150	253,000	235,500	217,000	203,000	8,900

International Federation of Red Cross and Red Crescent Societies

	1997	1998	1999	2000	2001	2002	2003
Guatemala[3]	30,000	251,300	146,000	102,600	129,000	129,000	11,600
Haiti	–	600	23,000	20,600	25,000	30,800	25,900
Honduras	–	–	–	–	–	–	1,400
Jamaica	–	–	–	–	–	–	500
Mexico	–	–	–	–	11,000	–	20,700
Nicaragua[3]	19,000	18,000	18,000	3,800	13,000	15,800	12,700
Panama	–	–	–	–	–	–	100
Peru	–	350	1,700	750	–	1,200	3,200
United States	–	–	–	–	–	–	300
Uruguay	–	–	–	–	–	–	600
Venezuela	–	–	–	–	–	–	3,000
Total	**12,295,000**	**12,733,150**	**12,511,350**	**14,692,150**	**14,493,000**	**12,174,600**	**11,142,000**

Source: US Committee for Refugees

Note: – indicates zero or near zero.

[1] These figures are provisional, as accurate estimates were unavailable at the time of publication.
[2] See note 3, Table 15.
[3] The Nicaraguan Adjustment and Central American Relief Act of 1997 (NACARA) covers many long-pending Salvadorean and Guatemalan asylum applicants. Those who apply under NACARA are granted permanent residence at a rate of 96 per cent. Those denied can still pursue asylum pursuant to a federal court settlement. USCR, therefore, considers that these populations have a durable solution and should no longer be counted as people in need of international protection.

Almost half of the world's refugees and asylum seekers in 2003 were either Palestinians or Afghans, despite the repatriation of more than 500,000 Afghans during the year. The number of refugees and asylum seekers from Colombia, Côte d'Ivoire, Myanmar (Burma), Liberia, Sudan and other countries increased during the year, while the number of refugees from Afghanistan, Angola, Bosnia and Herzegovina, Croatia, East Timor, Sierra Leone and other countries declined during the year.

Table 15 Refugees and asylum seekers by host country/territory (1997 to 2003)

	1997	1998	1999	2000	2001	2002	2003
Africa	**2,944,000**	**2,924,000**	**3,147,000**	**3,346,000**	**3,002,000**	**3,030,000**	**3,056,000**
Algeria	104,000	84,000	84,000	85,000	85,000	85,000	170,000
Angola	9,000	10,000	15,000	12,000	12,000	12,000	13,000
Benin	3,000	3,000	3,000	4,000	5,000	6,000	5,000
Botswana	–	–	1,000	3,000	4,000	4,000	4,000
Burkina Faso	2,000	–	–	–	–	–	–
Burundi	12,000	5,000	2,000	6,000	28,000	41,000	40,000
Cameroon	1,000	3,000	10,000	45,000	32,000	17,000	25,000
Central African Rep.[1]	38,000	47,000	55,000	54,000	49,000	50,000	50,000
Chad[1]	–	10,000	20,000	20,000	15,000	16,000	160,000
Congo, DR of[1]	255,000	220,000	235,000	276,000	305,000	274,000	180,000
Congo, Rep. of	21,000	20,000	40,000	126,000	102,000	118,000	90,000
Côte d'Ivoire[1]	202,000	128,000	135,000	94,000	103,000	50,000	50,000
Djibouti	22,000	23,000	23,000	22,000	22,000	23,000	25,000
Egypt	46,000	46,000	47,000	57,000	75,000	78,000	70,000
Eritrea	3,000	3,000	2,000	1,000	2,000	3,000	4,000
Ethiopia[1]	313,000	251,000	246,000	194,000	114,000	115,000	100,000
Gabon	1,000	1,000	15,000	15,000	20,000	20,000	19,000
Gambia	8,000	13,000	25,000	15,000	15,000	10,000	11,000
Ghana	20,000	15,000	12,000	13,000	12,000	41,000	50,000
Guinea	430,000	514,000	453,000	390,000	190,000	182,000	170,000
Guinea-Bissau	4,000	5,000	5,000	6,000	7,000	7,000	10,000
Kenya[1]	196,000	192,000	254,000	233,000	243,000	221,000	215,000
Liberia[1]	100,000	120,000	90,000	70,000	60,000	65,000	65,000
Libyan AJ	27,000	28,000	11,000	11,000	33,000	12,000	12,000
Malawi	–	–	–	–	6,000	13,000	13,000
Mali	17,000	5,000	7,000	7,000	9,000	4,000	–
Mauritania	5,000	20,000	25,000	25,000	25,000	25,000	26,000
Morocco	–	–	–	–	–	2,000	–
Mozambique	–	–	1,000	2,000	5,000	7,000	8,000
Namibia	1,000	2,000	8,000	20,000	31,000	26,000	15,000
Niger	7,000	3,000	2,000	1,000	1,000	–	–
Nigeria	9,000	5,000	7,000	10,000	7,000	7,000	10,000
Rwanda	28,000	36,000	36,000	29,000	35,000	32,000	36,000
Senegal	41,000	30,000	42,000	41,000	43,000	45,000	23,000
Sierra Leone[1]	15,000	10,000	7,000	3,000	15,000	60,000	70,000
South Africa	28,000	29,000	40,000	30,000	22,000	65,000	105,000
Sudan[1]	365,000	360,000	363,000	385,000	307,000	287,000	350,000
Swaziland	–	–	–	–	1,000	1,000	–
Tanzania[1]	295,000	329,000	413,000	543,000	498,000	516,000	480,000
Togo	12,000	11,000	10,000	11,000	11,000	11,000	12,000
Uganda	185,000	185,000	197,000	230,000	174,000	221,000	220,000
Zambia[1]	118,000	157,000	205,000	255,000	270,000	247,000	140,000
Zimbabwe[1]	1,000	1,000	1,000	2,000	9,000	10,000	10,000

International Federation
of Red Cross and Red Crescent Societies

	1997	1998	1999	2000	2001	2002	2003
East Asia and Pacific	**535,100**	**559,200**	**657,300**	**791,700**	**815,700**	**874,700**	**871,600**
Australia	18,000	15,000	17,000	16,700	21,800	25,000	23,300
Cambodia	–	200	100	50	1,000	300	100
China[2]	281,800	281,800	292,800	350,000	345,000	396,000	397,000
Hong Kong[2]	n.a.	n.a.	n.a.	n.a.	n.a.	–	–
Indonesia	100	100	120,000	120,800	81,300	28,700	300
Japan	300	500	400	3,800	6,400	6,500	7,900
Korea, Rep. of	–	–	–	350	600	–	–
Malaysia[1]	5,200	50,600	45,400	57,400	57,500	59,000	78,900
Nauru[1]	–	–	–	–	800	100	200
New Zealand	–	–	–	3,100	2,700	1,700	1,200
Papua New Guinea	8,200	8,000	8,000	6,000	5,400	5,200	7,800
Philippines	100	300	200	200	200	200	2,000
Solomon Islands	800	n.a.	–	–	–	-	–
Thailand	205,600	187,700	158,400	217,300	277,000	336,000	337,500
Viet Nam	15,000	15,000	15,000	16,000	16,000	16,000	15,400
South and central Asia	**1,743,000**	**1,708,700**	**1,689,000**	**2,655,600**	**2,702,800**	**2,188,600**	**1,873,500**
Bangladesh	40,100	53,100	53,100	121,600	122,000	122,200	119,900
India	323,500	292,100	292,000	290,000	345,800	332,300	317,000
Kazakhstan	14,000	4,100	14,800	20,000	19,500	20,600	15,800
Kyrgyzstan	15,500	15,000	10,900	11,000	9,700	8,300	8,200
Nepal	116,000	118,000	130,000	129,000	131,000	132,000	134,600
Pakistan	215,650	1,217,400	1,127,000	2,019,000	2,018,000	1,518,000	1,219,000
Tajikistan	3,800	5,500	4,700	12,400	4,600	3,500	3,200
Turkmenistan	13,000	500	18,500	14,200	14,000	13,700	14,100
Uzbekistan	1,250	3,000	38,000	38,400	38,000	38,000	41,700
Middle East	**5,708,000**	**5,814,100**	**5,849,000**	**6,035,300**	**6,830,200**	**5,290,300**	**4,107,000**
Gaza Strip	746,000	773,000	798,400	824,600	852,600	879,000	925,000
Iran	1,900,000	1,931,000	1,835,000	1,895,000	2,558,000	2,208,500	1,100,000
Iraq	110,000	104,000	129,400	127,700	128,100	134,700	124,000
Israel	–	–	400	4,700	4,700	2,100	2,000
Jordan[3]	1,413,800	1,463,800	1,518,000	1,580,000	1,643,900	155,000	160,000
Kuwait	90,000	52,000	52,000	52,000	50,000	65,000	65,000
Lebanon[3]	362,300	368,300	378,100	383,200	389,500	409,000	238,000
Saudi Arabia	116,750	128,300	128,600	128,500	128,500	245,400	240,000
Syrian Arab Rep.[3]	361,000	369,800	379,200	389,000	397,600	482,400	498,000
United Arab Emirates	500	200	–	–	–	–	–
West Bank	543,000	555,000	569,700	583,000	607,800	627,500	665,000
Yemen	64,900	68,700	60,000	67,600	69,500	81,700	90,000
Europe	**2,020,300**	**1,728,400**	**1,909,100**	**1,153,300**	**972,800**	**877,400**	**703,700**
Albania	–	25,000	5,000	500	400	100	100
Armenia	219,150	229,000	240,000	–	11,000	11,000	11,000
Austria	11,400	16,500	16,600	6,100	10,800	30,900	17,600
Azerbaijan	244,100	235,300	222,000	3,600	7,000	11,400	9,000

	1997	1998	1999	2000	2001	2002	2003
Belarus[1]	33,500	16,500	2,900	3,200	3,100	3,600	3,000
Belgium	14,100	25,800	42,000	46,400	41,000	30,300	21,000
Bosnia and Herzegovina	40,000	40,000	60,000	38,200	33,200	34,200	22,500
Bulgaria	2,400	2,800	2,800	3,000	2,900	1,200	800
Croatia	50,000	27,300	24,000	22,500	21,900	8,100	4,200
Cyprus	–	200	300	300	1,300	1,800	4,800
Czech Republic	700	2,400	1,800	4,800	10,600	6,300	3,900
Denmark	13,000	6,100	8,500	10,300	12,200	5,200	3,500
Finland[1]	1,600	2,300	3,800	2,600	2,100	1,200	1,000
France[1]	16,000	17,400	30,000	26,200	12,400	27,600	28,000
Georgia	100	300	5,200	7,600	7,900	4,200	3,900
Germany	277,000	198,000	285,000	180,000	116,000	104,000	90,800
Greece	2,100	2,800	7,500	800	6,500	1,800	3,000
Hungary	3,400	3,200	6,000	4,200	2,900	1,200	1,500
Iceland	–	–	100	50	–	–	–
Ireland	4,300	6,900	8,500	7,700	9,500	6,500	5,800
Italy[1]	20,000	6,800	24,900	13,700	9,600	5,200	5,000
Lithuania	100	100	100	150	300	200	100
Macedonia, FYR of	3,500	7,300	17,400	9,000	3,600	2,700	2,300
Malta	–	–	–	–	–	–	200
Moldova	–	–	–	–	300	300	–
Netherlands	64,200	47,000	40,000	29,600	31,000	17,200	12,400
Norway	3,100	2,500	9,500	8,600	13,200	5,900	11,000
Poland	1,200	1,300	1,300	2,300	1,800	300	1,500
Portugal	150	1,400	1,700	1,600	50	–	–
Romania	2,000	900	900	2,100	200	100	200
Russian Federation	324,000	161,900	104,300	36,200	28,200	17,400	11,500
Serbia and Montenegro	550,000	480,000	476,000	484,200	400,000	353,000	289,600
Slovak Republic	100	300	400	400	3,100	4,500	4,500
Slovenia	5,300	7,300	5,000	12,000	2,700	400	100
Spain	3,300	2,500	4,500	1,100	1,000	200	200
Sweden	8,400	16,700	20,200	18,500	18,500	24,900	25,600
Switzerland	34,100	40,000	104,000	62,600	57,900	44,200	38,300
Turkey	5,000	12,000	9,100	9,900	12,600	10,000	7,000
Ukraine	4,900	8,600	5,800	5,500	6,000	3,600	4,000
United Kingdom	58,100	74,000	112,000	87,800	69,800	79,200	55,700
Americas and Caribbean	**616,000**	**739,950**	**737,000**	**562,100**	**597,000**	**76,500**	**502,300**
Argentina	10,700	1,100	3,300	1,000	3,100	2,700	2,300
Bahamas	50	100	100	100	100	–	–
Belize	4,000	3,500	3,000	1,700	–	1,000	900
Bolivia	300	350	400	–	400	400	500
Brazil	2,300	2,400	2,300	2,700	4,050	3,700	3,800
Canada	48,800	46,000	53,000	54,400	70,000	78,400	70,200

	1997	1998	1999	2000	2001	2002	2003
Chile	300	100	300	300	550	400	500
Colombia	200	200	250	250	200	200	200
Costa Rica	23,100	23,100	22,900	7,300	10,600	12,800	13,600
Cuba	1,500	1,100	1,000	1,000	1,000	1,000	900
Dominican Republic	600	600	650	500	500	300	500
Ecuador	200	250	350	1,600	4,300	9,100	16,600
El Salvador	100	100	–	–	–	–	300
Guatemala	1,300	800	750	700	700	700	700
Honduras	–	100	–	–	–	–	–
Jamaica	–	50	50	50	–	–	–
Mexico	30,000	7,500	8,500	6,500	6,200	4,000	2,900
Nicaragua	700	150	500	300	–	–	300
Panama	300	1,300	600	1,300	1,500	1,700	1,800
Paraguay	–	–	–	–	50	–	–
Peru	–	–	700	750	750	900	700
United States[4]	491,000	651,000	638,000	481,500	492,500	638,000	203,200
Uruguay	–	–	150	50	100	100	100
Venezuela	300	150	200	100	400	1,100	182,300
Total	**14,479,550**	**13,566,400**	**13,988,000**	**14,543,700**	**14,921,000**	**12,337,500**	**11,114,000**

Source: US Committee for Refugees

Note: – indicates zero or near zero; n.a. not available, or reported estimates unreliable.

[1] These figures are provisional, as accurate estimates were unavailable at the time of publication.

[2] As of 1997, figures for Hong Kong are included in total for China.

[3] In the light of persistent protection gaps, USCR concluded in 2003 that the inclusion clause of Article 1D of the UN Refugee Convention brings Palestinian refugees under the Convention's application. Accordingly, USCR changed its statistical approach in 2003 by applying the Convention's definition of refugee status – including its cessation – to this population rather than UNRWA's registration criteria as before. The numbers in Lebanon were adjusted to reflect the acquisition of citizenship in Lebanon and other countries.

[4] Includes asylum applications pending in the United States; USCR estimates the number of individuals represented per case.

The total number of refugees and asylum seekers decreased in 2003. The decline was due to many factors, including refugee repatriations to several countries and to the unwillingness of many states, especially those in the developed world, to accept new refugees and asylum seekers. The number of refugees and asylum seekers remained relatively steady in Africa and east Asia during the year and decreased in the Americas, Europe, and south and central Asia as refugees returned to their homes or were deterred from seeking asylum. The Middle East continued to host almost 40 per cent of the world's refugees and asylum seekers. Almost half of the world's refugees and asylum seekers were found in just six countries or territories: Iran; the Gaza Strip and the West Bank; Pakistan; Syria; Tanzania; and China.

Table 16 Significant populations of internally displaced people (1997 to 2003)

	1997	1998	1999	2000	2001	2002	2003
Africa[1]	**7,590,000**	**8,958,000**	**10,355,000**	**10,527,000**	**10,935,000**	**15,230,000**	**12,009,000**
Algeria	n.a.	200,000	100,000	100,000	100,000	100,000	100,000
Angola	1,200,000	1,500,000	1,500,000	2,000,000	2,000,000	2,000,000	1,000,000
Burundi	500,000	500,000	800,000	600,000	600,000	400,000	500,000
Central African Republic	–	–	–	–	5,000	10,000	300,000
Congo, DR	100,000	300,000	800,000	1,500,000	50,000	2,000,000	2,000,000
Congo, Rep. of	–	250,000	500,000	30,000	2,000,000	100,000	60,000
Côte d'Ivoire	–	–	–	2,000	5,000	500,000	500,000
Djibouti	5,000	–	–	–	–	–	–
Eritrea	–	100,000	250,000	310,000	90,000	75,000	75,000
Ethiopia	–	150,000	300,000	250,000	100,000	90,000	200,000
Ghana	20,000	20,000	–	–	–	–	–
Guinea	–	–	–	60,000	100,000	20,000	50,000
Guinea-Bissau	–	200,000	50,000	–	–	–	–
Kenya	150,000	200,000	100,000	100,000	200,000	230,000	200,000
Liberia	500,000	75,000	50,000	20,000	80,000	100,000	500,000
Nigeria	50,000	3,000	5,000	–	50,000	50,000	57,000
Rwanda	50,000	500,000	600,000	150,000	–	–	–
Senegal	10,000	10,000	–	5,000	5,000	5,000	17,000
Sierra Leone	500,000	300,000	500,000	700,000	600,000	–	–
Somalia	200,000	250,000	350,000	300,000	400,000	350,000	350,000
South Africa	5,000	–	–	–	–	–	–
Sudan	4,000,000	4,000,000	4,000,000	4,000,000	4,000,000	4,000,000	5,000,000
Uganda	300,000	400,000	450,000	400,000	500,000	600,000	1,000,000
Zimbabwe	–	–	–	–	50,000	100,000	100,000
East Asia and Pacific	**800,000**	**1,150,000**	**1,577,000**	**1,670,000**	**2,266,000**	**1,349,000**	**1,972,000**
Cambodia	30,000	22,000	–	–	–	–	–
East Timor	–	–	300,000	–	–	–	–
Indonesia	–	–	440,000	800,000	1,400,000	600,000	720,000
Korea, DPR of	–	–	–	100,000	100,000	100,000	100,000
Myanmar	750,000	1,000,000	600,000	600,000	600,000	600,000	1,000,000
Papua New Guinea	20,000	6,000	5,000	–	1,000	–	1,000
Philippines	–	122,000	200,000	140,000	135,000	45,000	150,000
Solomon Islands	–	–	32,000	30,000	30,000	4,000	1,000
Europe	**3,695,000**	**3,685,000**	**3,993,000**	**3,539,000**	**2,785,000**	**2,560,000**	**3,088,000**
Armenia	70,000	60,000	–	–	50,000	50,000	50,000
Azerbaijan	550,000	576,000	568,000	575,000	572,000	576,000	575,000
Bosnia and Herzegovina	800,000	836,000	830,000	518,000	439,000	368,000	327,000
Croatia	110,000	61,000	50,000	34,000	23,000	17,000	13,000
Cyprus	265,000	265,000	265,000	265,000	265,000	265,000	265,000
Georgia	285,000	275,000	280,000	272,000	264,000	262,000	260,000

	1997	1998	1999	2000	2001	2002	2003
Macedonia	–	–	–	–	21,000	9,000	3,000
Russian Federation	375,000	350,000	800,000	800,000	474,000	371,000	368,000
Serbia and Montenegro	–	257,000	600,000	475,000	277,000	262,000	227,000
Turkey[1]	1,250,000	1,000,000	600,000	600,000	400,000	380,000	1,000,000
Americas and Caribbean	**1,624,000**	**1,755,000**	**1,886,000**	**2,176,000**	**2,465,000**	**2,518,000**	**2,742,000**
Colombia	1,000,000	1,400,000	1,800,000	2,100,000	2,450,000	2,500,000	2,730,000
Guatemala	250,000	–	–	–	–	–	–
Haiti	–	–	–	–	–	6,000	–
Mexico	14,000	15,000	16,000	16,000	15,000	12,000	12,000
Peru	360,000	340,000	70,000	60,000	–	–	–
Middle East[1]	**1,475,000**	**1,575,000**	**1,917,000**	**1,700,000**	**1,670,000**	**2,646,000**	**2,546,000**
Palestinian Territory, Occupied	–	–	17,000	–	20,000	26,000	26,000
Iraq	900,000	1,000,000	900,000	700,000	700,000	1,100,000	1,000,000
Israel	–	–	200,000	200,000	200,000	250,000	250,000
Jordan	–	–	–	–	–	800,000	800,000
Lebanon	450,000	450,000	350,000	350,000	250,000	300,000	300,000
Syrian Arab Rep.	125,000	125,000	450,000	450,000	500,000	170,000	170,000
South and central Asia	**2,253,500**	**2,130,000**	**1,617,000**	**1,542,000**	**2,402,000**	**2,023,000**	**1,614,000**
Afghanistan[1]	1,250,000	1,000,000	500,000	375,000	1,000,000	700,000	250,000
Bangladesh	–	50,000	50,000	60,000	100,000	60,000	61,000
India	200,000	520,000	507,000	507,000	500,000	600,000	650,000
Nepal[1]	–	–	–	–	–	100,000	150,000
Pakistan[1]	–	–	–	–	2,000	–	–
Sri Lanka	800,000	560,000	560,000	600,000	800,000	563,000	500,000
Tajikistan	3,500	–	–	–	–	–	–
Uzbekistan	–	–	–	–	–	–	3,000
Total	**17,437,500**	**19,253,000**	**21,345,000**	**21,154,000**	**22,523,000**	**26,326,000**	**23,971,000**

Source: US Committee for Refugees

Note: – indicates zero or near zero; n.a. not available, or reported estimates unreliable.

[1] Estimates of the size of internally displaced populations are frequently subject to great margins of error and are often imprecise, particularly in these countries and regions.

Approximately 2 million more people were internally displaced at the end of 2003 than at the end of 2002. Large internally displaced populations remained in Azerbaijan, Democratic Republic of the Congo, Côte d'Ivoire, India, Iraq, Myanmar (Burma), Russia, Turkey and elsewhere in 2003. Significant new displacement occurred in the Central African Republic, Colombia, Indonesia, Liberia, the Philippines, Sudan and Uganda, while some internally displaced people were able to return home in Afghanistan, Angola, Bosnia and Herzegovina, Republic of Congo, Rwanda, Sierra Leone and Sri Lanka. More than half of the world's internally displaced people were in Africa.

CHAPTER 9

Section
Two

**Tracking
the
system**

International Federation
of Red Cross and Red Crescent Societies

Reaching out across the world

This chapter contains contact details for the members of the International Red Cross and Red Crescent Movement (the International Federation, ICRC and National Societies) and the International Federation's network of regional and country delegations. Information correct as of 1 May 2004.

National Red Cross and Red Crescent Societies are listed alphabetically by International Organization for Standardization Codes for the Representation of Names of Countries, English spelling.

International Federation of Red Cross and Red Crescent Societies
P.O. Box 372
1211 Geneva 19
Switzerland
Tel.   +41 22 7304222
Fax   +41 22 7330395
E-mail secretariat@ifrc.org
Web http://www.ifrc.org

International Committee of the Red Cross
19 avenue de la Paix
1202 Geneva
Switzerland
Tel. +41 22 7346001
Fax +41 22 7332057
E-mail icrc.gva@gwn.icrc.org
Web http://www.icrc.org

Red Cross/European Union Office
Rue Belliard 65, bte 7
1040 – Brussels
Belgium
Tel.   +32 2 2350680
Fax   +32 2 2305465
E-mail infoboard@redcross-eu.net

Office of the Permanent Observer for the International Federation of Red Cross and Red Crescent Societies to the United Nations
800 Second Avenue
Third floor
New York, NY 10019
United States
Tel. +1 212 3380161
Fax +1 212 3389832
E-mail ifrcny02@ifrc.org

National Red Cross and Red Crescent Societies

Afghan Red Crescent Society
Afshar
P.O. Box 3066
Shar-e-Now
Kabul
Afghanistan
Tel.   +93 702 80698
Fax   +93 229 0097

Albanian Red Cross
Rruga "Muhammet Gjollesha"
Sheshi "Karl Topia"
C.P. 1511
Tirana
Albania
Tel.   +355 42 57532
Fax   +355 42 25855
Web http://www.kksh.org

Algerian Red Crescent
15 bis, Boulevard Mohammed V
Alger 16000
Algeria
Tel. +213 21 633952
Fax +213 21 633690
E-mail cra@algeriainfo.com
Web http://www.cra-dz.org

Andorra Red Cross

Prat de la Creu 22
Andorra la Vella
Andorra
Tel. +376 808225
Fax +376 808240
E-mail creuroja@creuroja.ad
Web http://www.creuroja.ad

Angola Red Cross

Rua 1° Congresso no 21
Caixa Postal 927
Luanda
Angola
Tel. +244 2 336543
Fax +244 2 372868
E-mail cruzvermelhangola@
      netangola.com

Antigua and Barbuda Red Cross Society

Old Parham Road
P.O. Box 727
St. Johns, Antigua W.I.
Antigua and Barbuda
Tel. +1 268 4620800
Fax +1 268 4609595
E-mail redcross@candw.org

Argentine Red Cross

Hipólito Yrigoyen 2068
1089 Buenos Aires
Argentina
Tel. +54 114 9527200
Fax +54 114 9527715
E-mail info@cruzroja.org.ar
Web http://www.cruzroja.org.ar

Armenian Red Cross Society

21 Paronian Street
375015 Yerevan
Armenia
Tel. +374 1 538367
Fax +374 1 583630
E-mail redcross@redcross.am

Australian Red Cross

155 Pelham Street
P.O. Box 196
Carlton South, VIC 3053
Australia
Tel. +61 3 93451800
Fax +61 3 93482513
E-mail redcross@nat.redcross.org.au
Web http://www.redcross.org.au

Austrian Red Cross

Wiedner Hauptstrasse 32
Postfach 39
1041 Wien
Austria
Tel. +43 1 589000
Fax +43 1 58900199
E-mail oerk@redcross.or.at
Web http://www.roteskreuz.at

Red Crescent Society of Azerbaijan

S. Safarov Street 2
Baku, Nesimi district
PC 370010
Azerbaijan
Tel. +994 12 938481
Fax +994 12 931578
E-mail azerb.redcrescent@azdata.net

The Bahamas Red Cross Society

John F. Kennedy Drive
P.O. Box N-8331
Nassau
Bahamas
Tel. +1 242 3237370
Fax +1 242 3237404
E-mail redcross@bahamas.net.bs

Bahrain Red Crescent Society

P.O. Box 882
Manama
Bahrain
Tel. +973 293171
Fax +973 291797
E-mail hilal@batelco.com.bh
Web http://www.batelco.com.bh/brcs

Bangladesh Red Crescent Society

684-686 Bara Maghbazar
G.P.O. Box 579
Dhaka – 1217
Bangladesh
Tel. +880 2 9330188
Fax +880 2 9352303
E-mail bdrcs@bdonline.com
Web http://www.bdrcs.org

The Barbados Red Cross Society

Red Cross House
Jemmotts Lane
P.O. Box 300
Bridgetown
Barbados
Tel. +1 246 4333889
Fax +1 246 4262052
E-mail bdosredcross@caribsurf.com

Belarusian Red Cross

35, Karl Marx Str.
220030 Minsk
Belarus
Tel. +375 17 2272620
Fax +375 17 2272620
E-mail brc@home.by

Belgian Red Cross

Ch. de Vleurgat 98
1050 Bruxelles
Belgium
Tel. +32 2 6454545
Fax +32 2 6454675 French;
      6456041 Flemish
E-mail info@redcross-fr.be
      documentatie@redcross-fl.be
Web http://www.redcross.be

Belize Red Cross Society

1 Gabourel Lane
P.O. Box 413
Belize City
Belize
Tel. +501 2 273319
Fax +501 2 230998
E-mail bzercshq@btl.net

International Federation
of Red Cross and Red Crescent Societies

Red Cross of Benin

B.P. No. 1
Porto-Novo
Benin
Tel. +229 212886
Fax +229 214927
E-mail crbenin@leland.bj

Bolivian Red Cross

Avenida Simón Bolívar N° 1515
Casilla N° 741
La Paz
Bolivia
Tel. +591 2 202930
Fax +591 2 359102
E-mail cruzrobo@caoba.entelnet.bo
Web http://www.come.to/
   cruzroja.org.bo

The Red Cross Society of Bosnia and Herzegovina

Titova 7
71000 Sarajevo
Bosnia and Herzegovina
Tel. +387 33 269 930
Fax +387 33 200 148
E-mail rcsbihhq@bih.net.ba

Botswana Red Cross Society

135 Independance Avenue
P.O. Box 485
Gaborone
Botswana
Tel. +267 352465
Fax +267 312352
E-mail brcs@info.bw

Brazilian Red Cross

Praça Cruz Vermelha No. 10/12
20230-130 Rio de Janeiro RJ
Brazil
Tel. +55 21 22210658
Fax +55 21 5071594
E-mail cvdobrasil@ig.com.br

Brunei Darussalam Red Crescent Society

P.O. Box 3065
KA1131 Kuala Belait
Brunei Darussalam
Tel. +673 2 380635
Fax +673 2 382797
E-mail bdrcs@netcad.com.bn

Bulgarian Red Cross

76, James Boucher Boulevard
1407 Sofia
Bulgaria
Tel. +359 2 8650595
Fax +359 2 8656937
E-mail secretariat@redcross.bg
Web http://www.redcross.bg

Burkinabe Red Cross Society

01 B.P. 4404
Ouagadougou 01
Burkina Faso
Tel. +226 361340
Fax +226 363121
E-mail croixrouge.bf@fasonet.bf

Burundi Red Cross

18, Av. de la Croix-Rouge
B.P. 324
Bujumbura
Burundi
Tel. +257 216246
Fax +257 211101
E-mail croixrougebdi@usan.net

Cambodian Red Cross Society

17, Vithei de la Croix-Rouge
   Cambodgienne
Phnom-Penh
Cambodia
Tel. +855 23 212876
Fax +855 23 212875
E-mail communications@crc.org.kh

Cameroon Red Cross Society

Rue Henri Dunant 2005
B.P. 631
Yaoundé
Cameroon
Tel. +237 2224177
Fax +237 2224177
E-mail croixrouge@camnet.com

The Canadian Red Cross Society

170 Metcalfe Street, Suite 300
Ottawa
Ontario K2P 2P2
Canada
Tel. +1 613 7401900
Fax +1 613 7401911
E-mail cancross@redcross.ca
Web http://www.redcross.ca

Red Cross of Cape Verde

Rua Andrade Corvo
Caixa Postal 119
Praia
Cape Verde
Tel. +238 611701
Fax +238 614174
E-mail cruzvermelhasg@
   mail.cvtelecom.cv

Central African Red Cross Society

Avenue Koudoukou Km, 5
B.P. 1428
Bangui
Central African Republic
Tel. +236 612223
Fax +236 613561
E-mail sida_crca@yahoo.fr

Red Cross of Chad

B.P. 449
N'Djamena
Chad
Tel. +235 523434
E-mail crftchad@intnet.td

Chilean Red Cross

Avenida Santa María No. 150
    Providencia
Comuna Providencia
Correo 21, Casilla 246 V
Santiago de Chile
Chile
Tel. +56 2 7771448
Fax +56 2 7370270
E-mail cruzroja@entelchile.net

Red Cross Society of China

53 Ganmian Hutong
100010 Beijing
China
Tel. +86 10 65124447
Fax +86 10 64029928
E-mail rcsc@chineseredcross.org.cn
Web http://www.chineseredcross.
    org.cn

Colombian Red Cross Society

Avenida 68 N° 66-31
Apartado Aéreo 11'110
Bogotá D.C.
Colombia
Tel. +57 1 4376339
Fax +57 1 4376365
E-mail mundo@
    cruzrojacolombiana.org
Web http://www.cruzrojacolombiana.
    org/cruzroja.html

Congolese Red Cross

8 rue Lucien Fourneau
Face Ministère de la Santé et
    Fonction Publique
Brazzaville
Congo
Tel. +242 688249
E-mail croixrouge_congobzv@
    yahoo.fr

Red Cross of the Democratic Republic of the Congo

41, Avenue de la Justice
Zone de la Gombe
B.P. 1712
Kinshasa I
Congo, D.R. of the
Tel. +243 1234897
Fax +243 8804151
E-mail secretariat@crrdc.aton.cd

Cook Islands Red Cross

P.O. Box 888
Rarotonga
Cook Islands
Tel. +682 22598
Fax +682 22598
E-mail nikratt@redcross.org.ck

Costa Rican Red Cross

Calle 14, Avenida 8
Apartado 1025
1000 San José
Costa Rica
Tel. +506 2337033
Fax +506 2337279
E-mail info@cruzroja.or.cr
Web http://www.cruzroja.or.cr

Red Cross Society of Côte d'Ivoire

P.O. Box 1244
Abidjan 01
Côte d'Ivoire
Tel. +225 20321335
Fax +225 20324381
E-mail crci@afnet.net

Croatian Red Cross

Ulica Crvenog kriza 14
10000 Zagreb
Croatia
Tel. +385 1 4655814
Fax +385 1 4655365
E-mail redcross@hck.hr
Web http://www.hck.hr

Cuban Red Cross

Calle 20#707
C.P. 10300
Ciudad de la Habana
Cuba
Tel. +53 7 228272
Fax +53 7 228272
E-mail crsn@infomed.sld.cu

Czech Red Cross

Thunovska 18
CZ-118 04 Praha 1
Czech Republic
Tel. +420 2 51104111
Fax +420 2 51104271
E-mail cck.zahranicni@iol.cz

Danish Red Cross

Blegdamsvej 27
P.O. Box 2600
DK-2100 Copenhagen Ö
Denmark
Tel. +45 35259200
Fax +45 35259292
E-mail drc@redcross.dk
Web http://www.redcross.dk

Red Crescent Society of Djibouti

B.P. 8
Djibouti
Djibouti
Tel. +253 352270
Fax +253 352451
E-mail crd@intnet.dj

Dominica Red Cross Society

Federation Drive
Goodwill
Dominica
Tel. +1 767 4488280
Fax +1 767 4487708
E-mail redcross@cwdom.dm

International Federation
of Red Cross and Red Crescent Societies

Dominican Red Cross

Calle Juan E. Dunant No. 51
Ens. Miraflores
Apartado Postal 1293
Santo Domingo, D.N.
Dominican Republic
Tel. +1 809 6824545
Fax +1 809 6823793
E-mail cruzrojadom@codetel.net.do

Ecuadorian Red Cross

Antonio Elizalde E 4-31
    y Av. Colombia (esq.)
Casilla 1701
2119 Quito
Ecuador
Tel. +593 2 2954587
Fax +593 2 2570424
E-mail difusio@attglobal.net
Web http://www.cruzroja-
    ecuador.org

Egyptian Red Crescent Society

Abd El Razek Al Sanhoury Street
8th District, Nasr City
7516 Cairo
Egypt
Tel. +20 2 6703979
Fax +20 2 6703967
E-mail erc@brainy1.ie-eg.com

Salvadorean Red Cross Society

17 C. Pte. y Av. Henri Dunant
Apartado Postal 2672
San Salvador
El Salvador
Tel. +503 2227749
Fax +503 2227758
E-mail crsalvador@vianet.com.sv
Web http://www.elsalvador.
    cruzroja.org

Red Cross of Equatorial Guinea

Alcalde Albilio Balboa 92
Apartado postal 460
Malabo
Equatorial Guinea
Tel. +240 9 3701
Fax +240 9 3701
E-mail crge@intnet.gq

Estonia Red Cross

Lai Street 17
0001 Tallinn
Estonia
Tel. +372 6411644
Fax +372 6411641
E-mail haide.laanemets@recross.ee

Ethiopian Red Cross Society

Ras Desta Damtew Avenue
P.O. Box 195
Addis Ababa
Ethiopia
Tel. +251 1 519074
Fax +251 1 512643
E-mail ercs@telecom.net.et

Fiji Red Cross Society

22 Gorrie Street
G.P.O. Box 569
Suva
Fiji
Tel. +679 3314133
Fax +679 3303818
E-mail redcross@connect.com.fj

Finnish Red Cross

Tehtaankatu 1a
P.O. Box 168
FIN-00141 Helsinki
Finland
Tel. +358 9 12931
Fax +358 9 1293226
E-mail forename.surname@redcross.fi
Web http://www.redcross.fi

French Red Cross

1, Place Henry-Dunant
F-75384 Paris Cedex 08
France
Tel. +33 1 44431100
Fax +33 1 44431101
E-mail communication@
    croix-rouge.net
Web http://www.croix-rouge.fr

Gabonese Red Cross Society

Place de l'Indépendance
Derrière le Mont de Cristal
Boîte Postale 2274
Libreville
Gabon
Tel. +241 766159
Fax +241 766160
E-mail gab.cross@internetgabon.com

The Gambia Red Cross Society

Kanifing Industrial Area
P.O. Box 472
Banjul
Gambia
Tel. +220 392405
Fax +220 394921
E-mail redcrossgam@gamtel.gm

Red Cross Society of Georgia

15, Krilov St.
380002 Tbilisi
Georgia
Tel. +995 32 961534
Fax +995 32 953304
E-mail georcs@hotmail.com

German Red Cross

General Sekretariat
Carstennstrasse 58
D-12205 Berlin
Germany
Tel. +49 30 85404-0
Fax +49 30 85404470
E-mail drk@drk.de
Web http://www.rotkreuz.de

Ghana Red Cross Society

Ministries Annex Block A3
Off Liberia Road Extension
P.O. Box 835
Accra
Ghana
Tel. +233 21 662298
Fax +233 21 661491
E-mail grcs@idngh.com

Hellenic Red Cross

Rue Lycavittou 1
Athens 106 72
Greece
Tel. +30 210 3621681
Fax +30 210 3615606
E-mail ir@redcross.gr
Web http://www.redcross.gr

Grenada Red Cross Society

Upper Lucas Street
P.O. Box 551
St. George's
Grenada
Tel. +1 473 4401483
Fax +1 473 4401829
E-mail grercs@caribsurf.com

Guatemalan Red Cross

3a Calle 8-40, Zona 1
Guatemala, C.A.
Guatemala
Tel. +502 25322027
Fax +502 25324649
E-mail crg@guate.net
Web http://www.guatemala.
    cruzroja.org

Red Cross Society of Guinea

B.P. 376
Conakry
Guinea
Tel. +224 13405237
Fax +224 414255
E-mail belly1961@yahoo.fr

Red Cross Society of Guinea-Bissau

Parça Herios Avacionais
Bissau
Guinea-Bissau
Tel. +245 201361
Fax +245 205202
E-mail cvgb@mail.gtelecom.gv

The Guyana Red Cross Society

Eve Leary
P.O. Box 10524
Georgetown
Guyana
Tel. +592 2 65174
Fax +592 2 77099
E-mail redcross@sdnp.org.gy
Web http://www.sdnp.org.gy/
    redcross/

Haitian National Red Cross Society

1, rue Eden
Bicentenaire
CRH–B.P. 1337
Port-au-Prince
Haiti
Tel. +509 5109813
Fax +509 2231054
E-mail croroha@haitiworld.com

Honduran Red Cross

7a Calle
    entre 1a. y 2a. Avenidas
Comayagüela D.C.
Honduras
Tel. +504 2378876
Fax +504 2380185
E-mail honducruz@datum.hn
Web http://www.honduras.
    cruzroja.org/

Hungarian Red Cross

Magyar Vöröskereszt
1367 Budapest 5, Pf. 121
Hungary
Tel. +36 1 3741338
Fax +36 1 3741312
E-mail intdept@hrc.hu

Icelandic Red Cross

Efstaleiti 9
103 Reykjavik
Iceland
Tel. +354 5704000
Fax +354 5704010
E-mail central@redcross.is
Web http://www.redcross.is

Indian Red Cross Society

Red Cross Building
1 Red Cross Road
110001 New Delhi
India
Tel. +91 112 3716424
Fax +91 112 3717454
E-mail indcross@vsnl.com
Web http://www.indianredcross.org

Indonesian Red Cross Society

Jl. Jenderal Datot Subroto Kav. 96
P.O. Box 2009
Jakarta
Indonesia
Tel. +62 21 7992325
Fax +62 21 7995188

Red Crescent Society of the Islamic Republic of Iran

Ostad Nejatolahi Ave.
Tehran
Iran, Islamic Republic of
Tel. +98 21 8849077
Fax +98 21 8849079
E-mail helal@mail.dci.co.ir
Web http://www.redcrescent.ir

Iraqi Red Crescent Society

Al-Mansour
P.O. Box 6143
Baghdad
Iraq
Tel. +964 1 8862191
Fax +964 1 5372519

Irish Red Cross Society
16, Merrion Square
Dublin 2
Ireland
Tel. +353 1 6765135
Fax +353 1 6614461
E-mail reception@redcross.ie
Web http://www.redcross.ie

Italian Red Cross
Via Toscana, 12
00187 Roma – RM
Italy
Tel. +39 06 4759263
Fax +39 06 4759223
E-mail webmaster@cri.rupa.it
Web http://www.cri.it

Jamaica Red Cross
Central Village, Spanish Town
St. Catherine
Kingston 5
Jamaica
Tel. +1 876 9847860
Fax +1 876 9848272
E-mail jrcs@infochan.com

Japanese Red Cross Society
1-3 Shiba Daimon, 1-Chome,
    Minato-ku
Tokyo-105-8521
Japan
Tel. +81 3 34377087
Fax +81 3 34358509
E-mail kokusai@jrc.or.jp
Web http://www.jrc.or.jp

Jordan National Red Crescent Society
Madaba Street
P.O. Box 10001
Amman 11151
Jordan
Tel. +962 64 773141
Fax +962 64 750815
E-mail jrc@index.com.jo

Kazakh Red Crescent Society
Kunaev Street 86
480100 Almaty
Kazakhstan, Republic of
Tel. +73272 916291
Fax +73272 918172
E-mail Kazrc2@yahoo.co.k

Kenya Red Cross Society
Nairobi South "C"
Belle Vue, off Mombasa Road
P.O. Box 40712
Nairobi
Kenya
Tel. +254 20 603593
Fax +254 20 603589
E-mail kenyaredcross@kenyaweb.org

Kiribati Red Cross Society
P.O. Box 213
Bikenibeu
Tarawa
Kiribati
Tel. +686 28128
Fax +686 21416
E-mail redcross@tskl.net.ki

Red Cross Society of the Democratic People's Republic of Korea
Ryonwa 1, Central District
Pyongyang
Korea, Democratic People's
    Republic of
Tel. +850 2 18333
Fax +850 2 3814644

The Republic of Korea National Red Cross
32 - 3ka, Namsan-dong
Choong-Ku
Seoul 100 – 043
Korea, Republic of
Tel. +82 2 37053705
Fax +82 2 37053667
E-mail knrc@redcross.or.kr
Web http://www.redcross.or.kr

Kuwait Red Crescent Society
Al-Jahra Street, Shuweek
P.O. Box 1359
Kuwait
Tel. +965 4815478
Fax +965 4839114
E-mail krcs@kuwait.net

Red Crescent Society of Kyrgyzstan
10, prospekt Erkindik
720040 Bishkek
Kyrgyzstan
Tel. +996 312 624814
Fax +996 312 662181
E-mail redcross@elcat.kg

Lao Red Cross
Impasse XiengNhune
Avenue Sethathirath
B.P. 650
Vientiane
Lao People's Democratic Republic
Tel. +856 21 242467
Fax +856 21 212128
E-mail lrchqod@laotel.com

Latvian Red Cross
1, Skolas Street
Riga, LV-1010
Latvia
Tel. +371 7336651
Fax +371 7336652
E-mail secretariat@redcross.lv

Lebanese Red Cross
Rue Spears
Beyrouth
Lebanon
Tel. +961 1 372802
Fax +961 1 378207
E-mail redcross@dm.net.lb
Web http://www.dm.net.lb/
    redcross/

Lesotho Red Cross Society

23 Mabile Road
Old Europe
Maseru 100
Lesotho
Tel. +266 22 313911
Fax +266 22 310166
E-mail redcross@redcross.org.ls

Liberian Red Cross Society

National Headquarters
107 Lynch Street
P.O. Box 20-5081
1000 Monrovia 20
Liberia
Tel. +888 330125
Fax +231 330125
E-mail lnrc@Liberia.net

Libyan Red Crescent

General Secretariat
P.O. Box 541
Benghazi
Libyan Arab Jamahiriya
Tel. +218 61 9095202
Fax +218 61 9095829
E-mail libyan_redcrescent@
    libyamail.net

Liechtenstein Red Cross

Heiligkreuz 25
FL-9490 Vaduz
Liechtenstein
Tel. +423 2322294
Fax +423 2322240
E-mail info@lieredcross.li

Lithuanian Red Cross Society

Gedimino ave. 3a
2600 Vilnius
Lithuania
Tel. +370 52 628037
Fax +370 52 619923
E-mail international@redcross.lt
Web http://www.redcross.lt

Luxembourg Red Cross

44 Bd Joseph II
L - 2014 Luxembourg
Tel. +352 450202
Fax +352 457269
E-mail siege@croix-rouge.lu
Web http://www.croix-rouge.lu/

The Red Cross of The Former Yugoslav Republic of Macedonia

No. 13
Bul. Koco Racin
91000 Skopje
Macedonia, The Former Yugoslav
    Republic of
Tel. +389 23 114355
Fax +389 23 230542
E-mail mrc@mol.com.mk

Malagasy Red Cross Society

1, rue Patrice Lumumba
Tsaralalana
B.P. 1168
Antananarivo
Madagascar
Tel. +261 20 2222111
Fax +261 20 2266739
E-mail crm@dts.mg

Malawi Red Cross Society

Red Cross House
Along Presidential Way
P.O. Box 30096
Lilongwe
Malawi
Tel. +265 1 775377
Fax +265 1 775590
E-mail mrcs@eomw.net

Malaysian Red Crescent Society

JKR 32, Jalan Nipah
Off Jalan Ampang
55000 Kuala Lumpur
Malaysia
Tel. +60 3 42578122
Fax +60 3 4533191
E-mail mrcs@po.jaring.my
Web http://www.redcrescent.org.my/

Mali Red Cross

Route Koulikoro
B.P. 280
Bamako
Mali
Tel. +223 244569
Fax +223 240414
E-mail crmalienne@afribone.net.ml

Malta Red Cross Society

104 St Ursula Street
Valletta VLT 05
Malta
Tel. +356 21222645
Fax +356 21243664
E-mail redcross@redcross.org.mt
Web http://www.redcross.org.mt

Mauritanian Red Crescent

Avenue Gamal Abdel Nasser
B.P. 344
Nouakchott
Mauritania
Tel. +222 5251249
Fax +222 5291221
E-mail croissant_mau@yahoo.fr

Mauritius Red Cross Society

Ste. Thérèse Street
Curepipe
Mauritius
Tel. +230 6763604
Fax +230 6748855
E-mail redcross@intnet.mu

Mexican Red Cross

Calle Luis Vives 200
Colonia Polanco
México, D.F. 11510
Mexico
Tel. +52 55 53955605
Fax +52 55 55575529
E-mail cruzroja@mexporta.com
Web http://www.mexico.
    cruzroja.org

Micronesia Red Cross

P.O. Box 2405, Kolonia
Pohnpei
Micronesia, Federated States of
Tel. +691 3207077
Fax +691 3206531
E-mail mrcs@mail.fm

Red Cross Society of the Republic of Moldova

67a, Ulitsa Asachi
MD-277028 Chisinau
Moldova, Republic of
Tel. +373 2 729644
Fax +373 2 729700
E-mail moldova-RC@mdl.net

Red Cross of Monaco

27, Boulevard de Suisse
98000 Monte Carlo
Monaco
Tel. +377 97 976800
Fax +377 93 159047
E-mail redcross@croix-rouge.mc
Web http://www.croix-rouge.mc

Mongolian Red Cross Society

Central Post Office
Post Box 537
Ulaanbaatar 13
Mongolia
Tel. +976 11 312578
Fax +976 11 320934
E-mail redcross@magicnet.mn

Moroccan Red Crescent

Palais Mokri
Takaddoum
B.P. 189
Rabat
Morocco
Tel. +212 37 650898
Fax +212 37 653280
E-mail crm@iam.net.ma

Mozambique Red Cross Society

Avenida Agostinho Neto 284
Caixa Postal 2986
Maputo
Mozambique
Tel. +258 1 490943
Fax +258 1 497725
E-mail cvm@redcross.org.mz

Myanmar Red Cross Society

Red Cross Building
42 Strand Road
Yangon
Myanmar
Tel. +95 1 296552
Fax +95 1 296551
E-mail mrcsem@mptmail.mm

Namibia Red Cross

Red Cross House
Erf 2128, Independence Avenue
Katutura
P.O. Box 346
Windhoek
Namibia
Tel. +264 61 235216
Fax +264 61 228949
E-mail namcross@redcross.org.na

Nepal Red Cross Society

Red Cross Marg
Kalimati
P.O. Box 217
Kathmandu
Nepal
Tel. +977 1 4270650
Fax +977 1 4271915
E-mail nrcs@nrcs.org
Web http://www.nrcs.org

The Netherlands Red Cross

Leeghwaterplein 27
2502 KC The Hague
Netherlands
Tel. +31 70 4455666
Fax +31 70 4455777
E-mail hq@redcross.nl
Web http://www.rodekruis.nl

New Zealand Red Cross

69 Molesworth Street
Thorndon
Wellington 6038
New Zealand
Tel. +64 4 4723750
Fax +64 4 4730315
E-mail national@redcross.org.nz
Web http://www.redcross.org.nz

Nicaraguan Red Cross

Reparto Belmonte
Carretera Sur, km 7
Apartado 3279
Managua
Nicaragua
Tel. +505 2 650380
Fax +505 2 651643
E-mail crnsalud@ibw.ni
Web http://www.nicaragua.
   cruzroja.org

Red Cross Society of Niger

B.P. 11386
N° 655, rue NB 045
Niamey
Niger
Tel. +227 733037
Fax +227 732461
E-mail crniger@intnet.ne

Nigerian Red Cross Society

11, Eko Akete Close
Off St. Gregory's Road
South West Ikoyi
P.O. Box 764
Lagos
Nigeria
Tel. +234 1 2695188
Fax +234 1 2691599
E-mail nrcs@wananet.net

Norwegian Red Cross

Hausmannsgate 7
Postbox 1 – Gronland
0133 Oslo
Norway
Tel. +47 22054000
Fax +47 22054040
E-mail documentation.center@
    redcross.no
Web http://www.redcross.no

Pakistan Red Crescent Society

Sector H-8
Islamabad
Pakistan
Tel. +92 51 9257404
Fax +92 51 9257408
E-mail hilal@comsats.net.pk
Web http://www.prcs.org.pk

Palau Red Cross Society

P.O. Box 6043
Koror 96940
Republic of Palau
Tel. +680 4885780
Fax +680 4884540
E-mail palredcross@palaunet.com

Red Cross Society of Panama

Albrook, Areas Revertidas
Calle Principal
Edificio # 453
Apartado 668
Zona 1
Panama
Tel. +507 3151389
Fax +507 3151401
E-mail cruzroja@pan.gbm.net
Web http://www.panama.
    cruzroja.org

Papua New Guinea Red Cross Society

Taurama Road
Port Moresby
P.O. Box 6545
Boroko
Papua New Guinea
Tel. +675 3258577
Fax +675 3259714
E-mail hqpngrcs@online.net.pg

Paraguayan Red Cross

Brasil 216 esq. José Berges
Asunción
Paraguay
Tel. +595 21 222797
Fax +595 21 211560
E-mail crpveids@uninet.com.py
Web http://www.cruzroja.org.py

Peruvian Red Cross

Av. Arequipa N° 1285
Lima
Peru
Tel. +51 1 2658783
Fax +51 1 4710701
E-mail cruzrojaperuana@
    cruzroja.org.pe
Web http://www.cruzroja.org.pe

The Philippine National Red Cross

Bonifacio Drive
Port Area
P.O. Box 280
Manila 2803
Philippines
Tel. +63 2 5278386
Fax +63 2 5270857
E-mail pnrcnhq@redcross.org.ph

Polish Red Cross

Mokotowska 14
P.O. Box 47
00-950 Warsaw
Poland
Tel. +48 22 3261286
Fax +48 22 6284168
E-mail head.office@pck.org.pl
Web http://www.pck.org.pl

Portuguese Red Cross

Campo Grande, 28-6th
1700-093 Lisboa
Portugal
Tel. +351 21 3905571
Fax +351 21 7822454
E-mail internacional@
    cruzvermelha.org.pt

Qatar Red Crescent Society

P.O. Box 5449
Doha
Qatar
Tel. +974 4 435111
Fax +974 4 439950
E-mail info@qrcs.net

Romanian Red Cross

Strada Biserica Amzei, 29
Sector 1
Bucarest
Romania
Tel. +40 21 2129862
Fax +40 21 3128452
E-mail crr@xnet.ro

The Russian Red Cross Society

Tcheryomushkinski Proezd 5
117036 Moscow
Russian Federation
Tel. +7 095 1265731
Fax +7 095 3107048
E-mail mail@redcross.ru

Rwandan Red Cross

B.P. 425, Kacyiru
Kigali
Rwanda
Tel. +250 585446
Fax +250 585449
E-mail rrc@rwandate11.com

International Federation
of Red Cross and Red Crescent Societies

Saint Kitts and Nevis Red Cross Society

National Headquarters
Horsford Road
P.O. Box 62
Basseterre
Saint Kitts and Nevis
Tel. +1 869 4652584
Fax +1 869 4668129
E-mail skbredcr@caribsurf.com

Saint Lucia Red Cross

Vigie
P.O. Box 271
Castries St Lucia, W.I.
Saint Lucia
Tel. +1 758 4525582
Fax +1 758 4537811
E-mail sluredcross@candw.lc

Saint Vincent and the Grenadines Red Cross

Halifax Street
Minister of Education Compound
Kingstown
P.O. Box 431
Saint Vincent and the Grenadines
Tel. +1 784 4561888
Fax +1 784 4856210
E-mail svgredcross@caribsurf.com

Samoa Red Cross Society

P.O. Box 1616
Apia
Samoa
Tel. +685 23686
Fax +685 22676
E-mail samoaredcross@samoa.ws

Red Cross of the Republic of San Marino

Via Scialoja, Cailungo
Republic of San Marino 47031
Tel. +37 8 994360
Fax +37 8 994360
E-mail crs@omniway.sm
Web http://www.tradecenter.sm/crs

São Tomé and Principe Red Cross

Avenida 12 de Julho No.11
B.P. 96
São Tomé
São Tomé and Principe
Tel. +239 12 22469
Fax +239 12 22305
E-mail cvstp@sol.stome.telepac.net

Saudi Arabian Red Crescent Society

General Headquarters
Riyadh 11129
Saudi Arabia
Tel. +966 1 4740027
Fax +966 1 4740430
E-mail redcrescent@zajil.net

Senegalese Red Cross Society

Boulevard F. Roosevelt
B.P. 299
Dakar
Senegal
Tel. +221 8233992
Fax +221 8225369
E-mail crspsc@sentoo.sn

The Red Cross of Serbia and Montenegro

Simina 19
11000 Belgrade
Serbia and Montenegro
Tel. +381 11 2623564
Fax +381 11 2622965
E-mail indep@jck.org.yu
Web http://www.jck.org/yu

Seychelles Red Cross Society

Place de la République
B.P. 53
Victoria, Mahé
Seychelles
Tel. +248 324646
Fax +248 321663
E-mail redcross@seychelles.net
Web http://www.seychelles.net/
   redcross

Sierra Leone Red Cross Society

6 Liverpool Street
P.O. Box 427
Freetown
Sierra Leone
Tel. +232 22 229854
Fax +232 22 229083
E-mail slrcs@sierratel.sl

Singapore Red Cross Society

Red Cross House
15 Penang Lane
Singapore 238486
Tel. +65 6 3360269
Fax +65 6 3374360
E-mail redcross@starhub.net.sg
Web http://www.redcross.org.sg

Slovak Red Cross

Grösslingova 24
814 46 Bratislava
Slovakia
Tel. +421 2 5296518
Fax +421 2 5292356
E-mail headq@redcross.sk

Slovenian Red Cross

Mirje 19
P.O. Box 236
SI-61000 Ljubljana
Slovenia
Tel. +386 1 2414300
Fax +386 1 2414344
E-mail rdeci.kriz@rks.si

The Solomon Islands Red Cross

P.O. Box 187
Honiara
Solomon Islands
Tel. +677 22682
Fax +677 25299
E-mail sirc@solomon.com.sb

Somali Red Crescent Society

c/o ICRC Box 73226
Nairobi
Kenya
Tel. +252 1 216049 Mogadishu
     +254 2 2713785 Nairobi
Fax +252 5943880 Mogadishu
     +254 2 2718 862 Nairobi
E-mail srcsnai@iconnect.co.ke
Web http://www.bishacas.org

The South African Red Cross Society

1st Floor, Helen Bowden Bldg
Beach Road, Granger Bay
P.O. Box 50696, Waterfront
Cape Town 8002
South Africa
Tel. +27 21 4186640
Fax +27 21 4186644
E-mail sarcs@redcross.org.za
Web http://www.redcross.org.za

Spanish Red Cross

Rafael Villa, s/n Vuelta Ginés
     Navarro
28023 El Plantio
Madrid
Spain
Tel. +34 91 3354637
Fax +34 91 3354455
E-mail informa@cruzroja.es
Web http://www.cruzroja.es

The Sri Lanka Red Cross Society

307, 2/1 T.B. Jayah Mawatha
P.O. Box 375
Colombo 10
Sri Lanka
Tel. +94 75 370725
Fax +94 75 367462
E-mail slrc@sri.lanka.net

The Sudanese Red Crescent

P.O. Box 235
Khartoum
Sudan
Tel. +249 11 772011
Fax +249 11 772877
E-mail srcs@sudanmail.net

Suriname Red Cross

Gravenberchstraat 2
Postbus 2919
Paramaribo
Suriname
Tel. +597 498410
Fax +597 464780
E-mail surcross@sr.net

Baphalali Swaziland Red Cross Society

104 Johnstone Street
P.O. Box 377
Mbabane
Swaziland
Tel. +268 4042532
Fax +268 4046108
E-mail bsrcs@redcross.sz

Swedish Red Cross

Hornsgatan 54
Box 17563
SE-118 91 Stockholm
Sweden
Tel. +46 8 4524600
Fax +46 8 4524761
E-mail postmaster@redcross.se
Web http://www.redcross.se

Swiss Red Cross

Rainmattstrasse 10
Postfach
3001 Bern
Switzerland
Tel. +41 31 3877111
Fax +41 31 3877122
E-mail info@redcross.ch
Web http://www.redcross.ch

Syrian Arab Red Crescent

Al Malek Aladel Street
Damascus
Syrian Arab Republic
Tel. +963 11 4429662
Fax +963 11 4425677
E-mail SARC@net.sy

Red Crescent Society of Tajikistan

120, Omari Khayom St.
734017 Dushanbe
Tajikistan
Tel. +7 3772 240374
Fax +7 3772 245378
E-mail rcstj@yahoo.com

Tanzania Red Cross National Society

Ali Hassan Mwinyi Road
Plot 294/295
P.O. Box 1133
Dar es Salaam
Tanzania, United Republic of
Tel. +255 22 2150881
Fax +255 22 2150147
E-mail logistics@raha.com

The Thai Red Cross Society

Terd Prakiat Building, 4th Floor
1871 Henry Dunant Road
Bangkok 10330
Thailand
Tel. +66 2 2564037
Fax +66 2 2553064
E-mail wmaster@redcross.or.th
Web http://www.redcross.or.th

Togolese Red Cross

51, rue Boko Soga
Amoutivé
B.P. 655
Lome
Togo
Tel. +228 2212110
Fax +228 2215228
E-mail crtogol@syfed.tg.refer.org

Tonga Red Cross Society
P.O. Box 456
Nuku'Alofa
South West Pacific
Tonga
Tel. +676 21360
Fax +676 21508
E-mail redcross@kalianet.to

The Trinidad and Tobago Red Cross Society
7A, Fitz Blackman Drive
Wrightson Road
P.O. Box 357
Port of Spain
Trinidad and Tobago
Tel. +1 868 6278128
Fax +1 868 6278215
E-mail ttrcs@carib-link.net

Tunisian Red Crescent
19, Rue d'Angleterre
Tunis 1000
Tunisia
Tel. +216 71 325572
Fax +216 71 320151
E-mail hilal.ahmar@planet.tn

Turkish Red Crescent Society
Atac Sokak 1 No. 32
Yenisehir, Ankara
Turkey
Tel. +90 312 4302300
Fax +90 312 4300175
E-mail international@kizilay.org.tr
Web http://www.kizilay.org.tr

Red Crescent Society of Turkmenistan
48 A. Novoi str.
744000 Ashgabat
Turkmenistan
Tel. +993 12 395511
Fax +993 12 351750
E-mail nrcst@online.tm

The Uganda Red Cross Society
Plot 28/30 Lumumba Avenue
Kampala
Uganda
Tel. +256 41 258701
Fax +256 41 258184
E-mail sgurcs@redcross.org

Ukrainian Red Cross Society
30, Pushkinskaya St.
252004 Kiev
Ukraine
Tel. +380 44 2350157
Fax +380 44 2465658
E-mail redcross@ukrpack.net
Web http://www.redcross.org.ua

Red Crescent Society of the United Arab Emirates
P.O. Box 3324
Abu Dhabi
United Arab Emirates
Tel. +9 712 6419000
Fax +9 712 6420101
E-mail hilalrc@emirates.net.ae

British Red Cross
9 Grosvenor Crescent
London SW1X 7EJ
United Kingdom
Tel. +44 207 2355454
Fax +44 207 2456315
E-mail information@redcross.org.uk
Web http://www.redcross.org.uk

American Red Cross
2025 E Street NW, 8th Floor
NW 8088C
Washington, DC 20006
United States of America
Tel. +1 202 3035279
Fax +1 202 3030054
E-mail postmaster@usa.redcross.org
Web http://www.redcross.org

Uruguayan Red Cross
Avenida 8 de Octubre, 2990
11600 Montevideo
Uruguay
Tel. +598 2 4802112
Fax +598 2 4800714
E-mail cruzroja@adinet.com.uy
Web http://www.uruguay.
cruzroja.org

Red Crescent Society of Uzbekistan
30, Yusuf Hos Hojib St.
700031 Tashkent
Uzbekistan
Tel. +988 712 563741
Fax +988 712 561801
E-mail RCUZ@uzpak.uz
Web http://www.redcrescent.uz

Vanuatu Red Cross Society
P.O. Box 618
Port Vila
Vanuatu
Tel. +678 27418
Fax +678 22599
E-mail redcross@vanuatu.com.vu

Venezuelan Red Cross
Avenida Andrés Bello, 4
Apartado 3185
Caracas 1010
Venezuela
Tel. +58 212 5714380
Fax +58 212 5761042
E-mail dirnacsoc@cantv.net
Web http://www.venezuela.
cruzroja.org

Red Cross of Viet Nam
82, Nguyen Du Street
Hanoï
Viet Nam
Tel. +844 8 225157
Fax +844 9 424285
E-mail vnrchq@netnam.org.vn
Web http://www.vnrc.org.vn

Yemen Red Crescent Society

Head Office, Building No. 10
26 September Street
P.O. Box 1257
Sanaa
Yemen
Tel. +967 1 283132
Fax +967 1 283131

Zambia Red Cross Society

2837 Los Angeles Boulevard
Longacres
P.O. Box 50001 Ridgeway 15101
Lusaka
Zambia
Tel. +260 1 253661
Fax +260 1 252219
E-mail zrcs@zamnet.zm

Zimbabwe Red Cross Society

Red Cross House
98 Cameron Street
P.O. Box 1406
Harare
Zimbabwe
Tel. +263 4 775416
Fax +263 4 751739
E-mail zrcs@ecoweb.co.zw

International Federation regional delegations

Yaoundé

Rue Mini-Prix Bastos
BP 11507
Yaoundé
Cameroon
Tel. +237 2217437
Fax +237 2217439
E-mail ifrccm04@ifrc.org

Beijing

Apt. 4-2-51 Building 4, Entrance 2,
    Floor 5, Apt.1
Jianguomenwai Diplomatic
    Compound
Chaoyang District
Beijing 100600
China
Tel. +8610 65327162
Fax +8610 65327166
E-mail ifrccn14@ifrc.org

Suva

P.O. Box 2507
Government Building
Suva
Fiji
Tel. +679 311855
Fax +679 311406
E-mail ifrcrds@is.com.fj

Budapest

Zolyomi Lepcso Ut 22
1124 Budapest
Hungary
Tel. +361 2483300
Fax +361 2483322
E-mail ifrchu01@ifrc.org

New Delhi

C-1/35 Safdarjung Development
    Area
New Delhi 110 016
India
Tel. +9111 26858671
Fax +9111 26857567
E-mail ifrcin01@ifrc.org

Amman

Al Shmeisani
Maroof Al Rasafi Street
Building No. 19
P.O. Box 830511 / Zahran
Amman
Jordan
Tel. +962 6 5681060
Fax +962 6 5694556
E-mail ifrcjo01@ifrc.org

Almaty

86, Kunaeva Street
480100 Almaty
Kazakhstan, Republic of
Tel. +732 72 918838
Fax +732 72 914267
E-mail ifrckz01@ifrc.org

Nairobi

Woodlands Road (off State House
    Road)
P.O. Box 41275
Nairobi
Kenya
Tel. +254 20 2714255
Fax +254 20 2718415
E-mail ifrcke01@ifrc.org

Panama

Clayton, Ciudad del Saber # 804 A/B
Ciudad de Panamá
Panama, República de Panamá
Tel. +507 317 1300
Fax +507 317 1304
E-mail ifrcpa50@ifrc.org

Lima

Los Naranjos 351
San Isidro, Lima
Peru
Tel. +511 2219006
Fax +511 4413607
E-mail ifrcpe07@ifrc.org

Dakar

VDN x Ancienne Piste, Mermoz
    Pyrotechnie
Boite Postale 25956
Dakar – Fann
Senegal
Tel. +221 869 36 40
Fax +221 860 20 02
E-mail ifrcsn20@ ifrc.org

International Federation
of Red Cross and Red Crescent Societies

Bangkok
18th Floor, Ocean Tower 2
75/26 Sukhumvit 19
Wattana
Bangkok 10110
Thailand
Tel. +662 6616933
Fax +662 6616937
E-mail ifrcth02@ifrc.org

Ankara
Cemal Nadir Sokak, No.9
Cankaya
Ankara 06680
Turkey
Tel. +90312 441 42 92
Fax +90312 441 3866
E-mail ifrctr06@ifrc.org

Harare
42 Bates Street
Milton Park
Harare
Zimbabwe
Tel. +2634 705166
Fax +2634 708784
E-mail ifrczw01@ifrc.org

International Federation country delegations

Afghanistan
Estgah Dawa Khana
Shash Darak, House 61
Kabul
Afghanistan
Tel. +873 382280530
Fax +873 382280534
E-mail kabuldel@wireless.ifrc.org

Angola
Caixa Postal 3324
Rua 1 Congresso de MPLA 27/27
Luanda
Angola
Tel. +2442 393652
Fax +2442 372868
E-mail ifrcao01@ifrc.org

Armenia
Gevorg Chaush St. 50/1
Yerevan 375088
Armenia
Tel. +3741 354649
Fax +3741 400491
E-mail ifrcam03@ifrc.org

Azerbaijan
S. Safarov Street 2
Baku, Nesimi District
PC 370010
Azerbaijan
Tel. +99412 983772
Fax +99412 985501
E-mail ifrcaz01@ifrc.org

Bangladesh
c/o Bangladesh Red Crescent
    Society
684-686 Bara Magh Bazar
Dhaka – 1217
Bangladesh
Tel. +8802 8315401
Fax +8802 9341631
E-mail ifrcbd@citecho.net

Belarus
Ulitsa Mayakovkosgo 14
Minsk 220006
Belarus
Tel. +375172 217237
Fax +375172 219060
E-mail ifrcby01@ifrc.org

Burundi
Avenue des Etats-Unis 3674A
B.P. 324
Bujumbura
Burundi
Tel. +254 20 2714255
Fax +257 20 2718415
E-mail ifrcke01@ifrc.org

Cambodia
17 Deo, Street Croix-Rouge
Central Post Office/P.O. Box 620
Phnom Penh
Cambodia
Tel. +855 23 210162
Fax +855 23 210163
E-mail ifrckh01@ifrc.org

Congo, Democratic Republic of the
21 Avenue Flamboyant
Place de Sefoutiers
Gombe, Kinshasa
Democratic Republic of the Congo
Tel. +871 763050365
Fax +871 763050366
E-mail hod@ficr.aton.cd

East Timor
Bidau-Santana Rua de Cristo Rei s/n
Dili
East Timor
Tel. +670 390 322778
Fax +670 390 322778
E-mail ifrc_east_timor01@ifrc.org

El Salvador
c/o Salvadorean Red Cross Society
Apartado Postal 1401
17 calle Poniente y
    Av. Henry Dunant
Centro de Gobierno, San Salvador
El Salvador
Tel. +503 2222166
Fax +503 2811932
E-mail ifrcsv11@ifrc.org

Eritrea
c/o Red Cross Society of Eritrea
Andnet Street
P.O. Box 575
Asmara
Eritrea
Tel. +2911 150550
Fax +2911 151859
E-mail ifrc@eol.com.er

Ethiopia

Ras Desta Damtew Avenue
P.O. Box 195
Addis Ababa
Ethiopia
Tel. +2511 514571
Fax +2511 512888
E-mail ifrcet04@ifrc.org

Georgia

54, Chavchavadze Ave., Apt. 18
380079 Tbilisi
Georgia
Tel. +99532 922248
Fax +99532 922248
E-mail ifrcge01@ifrc.org

Guatemala

c/o Guatemala Red Cross
3A Calle 8-40, Zona 1, 2no Nivel
Guatemala, C.A.
Guatemala
Tel. +502 2537351
Fax +502 2380091
E-mail fedecng@intelnet.net.gt

Guinea

Coleah, route du Niger
    (derrière la station Shell)
Près de l'Ambassade
    de Yougoslavie
B.P. No 376
Conakry
Guinea
Tel. +224 413825
Fax +224 414255
E-mail ifrc.gn01@ifrc.org

India

Red Cross Building
1 Red Cross Road
110001 New Delhi
India
Tel. +9111 23324203
Fax +9111 23324235
E-mail ifrcin65@ifrc.org

Indonesia

c/o Indonesian Red Cross Society
P.O. Box 2009
Jakarta
Indonesia
Tel. +6221 79191841
Fax +6221 79180905
E-mail ifrcid01@ifrc.org

Iran

c/o Iranian Red Crescent Society
Ostad Nejatollahi Avenue
Tehran
Islamic Republic of Iran
Tel. +98 21 889 0567
Fax +98 21 889 5346
E-mail ifrcir01@ifrc.org

Iraq

c/o Iraqi Red Crescent Society
P.O. Box 6143
Baghdad
Iraq
Tel. +964 1 7783628
Fax +964 1 5372519
E-mail ifrciq10@ifrc.org

Korea, DPR

c/o Red Cross Society of the
    DPR Korea
Ryonwa 1, Central District
Pyongyang
Korea, Democratic People's
Republic of
Tel. +8502 3814350
Fax +8502 3813490

Laos

c/o Lao Red Cross
P.O. Box 2948
Setthatirath Road, Xiengnhune
Vientiane
Lao People's Democratic Republic
Tel. +856 21215762
Fax +856 21215935
E-mail laoifrc@laotel.com

Lebanon

c/o Lebanese Red Cross
Rue Spears
Beyrouth
Lebanon
Tel. +961 1 365 374
Fax +961 1 365 046
E-mail ifrclb03@ifrc.org

Mongolia

c/o Red Cross Society of Mongolia
Central Post Office
Post Box 537
Ulaanbaatar
Mongolia
Tel. +97611 321684
Fax +97611 321684
E-mail ifrcmongol@magicnet.mn

Myanmar

c/o Myanmar Red Cross Society
42 Strand Road
Yangon
Myanmar
Tel. +951 297877
Fax +951 297877
E-mail ifrc@mptmail.net.mm

Nicaragua

c/o Nicaraguan Red Cross
Reparto Belmonte, Carretera Sur
Km 71/2
Apartado Postal P-48
    Las Piedrecitas
Managua
Nicaragua
Tel. +505 2650186
Fax +505 2652069

Nigeria

c/o Nigerian Red Cross Society
11, Eko Akete Close
Off St. Gregory's Road
South West Ikoyi
P.O. Box 764
Lagos
Nigeria
Tel. +2341 2695228
Fax +2341 2695229
E-mail ifrcng02@ifrc.org

International Federation
of Red Cross and Red Crescent Societies

Pakistan

c/o Pakistan Red Crescent Society
National Headquarters
Sector H-8
Islamabad
Pakistan
Tel. +9251 9257122
Fax +9251 4430745
E-mail ifrcpk@ifrc.org

Palestine

P.O.Box 18646
Jerusalem 91184
Israel
Tel. +972 2 2400485
Fax +972 2 2400484
E-mail ifrcpal01@ifrc.org

Papua New Guinea

c/o PNG Red Cross
P.O. Box 6545
Boroko
Papua New Guinea
Tel. +675 3112277
Fax +675 3230731

Russian Federation

c/o Russian Red Cross Society
Tcheryomushkinski Proezd 5
117036 Moscow
Russian Federation
Tel. +7095 9375267
Fax +70959375263
E-mail moscow@ifrc.org

Rwanda

c/o Rwandan Red Cross
B.P. 425, Kacyiru
Kigali
Rwanda
Tel. +250 585447
Fax +250 585447
E-mail ifrcrw01@ifrc.org

Serbia and Montenegro

Simina Ulica Broj 21
11000 Belgrade
Serbia and Montenegro
Tel. +381 11 3282202
Fax +381 11 3281791
E-mail telecom@ifrc.org.yu

Sierra Leone

c/o Sierra Leone Red Cross Society
6, Liverpool Street
P.O. Box 427
Freetown
Sierra Leone
Tel. +23222 227772
Fax +23222 228180
E-mail ifrcsl01@ifrc.org

Somalia

c/o Regional Delegation Nairobi
Woodlands Road, off
    State House Road
P.O. Box 41275
Nairobi
Kenya
Tel. +254 20 2728294
Fax +254 20 2718415
E-mail ifrcso01@ifrc.org

South Africa

c/o South African Red Cross
1st Floor, Helen Bowden Bldg
Beach Road, Granger Bay
P.O. Box 50696, Waterfront
Cape Town 8002
South Africa
Tel. +27 21 4186640
Fax +27 21 4186644
E-mail ifrcsa15@ifrc.org

Sri Lanka

3rd floor, 307 T B Jayah Mawatha
LK Colombo
Sri Lanka
Tel. +9411 4715977
Fax +9411 4715978
E-mail ifrclk01@srilanka.net

Sudan

Al Mak Nimir Street/
    Gamhouria Street
Plot No 1, Block No 4
P.O. Box 10697
East Khartoum
Sudan
Tel. +24911 771033
Fax +24911 770484
E-mail ifrcsd01@ifrc.org

Tajikistan

c/o Tajikistan Red Crescent Society
120, Omar Khayom St.
734017 Dushanbe
Tajikistan
Tel. +992372 245981
Fax +992372 248520
E-mail ifrcdsb@ifrc.org

Tanzania

c/o Tanzania Red Cross Society
Ali Hassan Mwinyi Road
Plot No. 294/295
P.O. Box 1133
Dar es Salaam
Tanzania, United Republic of
Tel. +255 22 2116514
Fax +255 22 2117308
E-mail ifrctz02@ifrc.org

Viet Nam

19 Mai Hac De Street
Hanoï
Viet Nam
Tel. +844 9438250
Fax +844 9436177
E-mail ifrc@hn.vnn.vn

International Federation
of Red Cross and Red Crescent Societies

International Conference prioritizes risk reduction

The 28th International Conference of the Red Cross and Red Crescent took place in Geneva from 6 to 8 December 2003. The International Conference brings together all the components of the Red Cross and Red Crescent Movement: 181 National Societies, their International Federation, the International Committee of the Red Cross (ICRC) and the 191 states party to the Geneva Conventions. Together they examine and decide upon humanitarian matters of common interest and any other related matter.

The International Conference resulted in a declaration, an "Agenda for Humanitarian Action" and pledges on individual or collective action. The Agenda for Humanitarian Action focuses on the main theme and overall goal of the International Conference, namely "Protecting Human Dignity", and sets out action-oriented goals and measures that states and the components of the International Red Cross and Red Crescent Movement can undertake to protect human dignity.

Four humanitarian concerns are addressed in the Agenda, the third of which is "to reduce the risk and impact of disasters and improve preparedness and response mechanisms".

This concern builds on long Red Cross and Red Crescent experience of the importance of improving disaster preparedness and response, and at the same time reducing risk and increasing capacity in a national context. Reducing risk was the theme explored and analysed in the *World Disasters Report 2002: Focus on risk reduction*. This year's *World Disasters Report* develops the same theme by arguing that building on people's capacity and supporting resilience is an underestimated area, demanding increased attention.

The objective, goals and actions for reducing disaster risks and impacts proposed in the Agenda for Humanitarian Action are quoted in full below. They form a strong recommendation to the United Nations' World Conference on Disaster Reduction, to be held in Kobe/Hyogo, Japan, in January 2005, ten years after the first World Conference on Disaster Reduction in Yokohama.

Photo opposite page: Devastating floods swept through Haiti and the Dominican Republic in late May 2004, killing at least 2,000 people and destroying crops and homes. Reducing disaster risks through better preparedness and response is vital to safeguard development in the world's poorest regions.

Marko Kokic/ International Federation.

Reducing the risk
and impact of disasters

General Objective 3 – Minimize the impact of disasters through implementation of disaster risk reduction measures and improving preparedness and response mechanisms

The aim is to protect human dignity, lives and livelihoods from the devastating impact of disasters:

- by fully integrating disaster risk reduction into national and international planning and policy instruments and implementing appropriate operational measures to reduce risks, and
- by implementing appropriate legal, policy and operational measures to facilitate and expedite effective responses to disasters,
- in order to reduce the risks and effects of disasters on marginalized and vulnerable populations.

Final Goal 3.1 – Acknowledge the importance of disaster risk reduction and undertake measures to minimize the impact of disasters on vulnerable populations

Comprehensive disaster risk reduction, including disaster management, prevention and mitigation can be achieved through education and awareness-raising activities. Other measures to minimize the impact of disasters include: effective management of natural resources and protection of the environment; the implementation of early warning systems; ensuring that building codes, particularly in disaster prone countries, are implemented and enforced to limit suffering caused by structural damage; supporting sustainable recovery; and optimising capacity-building opportunities for vulnerable populations.

Of particular importance is directing such efforts towards populations that are most at risk, including those marginalized because of poverty, discrimination or social exclusion, or those that do not have access to disaster preparedness and response services as a consequence of their circumstances or legal status.

Actions proposed

3.1.1 States should, in accordance with the United Nations International Strategy for Disaster Reduction, review their existing legislation and policies to fully integrate disaster risk reduction strategies into all relevant legal, policy and planning instruments in order to address the social, economic, political and environmental dimensions that influence vulnerability to disasters.

International Federation
of Red Cross and Red Crescent Societies

3.1.2 State authorities should take appropriate operational measures to reduce disaster risks at the local and national levels, including sustainable natural resource, environmental and land-use management, appropriate urban planning, and enforced building codes. States should, in cooperation with National Societies and other concerned agencies, implement disaster risk awareness programmes, public education programmes, early-warning systems, contingency planning, disaster management training and other mitigation and preparedness measures, based on risk, vulnerability and capacity assessments.

3.1.3 States, in cooperation with National Societies, are urged to incorporate risk reduction as a central feature in national development plans, poverty-reduction strategies and post-disaster recovery plans, be it on their own territory or through their development and cooperation assistance in a bilateral, multilateral or regional context, with a special emphasis on reducing the vulnerability of populations in hazard-prone areas or otherwise at risk owing to poverty, marginalization, social exclusion or discrimination.

3.1.4 States are strongly encouraged to prioritise and provide resources to implement comprehensive disaster risk reduction measures, including measures to address issues relating to climate change and variability. National Societies will increase their cooperation with States and experts in the area of climate change in order to limit the potential negative impact on vulnerable populations. In so doing, they may draw on the recommendations outlined in the report "Preparedness for climate change" as requested by the Plan of Action of the 27th International Conference in 1999.

3.1.5 States, recognizing the importance of the independent and auxiliary role of National Societies with respect to the public authorities in providing humanitarian services in the field of disaster management, should negotiate clearly defined roles and responsibilities with their respective National Societies in risk reduction and disaster management activities. This may include National Society representation on relevant national policy and coordination bodies as collaborative partners with States. States should also take specific legal and policy measures to support and assist National Societies in building sustainable volunteer and community capacity, particularly promoting the participation of women, in the areas of risk reduction and disaster management.

3.1.6 The components of the Movement, in cooperation with States, will prioritise and scale up efforts to build sustainable capacity and improve performance in the area of disaster risk reduction, including disaster management, awareness-raising and advocacy activities at the local, national and regional levels. This will include an emphasis on building effective and inclusive partnerships with populations that live in hazard-prone areas or are otherwise vulnerable owing to poverty, marginalization, social exclusion or other forms of discrimination and will involve all relevant partners.

3.1.7 The International Federation will support the efforts of National Societies to strengthen their capacity in the field of disaster risk reduction through continued knowledge sharing on best practices, resource mobilization and advocacy on disaster risk reduction issues with States and other relevant international, regional and national actors, including with the private sector.

Final Goal 3.2 – Enhance international disaster response through support for the compilation and application of the laws, rules and principles applicable to international disaster response

It is essential to provide neutral and impartial assistance to all populations affected by disasters, without discrimination and on the basis of vulnerability and need. Experience has shown that achieving this goal depends to a significant extent on improved understanding of the regulatory framework within which international disaster response is provided. Global research conducted as part of the International Federation's IDRL Project identified that there are many instruments aimed at improving international disaster response but that awareness of them is often lacking and implementation inconsistent.

Actions proposed

3.2.1 All members of the Conference welcome the work undertaken by the International Federation in cooperation with National Societies, States, the United Nations and other bodies to collate and examine the effectiveness of laws, rules and principles applicable to international disaster response, as noted in United Nations General Assembly Resolution on strengthening the effectiveness and coordination of international urban search and rescue assistance (A/RES/57/150).

3.2.2 All members of the Conference recognize that improved awareness, clarification, application and development of laws, rules and principles applicable to international disaster response will assist in facilitating and improving the coordination, timeliness, quality and accountability of international disaster response activities and can therefore make a major contribution to the protection of human dignity in situations of disasters.

3.2.3 States and the components of the Movement are encouraged to work together to ensure the fullest possible consideration and application, where appropriate, of the laws, rules and principles that pertain to international disaster response, as well as the recommendations of Resolution 6 of the 23rd International Conference of the Red Cross and Red Crescent on measures to expedite international relief and United Nations General Assembly Resolution on strengthening the coordination of emergency humanitarian assistance of the United Nations and its accompanying Annex (A/RES/46/182).

3.2.4 States, recognizing the importance of the independent and auxiliary role of National Societies with respect to the public authorities in providing humanitarian services in the event of disaster, are encouraged to work in cooperation with their respective National Societies and the International Federation to review existing disaster management laws and operational instruments at the national, regional and international levels so as to enhance harmonization with relevant laws, rules and principles, and where feasible, guidelines applicable to international disaster response.

3.2.5 States that have not yet done so are encouraged to consider acceding to and implementing the Tampere Convention on the Provision of Telecommunication Resources for Disaster Mitigation and Relief Operations in order to facilitate the effective use of telecommunications in disaster and emergency relief operations. States will, as appropriate, also implement the relevant resolutions of the International Conference of the Red Cross and Red Crescent, International Telecommunication Union and United Nations related to the use of telecommunications in disasters, as well as access and protection of disaster response and mitigation workers.

3.2.6 The International Federation and National Societies will continue to lead collaborative efforts, involving States, the United Nations and other relevant bodies, in conducting research and advocacy activities relating to the compilation of the laws, rules and principles applicable to international disaster response. This includes identifying any outstanding needs in terms of the legal and regulatory framework and the development of models, tools and guidelines for practical use in international disaster response activities. This also includes the active promotion of the awareness, dissemination, clarification and application, where appropriate, of the laws, rules and principles applicable to international disaster response, as well as applicable guidelines by States and the international community at all levels. The International Federation will submit a progress report to the International Conference of the Red Cross and Red Crescent in 2007.

Index

International Federation
of Red Cross and Red Crescent Societies

community grain fund(s) 66, 67

community-led 58, 117

cold waves 46, 47
   see also extreme temperatures

coping strategies 12, 17, 24, 32, 117, 123, 126, 127, 149, 157

conflict(s) 13, 85, 161, 167, 170, 171, 173

cyclone(s) 16, 27, 57, 59, 62, 64, 65

dalit(s) 23, 59
   see also caste(s)

Deccan Development Society (DDS) 66-68, 74-76

deforestation 19, 63, 101, 110, 112, 154

Department for International Development (DFID) 126, 167

development 18, 21, 22, 32-34, 57, 59, 62, 64-69, 72, 75, 92, 96-98, 102, 103, 105, 106, 109-117, 126-128, 130, 131, 138, 150, 154-157, 173-176, 181-184, 221, 223-225
   see also economic development
   see also sustainable development

development agency(ies) 57
   see also aid agency(ies)/organization(s)
   see also humanitarian
   agency(ies)/organization(s)

Development Assistance Committee (DAC) 165, 167, 168
   see also Organisation for Economic
   Co-operation and Development
   (OECD)

de Waal, Alex 12, 125, 126

disaster(s) 11-33, 57, 59, 64, 73, 86, 88, 89, 91-93, 95-97, 101-104, 106, 107,110-112, 115, 117, 144, 149, 152, 157, 161-201, 221, 222, 224, 225
   see also hazards
   see also natural disaster(s)
   see also technological disaster(s)

disaster data 102, 161, 171, 172

disaster management 17, 24, 25, 65, 73, 85, 86, 93, 95, 96, 104, 108, 114, 115, 117, 150, 222, 223, 225

disaster mitigation 21, 64, 72, 108, 111, 114, 117, 225

Disaster Mitigation Institute (DMI) 21

disaster preparedness (DP) 16, 17, 25, 30, 32, 64, 65, 79, 92, 93, 98, 101, 104, 105, 107-109, 113-117, 153, 163, 169, 172, 221, 222

disaster prevention 53
   see also risk reduction

disaster-proof 30, 57, 59, 62

disaster response 65, 84, 85, 103, 224, 225
   see also search and rescue

disease(s) 22, 25, 27, 59, 60 61, 85, 103, 128, 129, 134, 135, 143, 146, 161, 171, 173

donor(s) 14, 18, 27, 32, 34, 90, 91, 96, 97, 108, 114, 115, 118, 125, 128, 130, 131, 134, 139, 154, 155, 166, 167, 172

drought(s) 13, 15, 17-20, 22, 23, 57, 58, 63, 66, 67, 69, 71, 75, 96, 102, 116, 122, 127, 163, 165, 171, 177-184

drought-resistant 19, 23, 66, 67, 116

early warning system(s) 16, 154, 163

earthquake(s) 11, 12, 16, 19, 20, 21, 26, 27, 31, 57, 69, 73, 79-98, 101, 144, 150, 151, 155, 162-164, 171, 174, 176-184, 192

earthquake-safe 70, 74, 98

economic development 65, 130, 164
   see also development
   see also sustainable development

elderly 23, 26, 29, 112, 127

EM-DAT 169, 171-184
   see also Centre for the Epidemiology of
   Disasters (CRED)

epidemic(s) 131, 133, 161, 171, 173
   see also HIV/AIDS

Eshghi Sassan 82-84, 94

Europe 13, 23, 37-53, 86, 162, 164, 173-176, 180-184, 189, 191, 192, 194, 197, 199, 200

European Union (EU) 47

International Federation
of Red Cross and Red Crescent Societies

INDEX

International Federation
of Red Cross and Red Crescent Societies

INDEX